W9-BTB-656

CAREERS in

BUSINESS

Professional Careers Series

BUSINESS

LILA B. STAIR
LESLIE STAIR

FIFTH EDITION

McGraw·Hill

New York   Chicago   San Francisco   Lisbon   London   Madrid   Mexico City
Milan   New Delhi   San Juan   Seoul   Singapore   Sydney   Toronto

The McGraw·Hill Companies

Library of Congress Cataloging-in-Publication Data

Stair, Lila B.
      Careers in business / by Lila B. Stair, Leslie Stair.—5th ed.
          p.   cm. — (McGraw-Hill professional careers series)
      ISBN 0-07-144855-1 (alk. paper)
      1. Business—Vocational guidance—United States.   I. Stair, Leslie.   II. Title.

      HF5382.5.U5S66   2006
      650.1—dc22   2005007794

1 2 3 4 5 6 7 8 9 0   DOC/DOC   0 9 8 7 6 5

ISBN 0-07-144855-1

McGraw-Hill books are available at special quantity discounts to use as premiums and sales promotions, or for use in corporate training programs. For more information, please write to the Director of Special Sales, Professional Publishing, McGraw-Hill, Two Penn Plaza, New York, NY 10121-2298. Or contact your local bookstore.

The editors would like to acknowledge Josephine Scanlon, a professional writer specializing in career books, for revising this fifth edition.

This book is printed on acid-free paper.

CONTENTS

JOB INDEX

JOB TITLE	CHAPTER

JOB TITLE	CHAPTER

JOB TITLE	CHAPTER

JOB TITLE	CHAPTER

BUSINESS

C H A P T E R

CHOOSING A CAREER IN A DYNAMIC BUSINESS ENVIRONMENT

After reading this chapter, you will be able to:

- Describe the concepts "career" and "career development"
- Discuss the nature of the entry-level position and job mobility
- List some economic factors likely to affect business careers today
- Relate the process of self-evaluation to a successful career
- Identify critical factors in career decision making
- Adapt your own open career decision-making model

PLANNING A CAREER FOR THE TWENTY-FIRST CENTURY

When you begin to plan your career, you take a big step forward from relying on an employer to determine your path. Career planning involves assuming responsibility for the development of your career path amid considerations of expanding knowledge, technological change, and corporate restructuring. Employees today must continue to acquire new skills and knowledge throughout their careers. Self-development is important not only since it contributes to job stability and mobility but also to compensation as well. Participating effectively as part of a team will help to improve job skills while you form corporate alliances at the same time. This is important because layoffs and outsourcing are common in corporate restructuring, and who goes and who stays is sometimes determined by these alliances. Many large U.S. companies have outsourced at least one major part of their operations.

Knowing what the marketplace values in terms of knowledge and skills is the first step in planning a career. Desired skills, technological literacy, self-reliance, and flexibility on the part of professional, technical, and other skilled workers are indispensable. Keeping current in your field without being overwhelmed by the volume of information available poses a challenge. Obtaining an academic degree is only the first step in a lifetime of learning. This book is structured to help you use a variety of resources to make your career choices and plans. First, it is important to understand what a "career" is.

A CAREER IS NOT JUST A JOB

The concept of a career implies much more than a specific job or the type of work you perform. A career will span your entire working life and includes not only your behavior, but also your attitudes toward work. Your career will develop in accordance with these attitudes and behaviors. In this sense, you do not select a career itself, but rather choose educational and work experiences that will be the foundation of your career development.

For example, you may choose accounting as a field, major in it in college, and accept an entry-level position with a public accounting firm upon graduation. From that point you may choose several paths along which you will develop your career. You may start an independent practice, switch to private industry and ultimately become a chief executive of the company, or become fascinated with information systems and return to school for an advanced degree in that field. Figure 1.1 shows a sample career path of a college graduate. The choices are all yours!

THE NATURE OF THE ENTRY-LEVEL POSITION

As a college graduate you are more likely to be hired for your potential contribution to the organization over time than for your immediate produc-

Figure 1.1

Sample career path of a college graduate

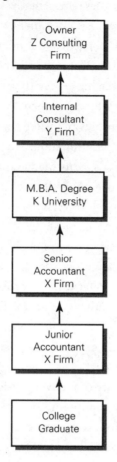

tive capabilities. In this sense, the entry-level position is a testing ground of sorts. It is used by the organization to observe the level of competence of new employees to determine which of them possess the talent to assume a leadership role within the organization and contribute substantially to it.

A business professor tells a story about following up with his former students to see how their careers are progressing. One of his most ambitious and academically skilled students took an entry-level position in the sales force of a major national organization—a very common position for a new graduate from a business school. When the professor asked his former student, John, how things were going after six months with the company, John answered, "Not very well."

Puzzled by this response, the professor spoke to John's supervisor, who indicated two problem areas: First, John's sales were considerably lower than those of the other new sales representatives, perhaps because he wasn't calling on enough potential new customers; and second, John's rapport with his coworkers was not particularly good, which limited the learning and growth on the job that usually result from association with other members of the sales force. After his talk with the supervisor, the professor shared these remarks with John over lunch.

Three months later, the professor visited the same company to do some consulting. He asked the supervisor about John's progress. The supervisor was obviously pleased with his performance and said that John had shown tremendous improvement over the past three months. In passing, the professor mentioned his luncheon conversation with John, at which point the supervisor accused angrily, "You cheated!"

How do you interpret that accusation? The point is that the supervisor expected John to have enough insight to identify his problems for himself as well as the intelligence to determine how to solve them. New employees are often similarly tested. Perhaps John was finding the college-to-work adjustment rather difficult. Or John's problem may have been that his expectations for employment exceeded his position in sales, and his disappointment may have been part of the reason for his poor initial performance. Still, this is the nature of many entry-level positions.

From the organization's standpoint, the entry-level position is intended to smooth the transition from college to work, to orient the new employee to the organization and its values, and to open career paths within the company that would be unavailable to the employee without the entry-level experience. It is wise to be realistic about entry-level job experiences and to evaluate them as short-term objectives that can help you reach long-term career goals.

Most organizations view the first year of employment after college as a distinct career stage. It is important for the newly hired employee to understand this view of the first year as separate from the rest of the career ladder in order to make sense of the business world. Research suggests that future salary, advancement, and job satisfaction are all affected by how graduates approach the first year of employment.[1]

New employees must adjust to a number of factors that affect the nature of the entry-level job experience. The most important is the human organization of the company and the new employee's ability to adapt to and work with it on an emotional level. For example, new employees must adopt the right attitudes for the workplace and consider the impressions that they make. They might have to adjust their expectations to fit the reality of the entry-level position.

Understanding trends in the job market is particularly important for entry-level job seekers. Major transformations have occurred in American businesses over the past two decades. Changes that have impacted business careers include:

- The shift to a service economy
- The globalization of business
- The downsizing of corporations
- The outsourcing of company operations
- The acceleration of high technology
- The rapid increase in temporary and contract workers
- The variations in lifestyles of American families

These transformations affect the types of products offered, the nature of jobs involved in producing and marketing those products, the demand for individuals with certain skills, the salaries offered workers, and the size and locations of businesses themselves. Throughout this book, we have highlighted trends affecting specific fields, cited salary and demand statistics, and discussed opportunities that are available.

JOB MOBILITY

In today's job market, job mobility is the norm. Movement from one job to another—upward, downward, or laterally—or from one field to another are common steps in career development. While upward mobility has always been regarded as desirable or indicative of success, this has not always been the case with other types of movement. With restructuring and downsizing trends in full swing, mobility of all types is likely to be considered indicative of job market factors or personal development rather than instability. Job mobility in itself is neither good nor bad—it depends on the individual's circumstances. Ambition, quality of life or lifestyle considerations, and desire for new challenges may all affect job mobility. Graduates preparing to enter the workforce appear to be prepared for mobility in their careers. In a 2003 survey conducted by the National Association of Colleges and Employers, students indicated that they expect to stay at their first job an average of 4.9 years.[2]

There has been much restructuring of American corporations over the past three decades. Acquisitions and buyouts have changed many corporate identities. Hundreds of thousands of managers and professionals were forced to change jobs or to retire early, and management-level vacancies were not refilled. While 12 to 15 levels of supervision were typical in large corporations in the 1970s, today five or fewer is more common. The reduction in numbers of midlevel managers makes advancement in the corporate hierarchy increasingly competitive.

The upside of this issue is that entry-level jobs are more varied and challenging. Managers with too much to do are forced to delegate many tasks to lower-level and beginning employees. Many entry-level employees just completing college possess more current technology skills than older workers. Project teams are being used more widely as companies attempt a more entrepreneurial approach to product development. Work is less structured. More freedom, as a result of reduced numbers of supervisors, enables employees to take more initiative early in their careers and show what they are able to do.

In addition, the current economic upturn is leading employers to actively recruit new employees on college campuses. Corporate recruiting is expected to increase by about 20 percent at business schools around the country. Many companies also need to fill jobs left empty through attrition, and the expected retirement of many baby boomers within the next decade will leave even more jobs unfilled.[3]

Though this book suggests many ways to advance to positions higher in the company, it also addresses ways employees already in satisfying jobs—content to remain in the same position throughout their careers—can develop and grow as they become more proficient in their specific job.

The choice of whether or not to vie for management positions depends on the values, educational background, and abilities of the individual employee. Advancement from one position to another can often depend on your willingness to gain additional education. You may choose to work toward an advanced degree to increase the chance of entering management ranks. Sometimes the company will pay for this additional education. Because more people today are earning bachelor's degrees in business, employers are beginning to hire only these degree holders for many of the positions described in this book. Some positions also require graduate degrees. There are, however, still some positions in business for people with only an associate degree, as you will see in the following chapters. High school graduates with no further education are unlikely to go far in today's business world, unless they become successful entrepreneurs.

Each chapter of this book describes specific career areas and contains information regarding career mobility. This information will enable you to use the career decision-making model in a forward-looking way. Instead of merely opting for an entry-level position, you can focus on a possible career path right away.

BUSINESS CAREERS IN TODAY'S ECONOMY

Today's economy is characterized by low inflation and record employment. The U.S. Bureau of Labor projects employment to increase by 21.3 million jobs, or 15 percent, through 2012. Professional and related occupations as well as service occupations are projected to increase the fastest, accounting for more than half the total job growth during this period.

We live in a service-oriented economy with four times as many jobs in services-providing industries than in goods-providing industries. A service is an activity performed for an individual or a firm. And while a physical product (a good) is impersonal, a service is usually personal. Service industries may be equipment-based, people-based, or a combination of both. For example, the top ten industries with the fastest wage and salary employment growth include software publishing, management and technical consultants, computer systems design, Internet services, data processing, and other information services.

Services are intangible. Banks and airlines cannot give samples or claim qualities that outlast those of the competition. Services cannot be repossessed if bills are unpaid. Although services cannot be stored as inventory, they must be produced on demand. Long lines or an inability to accommodate customers can seriously impair a service business. Services cannot be mailed; they must be delivered on the spot at a convenient location. Quality is very hard to control—similar services can vary greatly from organization to organization, employee to employee, and even for the same employee. Because of the person-to-person interactions of many service jobs, the term "emotional quotient" (EQ) has been coined to measure the kind of ability service workers need to deal with people, in contrast with "intelligence quotient" (IQ), which measures the ability of employees in the goods-providing industry to develop new and better goods. Most new college graduates will be employed in service industries.

Advances in information and communications technology have revolutionized the workplace and have created opportunities for companies and individuals that did not exist a decade ago. Computers are faster, cheaper, smaller, and more versatile than ever before. They impact every aspect of business today. Managers have immediate access to information that enables them to make better business decisions. Vast communications networks connect every aspect of company operations and allow head offices to remain in close contact with their branches all over the world. The Internet alone has created a host of new job opportunities. Business majors who are not able to use these new technologies to enhance performance in a business environment will miss many career opportunities.

Not only has the economy of the United States become both service- and technology-oriented, it has become globally oriented as well. Competition from European and Asian markets has caused U.S. companies to expand their operations abroad, start new ones, or enter foreign markets through acquisitions and mergers instead of by merely exporting their products. The 1992 integration of the European Community removed trade barriers from country to country throughout Europe. Closer to home the North American Free Trade Agreement (NAFTA) with Mexico, similar to the agreement between the United States and Canada, eliminated such trade barriers as protective tariffs and created a unified North American economy.

Many U.S.-based companies have been multinational for years—that is, they have operations in other countries. Such companies as General Electric, Wal-Mart, Dell, Microsoft, FedEx, Home Depot, and Pfizer are only a few that have prospered globally. Although multinational companies fill many positions with nationals, they also employ qualified American workers in many key positions abroad. All of these changes have affected the nature of the global marketplace and have created many new opportunities both at home and abroad for business graduates.

PERSONAL FACTORS TO CONSIDER IN CAREER PLANNING

In addition to the economic factors, personal factors should play an important role in planning your career. Lifestyle preferences and personal attributes affect career success and happiness. Increasingly, people are viewing work as a way of maintaining a lifestyle rather than developing lifestyles consistent with their work. Family dynamics have changed in keeping with people's career choices and demands. In families with two-career couples, both partners share in family responsibilities. The role of fathers has changed as more mothers are building careers. While studies show that it is still the mothers who miss work more frequently when children are ill, fathers are definitely doing more shopping. Statistics also show that the divorce rate is decreasing. All these changes affect how people plan their careers and balance work and family responsibilities.

Opportunities in business careers exist everywhere, in companies of all sizes. However, considerable trade-offs in terms of quality of life, cost of living, and the merits of the job must all be considered. Salaries tend to be highest where the cost of living is greatest. The location of a job either adds to or detracts from its desirability, depending on personal values and priorities. A growing economy is likely the catalyst for work-related moves as more companies are willing to hire new employees or move current ones. Physically relocating for a job is a major consideration for most workers—particularly those with families or with a spouse or partner who is also employed. In a 2004 survey by personnel consulting firm DMB Inc., 34 percent of 1,100 job seekers indicated a willingness to move for a new job. In contrast, 82 percent of respondents were willing to change industry and 66 percent indicated that they would sign on for less pay than their previous salary rather than relocate.[4] Professionals with working spouses and children are more likely to refuse promotions that require moving to another or less desirable city.

Many professionals start their own businesses for both personal and professional reasons. Women with children often work or run their own businesses from the home. The ability to work from home is now possible for more employees as a result of advances in information and communications technology.

THE ROLE OF SELF-EVALUATION IN CAREER CHOICE

Accurate self-evaluation is an important part of your career development. Self-evaluation is, for the most part, a do-it-yourself project. Although you may seek the help of friends, family, and professional counselors, you are the ultimate authority on yourself. The development of a satisfying career can greatly affect your feelings of self-worth and the attainment of a desired lifestyle.

Self-concept develops in an interesting way. An individual is mirrored, to an extent, by others; that is, other people's perceptions of you are reflected in their messages, which contribute in part to your development of self-concept. But it is your translation of these messages that is most significant in the development of self-concept.

A person's self-concept is very much involved in career choice. It is affected by past successes and failures. We tend to develop our careers by building on past successes, which are related to our abilities, values, and personality characteristics. The purpose of this section is not psychoanalytical but practical, because you must be realistic about yourself in order to use the following career decision-making model in the most meaningful way.

AN OPEN MODEL FOR CAREER DECISION MAKING

So many factors determine career decisions that the only sensible, systematic approach for making these decisions is through a model that incorporates significant personal factors to the decision maker. The career decision-making model shown in Figure 1.2 includes the most common factors usually considered in these decisions. It is "open," providing space for you to add any other significant factors; thus you are adapting the model to yourself.

The model is divided into internal factors and external factors. The internal factors include those things about your personal makeup that will have an impact on your career choice. The external factors include those outside forces—family, economy, and society—that impact career decisions.

Internal Factors

The first category is Aptitudes and Attributes. Items in this category reveal answers to the question, "What am I able to do given the talents and characteristics that I have?" The talents and characteristics you possess will be consistent with demands for success in some jobs more than in others.

The second category is Interests. Items in this category answer the question, "What would I like to do on the job?" Does pressure stimulate you intellectually or cause you anxiety? Would you prefer to work in a variety of areas (generalist) or would you rather be an expert in one area (specialist)? Do you prefer greater structure or more freedom on the job?

The final category is Values. These items answer the question, "What do I need for job satisfaction?" Values vary greatly from individual to individual. This is one area in particular where you might want to add some factors to the model in the space provided.

External Factors

The first category, Family Influence, refers to expectations that your family might have of you or that you might have of yourself, instilled by your ethnic background, the socioeconomic level at which you grew up, or the occupations of your parents.

Figure 1.2

Career decision-making model

Internal factors	External factors
Aptitudes and attributes _____ Academic aptitudes and achievement _____ Occupational aptitudes and skills _____ Social skills _____ Communication skills _____ Leadership abilities _____ _____ _____ _____ _____ _____ _____ _____	**Family influence** _____ Family values and expectations _____ Socioeconomic level _____ _____ _____ _____ _____ _____ _____ _____ _____ _____ _____ _____
Interests _____ Amount of supervision _____ Amount of pressure _____ Amount of variety _____ Amount of work with data _____ Amount of work with people _____ _____ _____ _____ _____ _____	**Economic influence** _____ Overall economic conditions _____ Employment trends _____ Job market information _____ _____ _____ _____ _____ _____ _____ _____

Values
 	
_____ Salary
_____ Status/prestige
_____ Advancement opportunity
_____ Growth on the job
_____ _____
_____ _____
_____ _____
_____ _____
	Societal influence
	
	_____ Perceived effect of race, sex, or
	       ethnic background on success
	_____ Perceived effect of physical or
	       psychological disabilities on success
	_____ _____
	_____ _____
	_____ _____

The second category is Economic Influence, an area that is constantly changing and one that you should carefully consider in making any career decisions. What do overall economic conditions tell you about your future in a certain industry? How consistent is your background with trends in employment? What effect will advancing technology have on your ability to advance in your job or in the industry in which you are employed? Is the job market an employer's or a job-seeker's market in your area? What are the chances of employment in your chosen field after graduation?

The last external factor is Societal Influence. How successful are women and minorities in your chosen field? Will your sex, race, and ethnic background help or hinder you in getting the job you want and advancing in it? To what extent will impaired hearing or vision or any other disability limit you in the career area of your choice?

Adapting the Model to Yourself

To prepare this model for use in evaluating the career options described throughout this book, you must do the following:

1. Add any additional factors that you feel are relevant to your individual career decision-making process in the spaces provided.
2. Weigh each factor, including the ones that you added to the model, by entering a weight—according to the following scale— of between 0 and 5 in the space to the left of the factor.

0 Totally unimportant to career decisions
1 Slightly important to career decisions
2 Somewhat important to career decisions
3 Moderately important to career decisions
4 Substantially important to career decisions
5 Extremely important to career decisions

To help you do this, let's consider each factor. Make sure to add any factors to your model as you review each area. Beginning with internal factors, under Aptitudes and Attributes, consider the explanations and assign a weight to each factor as you proceed.

- **Academic aptitudes and achievement.** This refers to how well you have done or can do in school and where your strong and weak areas are. To what extent do you think that your academic aptitudes and achievement will affect your choice of a career?

- **Occupational aptitudes and skills.** This refers to how well you can perform or learn to perform certain job-related tasks. How important do you think that your occupational aptitudes and skills are in your choice of a career?

- **Social skills.** This refers to how well you are able to get along with people—your human relations skills. To what extent do you think your social skills will affect your career choice?

- **Communication skills.** This refers to how well you are able to communicate with others through speaking, writing, and body language. How important are communication skills to you in choosing a career?

- **Leadership abilities.** This refers to how well you are able to influence others to think or act in a certain way or to follow your lead. To what extent will your leadership abilities affect your choice of a career?

- **Other.** Assign a weight to any factors that you have added to your model in the space provided under Aptitudes and Attributes.

Under Interests, consider the following explanations and weigh the factors as you proceed.

- **Amount of supervision.** This refers to the extent to which you take orders from someone else or work on your own. If you have no preference one way or the other, assign a weight of 0 to the factor. If you prefer more or less supervision, assign a weight between 1 and 5, depending on how important the amount of supervision is to your career choice.

- **Amount of pressure.** This refers to the pressure that is part of most jobs. Which would you prefer: low-pressure or high-pressure? Weigh this factor according to how important the amount of pressure on the job might be to your career choice.

- **Amount of variety.** Some jobs have many varied duties; some have only a few specific duties. Some jobs have duties that change periodically, while others are fairly routine. To what extent will the amount of variety affect your career choice?

• **Amount of work with data.** Although all careers in business require working with raw data or with data that have been processed into information, some business careers are based primarily on working with data rather than with people. To what extent will the amount of work with data affect your career choice?

• **Amount of work with people.** Although all careers in business require working with people to some extent, some careers involve primarily working with people. How important is the amount of time spent working with people in choosing your career?

• **Other.** Assign a weight to any factors that you have added to your model in the spaces provided under Interests.

Under Values, consider the following explanations and weigh these factors as you proceed.

• **Salary.** How important is the salary you will receive to your career choice?

• **Status/prestige.** Status or prestige suggests the need to feel important among colleagues. To what extent will this factor affect your career choice?

• **Advancement opportunity.** Some careers afford much opportunity for advancement, while others provide little. How important is advancement opportunity in your career choice?

• **Growth on the job.** Many career areas offer training, education, and special opportunities for growth or professional development. How important are these to you in considering a career?

• **Other.** Assign a weight to any factors that you have added to your model in the spaces provided under Values.

Now let's consider external factors. Under Family influence, consider the explanations and weigh the following factors.

• **Family values and expectations.** Consider the expectations that your family has of you. The values that they possess define these expectations. Are you expected to follow in your father's or mother's footsteps or to enter the family business? Do you currently have or anticipate having a family of your own? Are you a partner in a dual-career couple relationship? To what extent do the values and expectations of your family play a part in your choice of a career?

• **Socioeconomic level.** You have grown up in a certain economic level of society, which was established to some extent by your parents' occupations and income. Do you want to continue living in the style to which you are accustomed, or would you like to become accustomed to a more affluent or less affluent style of living? To what extent does the socioeconomic level of your family affect your career choice?

• **Other.** Assign a weight to any factors that you have added to your model in the spaces provided under Family Influence.

Under Economic Influence, consider the explanations and weigh the following factors.

• **Overall economic conditions.** Overall economic conditions affect some careers more than others. For example, retail sales tend to drop during economic downturns. To what extent do you think that overall economic conditions will affect your choice of a career?

• **Employment trends.** Many trends have an impact on patterns of employment. Changing technology often changes the nature of careers. As some knowledge becomes obsolete and other knowledge is in demand, the preparation for careers changes. Some careers vanish and others appear. To what extent do you think this knowledge of employment trends is important in selecting your career?

• **Job market information.** Available job opportunities can be found in a number of sources, such as the *Occupational Outlook Handbook* published by the U.S. government. This job market information gives an indication of the number of annual openings expected in various career areas and the competition for those openings. How important is this job market information to your choice of a career?

• **Other.** Assign a weight to any factors that you have added in the spaces provided under Economic Influence.

Under Societal Influence, consider the following explanations and weigh these factors as you proceed.

• **Perceived effect of race, sex, or ethnic background on success.** This factor refers to what effect you feel your race, sex, or ethnic background will have on your success in certain business careers. How important is this factor in your choice of a career?

• **Perceived effect of physical or psychological disabilities on success.** There are some careers that would be difficult to handle for people with certain kinds of disabilities. If you are physically disabled or have a psychological disability—such as a tendency to break down under stress—you would want to include this factor in your career decision-making model. The degree to which the disability might affect success will probably differ from one career to the next. If you have no physical or psychological disabilities, assign a weight of 0 to this factor.

• **Other.** Assign a weight to any factors that you have added in the spaces provided under Societal Influence.

No One Said This Was Going to Be Easy

This model may seem complicated to you, but so is choosing a career. As you read the material in each chapter and use the career decision-making model to evaluate the particular area described, you will have to use a good bit of judgment. You may have to do some additional research to complete the evaluation, particularly if you have added some factors that might not be addressed in the chapter. For the most part, the information in the following chapters will enable you to use the model effectively.

Note that getting career decision making down to a science does not reduce the amount of time you should spend in thoughtful consideration of the way you weigh the factors, the information you acquire from this book, and producing your own self-evaluation.

If you encountered any difficulties weighing factors in the model, you might find some of the following activities helpful:

- Activity A. Write ten statements that begin with "I am . . ."
- Activity B. List ten things that you would like to do before you die.
- Activity C. List ten conditions that mean the most to you in your work.

These simple activities are designed to assist you in self-evaluation. Through them, you might define some priorities in your life, which would suggest factors that should be added to your decision-making model.

GETTING DOWN TO BUSINESS

Exploring careers in business is fascinating because of the variety of possibilities that exist. Beginning with the interest in business that you have already demonstrated (you found this book!), you will be increasingly surprised, even bewildered, by the myriad of choices available to you. Each of the following nine chapters will explore a field in business usually related to a college major. Each chapter will describe various positions in the field, career paths, salaries, trends, job opportunities, aptitudes and attributes needed for success, and sources of additional information. At the end of each chapter, you will evaluate that career area using your weighted career decision-making model.

NOTES

1. Ed Holton, "The Critical First Year on the Job," *National Association of Colleges and Employers, Job Choices: Diversity Edition* (2005): 53–54.
2. Mimi Collins and Pattie Giordani, "The Class of 2003: Opinions and Expectations," *NACE Journal* (Spring 2003): 24.
3. Jennifer Merritt, "For 2005 Grads, Job Offers are Rolling In," *BusinessWeek* (December 6, 2004): 44.
4. Adam Geller, "In Need of a Job, Workers Hit Road," *Rocky Mountain News* (July 10, 2004): 7C.

CHAPTER 2

CAREERS IN ACCOUNTING

After reading this chapter, you will be able to:

- Describe the work of accountants
- Discuss the impact of trends on accounting careers
- Diagram career paths for accountants in government, public accounting firms, and private industry
- Discuss job opportunities within the accounting field today
- List the educational preparation and skills required to enter the field of accounting
- Evaluate accounting careers according to your individualized career decision-making model

Only two accountants at Price Waterhouse know who will win the Academy Awards each year before the announcements. Academy members return their ballots to the firm in specially numbered envelopes. Upon receipt these ballots are locked in a safe in the downtown Los Angeles office known as "Fort Waterhouse." Ballots are then counted manually by six employees to assure total security. These subtotals are then totaled by two accountants who must memorize the names of the winners, dress in tuxedos, and be on hand at the Academy Award ceremony just in case something goes wrong. While most accounting jobs are not that glamorous, individuals entering the field can establish careers that are secure and lucrative.

This chapter will enable you to look closely at accounting as a prospective career, and it includes the following information:

- What services accountants provide
- Who employs them
- Salaries and career paths
- Latest trends
- Job opportunities
- Education and skills needed to pursue a career in accounting
- Sources of additional information on accounting careers

ACCOUNTING

An accountant may work in a number of different areas throughout the course of a career. Many people who work in accounting have broadened their job functions due to the increased capacity of computers. Computers are now capable of performing time-consuming tasks, allowing accountants to do much more. Even with these new technologies there is a tendency to specialize in one area. Some areas in which accountants work are discussed in the following sections.

Auditing

Auditors test the accuracy of accounts and determine whether established procedures and systems were followed. They may detect waste and fraud. An auditor is responsible for checking the accounts periodically and for giving a professional opinion as to whether they accurately reflect the company's financial position. With the heightened amount of fraud that has occurred in the accounting arena, the job of an auditor has become even more important. Audits may be conducted by internal auditing personnel or by external auditors, that is, certified public accountants (CPAs) from public accounting firms. CPAs report their findings to top-level company executives and outside groups such as the Internal Revenue Service (IRS) and the Securities and Exchange Commission (SEC). Audits are required by the SEC for all companies offering stock for sale to the public.

Internal auditors review company operations in terms of their compliance with corporate policies and government regulations. This area of accounting is becoming more valuable to management. Computer systems enable internal auditors to provide top management with up-to-date information on which to base their decisions. Auditors sometimes specialize in such areas as environmental auditing, electronic data processing, health care auditing, investigative auditing, legal auditing, bank auditing, and others. Today auditors must be highly proficient with computers and familiar with a variety of software.

Tax Accounting

Tax accountants plan tax strategies based on company operations, prepare tax returns, research tax problems to identify maximum tax advantages, and confer with Internal Revenue Service examiners on behalf of employers and individuals. They may be internal accountants or CPAs employed outside the company. Most CPAs in public accounting firms are involved in tax accounting. Tax accountants must keep current, since the tax laws change annually, and help clients make wise and timely decisions with respect to these changes.

Another area of tax accounting includes tax examining and collections. These accountants ensure that the government obtains revenues from individuals and businesses. Entry-level tax examiners deal with the simpler tax returns of individual taxpayers while revenue agents specialize in the complicated returns of businesses and large corporations. Many tax examiners work forty hour workweeks, plus some overtime during tax season. Both tax examiners and revenue agents must pay strong attention to detail, have analytic and organizational skills, and must respond well to deadlines. Frequently they work independently. In addition to tax examining, estate and retirement planning to minimize or delay taxes offers many new opportunities for tax accountants, particularly as the population ages.

Systems and Procedures Accounting

The responsibility of a systems and procedures accountant is to design and install accounting systems, usually computerized, that enable a firm to keep good financial records. As the business grows or the laws change, these accountants review and expand the accounting systems and procedures. They are involved in the purchase, installation, and use of computers and information systems.

Cost Accounting

Cost accountants work primarily with production records and inventory accounts. They are responsible for measuring, allocating, and assigning production and overhead costs to units of inventory, which enables management to make decisions concerning whether existing products should continue to be produced or new ones should be made, and for how much they should be sold. Cost-benefit analyses are frequently conducted in business to get to the proverbial bottom line.

Budget and Forecast Accounting

A budget and forecast accountant plans for the future, prepares both short- and long-term budgets, provides for the organization's cash requirements, projects market forecasts, and accumulates a variety of other analytical information needed by management to make sound financial decisions. Budget and forecast accountants are widely employed in the private and public sectors, and nonprofit organizations. In addition to preparing and analyzing annual budgets and proposals, budget analysts monitor the budget periodically to make sure funds have been spent in the proper places and everything is on track. Long work hours are common, usually more than forty hours a week, and most of the time is spent working independently analyzing data and preparing proposals.

General Accounting

General accountants perform some or all of the activities described for other specialties, including daily recordkeeping, developing and supervising accounting practices, and preparing financial statements and special reports such as balance sheets and income statements, profit and loss statements, cash flow statements, and cost-benefit analyses.

Management Accounting

A management accountant provides operational advice to management on a variety of matters and is considered a member of the management team. Duties include analyzing financial information, budgeting, evaluating performance, and participating in asset and cost management. Financial decisions involving mergers and acquisitions, long-term financing, capital budgets, and major corporate decisions are analyzed in conjunction with marketing and finance specialists. Management accounting involves a lot of teamwork and collaborating with various departments in the company. The top accounting position in an organization is the controller. The controller directs the entire accounting program, including all of the activities previously described. Computer-oriented management consulting is offered through the consulting divisions of major accounting firms. Many managerial accountants find positions with such firms.

Public Accounting

CPAs are employed by public accounting firms, all types of organizations, the government, or work in independent practice. They perform one or all of the services described for other accounting specialties for their clients or employers, usually on a repeat basis. Much of the work performed by CPAs involves auditing and tax accounting. Today, large public accounting firms are offering more services to more types of organizations than ever before. Specialization by industry or accounting function is common. International specialization offers many opportunities for those who have a CPA license and expertise in another language. For diversity of experience, public accounting offers the most opportunity since CPAs work with a variety of people and companies. Pressure, travel, and seven-day workweeks often go with the job.

Government Accounting

Many accountants who choose to work in the government sector are employed by the federal, state, and local governments. Duties include maintaining records of many government agencies, and auditing individuals and private businesses who are subject to government regulation. They verify that revenues and expenditures are in accordance with the law. To aid in their position and job growth, many government accountants, in addition to other certifications, choose to earn the Certified Government Financial Manager (CGFM) credential, which is granted by the Association of Government Accountants.

CURRENT TRENDS

The role of the accountant is changing in a number of ways. With many recent accounting scandals and closer scrutiny of company finances, the accountant's job has become extremely important. As a result of these scandals, federal legislation that creates opportunities for accountants to be more thorough in eliminating fraud has increased. The trend toward downsizing and restructuring in corporations places the accountant in the critical position of determining the most cost-effective way to organize the company's operations. Determining which operations need overhauling, which should be eliminated, and which should be outsourced, as well as explaining in financial terms the rationale for these decisions to management is up to the accountant. The accountant's new role as full member of the management team increases the need for communication skills. The increased involvement of the accountant in organizational change includes planning and controlling, designing information systems, and suggesting responsibility.

With the U.S. national debt and the overwhelming task of streamlining federal government spending, today's CPA is expected to go beyond the financial audit and tackle measuring the efficiency, effectiveness, and economy of government programs. CPAs have recently been placed in the forefront of this national issue. The accountant must learn new standards and techniques of measurement. While computers have simplified many of the routine tasks, greater communication with employees in the programs is required.

New Technology

The information and technology revolution has changed the nature of the accountant's job and has brought about the need for changes in financial statement models. Today's accountants are dealing with volatile prices, currency fluctuations, and changing property values—all of which can be transmitted instantaneously at the computer keyboard and have immediate impact on financial markets. In addition, more complex financial transactions and instruments make the field even more challenging. Opportunities will abound for accountants with the ability to use the new accounting systems and information technologies to the utmost advantage.

Specialization

As the work of the accountant becomes more complicated, the tendency to specialize becomes greater. In business careers, such specialists as tax accountants, systems and forecast accountants, and internal auditors complement the activities of cost and managerial accountants. In public accounting, specialist areas outside the main function of general auditing include tax accounting, management consulting, systems development, marketing, research and training, and international accounting. There is also a tendency in public accounting to specialize by industry.

The increase of accounting scandals and fraud has even created another type of specialization. A new area of accounting called forensic accounting focuses on detecting illegal financial activity in individuals, companies, and organized crime rings. With computer technology increasing, the number of computer-related crimes is also increasing. Forensic accountants use special software and surveillance technology to track down these criminals.

The advantages of specialization are high initial salaries and a great demand for services. An accountant can spend two or three years in a specialist field without restricting opportunities to get back into the mainstream of auditing or financial management. However, a longer time as a specialist might restrict these opportunities by limiting the range of the accountant's experience. It is important to identify both the short- and long-term career goals in the field of accounting.

JOB OPPORTUNITIES

Much of the demand for accounting services is created by the passage of new laws and regulations. For example, tax laws change so frequently and are so complex that every year fewer Americans attempt to prepare their own tax returns. Also, every year the SEC makes additional requirements for record keeping and disclosure practices in corporations who sell their stock to the public. This causes an increased demand for CPAs. New auditing requirements for pension plans and for public campaign fund records further increase the need for CPAs. The 1986 Tax Reform Act, which purported to simplify the tax laws, and the continued subsequent changes have confused both individuals and companies, also increasing the need for accountants. And the growth of international business has increased demand for accountants who work in international trade, which should subsequently increase the jobs for these types of accountants as well.

In addition, as more states adopt the 150-hour rule, which requires CPA candidates to complete thirty hours of additional course work beyond the bachelor's degree, it will become more difficult to earn the certification.

Numerous new financial instruments have created the need for money managers who may have backgrounds in either accounting or finance. Information technology has motivated many accounting firms to create management information systems departments that offer consulting services to assist companies in the design and implementation of accounting information systems.

Beware of the job market, as it is constantly fluctuating. Often when demand in a particular area is great, more students major in that area to be assured of a good job after graduation. A pendulum effect occurs. When too many job seekers flock to a hot demand area, the market becomes glutted, the pendulum swings to the other extreme, and demand falls to a low point. There is then a cooling-off period when fewer students enter academic programs, and fewer new applicants enter the field over a period of years. This causes supply to decrease and the pendulum swings again.

One factor that might keep the accounting market from being glutted is the casualty rate among would-be accounting majors. Many students lack the analytical abilities and the persistence for accuracy with numbers required for success in an accounting program, thus the casualty rate is sizable. Don't become a casualty statistic! Be sure you have the necessary aptitudes and characteristics for success before choosing accounting as your major.

Equal Opportunity

Women have done well in the accounting profession. Involved in professional organizations, women have begun two societies for female accountants, the American Society of Women Accountants (ASWA) and the American Woman's Society of Certified Public Accountants (AWSCPA). Further evidence of the high degree of professionalism among female accountants is the high percentage of women involved in continuing education programs and in professional activities such as writing articles and giving speeches. If you are female you will be happy to hear that preliminary surveys indicate that a larger percentage of women than men pass the

CPA exam the first time around. If you are male know that you are in for some competition from women. An increasing number of women are moving into management and being promoted to partner in large accounting firms.

Fewer than 5 percent of CPAs are minorities. The National Association of Black Accountants (NABA) estimates that of over 200,000 practicing African American accountants, only five thousand are CPAs.[1] The association has established the Center for Advancement of Minority Accountants (CAMA). It sponsors annual conferences for members as well as provides job information. The American Institute of Certified Public Accountants (AICPA) also offers scholarships to minority accounting students in undergraduate and graduate programs.

APTITUDES AND ATTRIBUTES NEEDED FOR SUCCESS

The field of accounting requires specific education and training. The requirements you will need to fulfill in order to succeed are explored in this section.

Education

To prepare for a career in accounting, you must complete a college program with a major in accounting and earn a bachelor of arts (B.A.) or bachelor of science (B.S.) degree. Many professional accounting programs are five-year programs, and were established for the following reasons:

- The expansion of knowledge required in accounting today
- The increase of complex interrelationships between business, government, and society
- The increased need for communication skills
- The increased need for computer skills
- The 150-hour requirement for CPA candidates

A master of business administration (M.B.A.) degree with an accounting undergraduate degree, or a master of accounting degree can increase your chances of being hired, particularly by a big public accounting firm. Many accounting professors feel that students who ultimately make partner in large accounting firms or rise to leadership positions in government and industry are those who have completed a master's degree or professional accounting program.

A college program should include a core of liberal arts courses with emphasis on written and oral communications, and at least the following accounting and finance courses:

- The two beginning accounting courses
- An intermediate course
- Cost accounting
- Courses in auditing and tax
- A beginning course in the principles of finance
- Computer science or information systems courses

Liberal arts graduates with courses in economics, calculus, statistics, and computer science may be recruited by large public accounting firms and put through a demanding training program. Some universities offer highly competitive twelve- to fifteen-month accounting programs. Acceptance into such a program is often contingent on an employment offer from a public accounting firm.

Internships. Internships in accounting are available with accounting firms, corporations, and government agencies. These internships may be found through college and university placement offices, professors, state CPA societies, or direct contact with companies. Large public accounting firms and the U.S. General Accounting Office select college juniors and seniors for internship programs.

Extracurricular activities. Although your grade point average is important, other qualifications carry equal weight. Many interviewers, particularly from public accounting firms, highly regard extracurricular involvement in student organizations. If you hold an office in a student organization, this indicates that you work well with others and are able to gain their confidence and respect. These qualities are essential for success in public accounting since you must be able to sell your skills to clients.

Aptitudes and attributes necessary for success in a college accounting program as well as in an accounting position after graduation include:

- Analytical ability
- Communications skills

- Strong organizational skills
- Creativity
- Patience and persistence to work with detail
- A natural tendency toward orderliness
- Ability to handle pressure in meeting deadlines
- Strong decision-making skills
- Computer and information systems skills

Certification. A recent survey found that over half the corporations hiring accountants considered the Certified Public Accountant (CPA) and the Certified Management Accountant (CMA) certifications important to have. Certainly, the widest range of job opportunities in public accounting are offered to those who pass the Uniform CPA Examination, which is used in all states. This examination provides a challenge for those wanting to enter public accounting. Included in the two-day exam are four sections in the areas of accounting practices, auditing standards, accounting theory, and business law. The failure rate is high on this exam. Those passing two sections with a minimum overall score may retake the other two at a later time. Those who do not achieve this minimum requirement must retake the entire exam. After successfully passing all parts of the exam, accountants may be eligible to receive the CPA certificate, which earns them a permit to practice issued by their resident state board of accountancy. Many states require that individuals have one or two years of experience in accounting before receiving the CPA certificate. The CPA exam is administered by the American Institute of Certified Public Accountants (AICPA); contact information is given at the end of this chapter. With the CPA designation you also have the opportunity to focus on an area of expertise and to receive the Accredited in Business Valuation (ABV), Personal Financial Specialist (PFS), and Certified Information Technology Professional (CITP) credentials.

The Certified Management Accountant (CMA) certification is issued by the Institute of Management Accountants (IMA) to those who successfully complete a four-part exam, have a minimum of two years' experience in management or financial accounting, agree to meet continuing education requirements, and comply with standards of professional conduct.

The Certified Internal Auditor (CIA) certification is conferred by the Institute of Internal Auditors (IIA) to candidates who successfully complete a four-part exam and who have a minimum of two years' experience in internal auditing.

The Certified Information Systems Auditor (CISA) designation is conferred by the Information Systems Audit and Control Association (ISACA) upon candidates who pass an examination and have five years' experience in auditing electronic data processing systems.

CAREER DEVELOPMENT AND COMPENSATION

Because the same functions are performed by accountants employed by public accounting firms, organizations, and government, there is considerable lateral mobility as well as upward mobility for accountants with the training, talent, and drive to strive for the highest positions. Figure 2.1 indicates the various positions in which you might be employed as an accountant and the patterns of mobility. Note that the different types of arrows reflect the frequency of occurrence of the upward and lateral mobility.

Typically, but not always, accountants who work for the federal government, major corporations, and multinational public accounting firms earn higher salaries than those accountants in local public accounting firms, small companies, and state and local governments. In those industries that employ the largest number of accountants and auditors, median annual earnings in 2002 were as follows:

Federal government	$51,070
Accounting, tax preparation, bookkeeping, and payroll services	$49,520
Management of companies and enterprises	$49,110
Local government	$44,690
State government	$42,680

According to a salary survey conducted by the National Association of Colleges and Employers (NACE), bachelor's degree candidates in accounting received starting offers of around $40,647 a year in 2003; master's degree candidates in accounting were initially offered $42,241.

A salary survey conducted in 2003 by Robert Half International, a staffing services firm specializing in accounting and finance, indicates that accountants and auditors with up to one year of experience earned between

$29,500 and $40,500. Those with one to three years of experience earned between $34,000 and $49,500. Senior accountants and auditors earned between $41,000 and $61,500; managers earned between $47,500 and $78,750; and directors of accounting and auditing earned between $66,750 and $197,500 a year. The variation in salaries reflects differences in the size of firm, location, level of education, and professional credentials.

Figure 2.1

Accounting positions and mobility

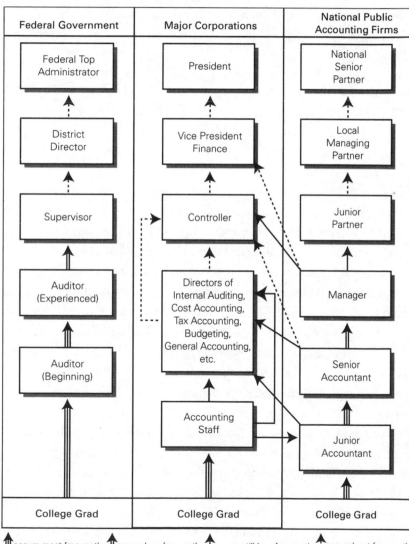

Federal Government	Major Corporations	National Public Accounting Firms
Federal Top Administrator	President	National Senior Partner
District Director	Vice President Finance	Local Managing Partner
Supervisor	Controller	Junior Partner
Auditor (Experienced)	Directors of Internal Auditing, Cost Accounting, Tax Accounting, Budgeting, General Accounting, etc.	Manager
Auditor (Beginning)		Senior Accountant
	Accounting Staff	Junior Accountant
College Grad	College Grad	College Grad

occurs most frequently � occurs less frequently occurs still less frequently occurs least frequently

In the federal government, the starting annual salary for junior accountants and auditors was $23,442 in 2003. Candidates who had a superior academic record might start at $29,037, while applicants with a master's degree or two years of professional experience usually began at $35,519. Accountants employed by the federal government averaged $69,370; auditors averaged $73,247.

Mobility and salary are only two factors to consider in comparing job offers, however. Government work, though lower in salary, offers numerous fringe benefits and is usually more stable. Likewise, though accountants who are self-employed may not always earn as much as those employed by large companies, they have a great deal of freedom.

The largest and most prestigious multinational public accounting firms are:

1. Ernst & Young LLP
2. Deloitte & Touche LLP
3. PricewaterhouseCoopers LLP
4. KPMG LLP

The big firms get many of the top accounting graduates. Tough competition eliminates some of the new recruits within three years. Why are these beginners willing to face these odds and this type of pressure? The large firms invest millions of dollars in training, giving junior accountants invaluable education and experience in sophisticated accounting techniques. Even if you leave a large company within the first three years, you take this education and experience away with you and into your next job. Those who never make partner in these firms eventually become partners in smaller firms, go into independent practice, join private industry financial staffs, or enter government jobs.

There is a great deal of prestige attached to working with a big public accounting firm or working at an executive level in an organization. There is also a great deal of pressure. Recall that accountants in private industry do very well moving up the corporate ladder. Some of those who leave a big public accounting firm end up on the staff of one of the firm's clients, so they begin in many cases with the advantage of knowing the accounting system and a good bit about their new employer.

One strategy of college graduates is to try to find a job with one of the large public accounting firms for the education and experience, then go

into private practice or work in corporate America. A big plus for beginning accountants is successful completion of an internship program in one
of three broad areas—auditing, tax/financial accounting, or management
accounting. Because much of accounting involves working as part of a
team, communication skills are important. Computer and analytical skills
are vital.

SOURCES OF ADDITIONAL INFORMATION

If you like what you have read and would like more information on careers
in accounting, contact the following professional organizations:

American Accounting Association
5717 Bessie Drive
Sarasota, FL 34233-2399
aaahq.org

American Institute of Certified Public Accountants (AICPA)
1211 Avenue of the Americas
New York, NY 10036-8775
aicpa.org

American Society of Women Accountants (ASWA)
8405 Greensboro Drive, Suite 800
McLean, VA 22102-5120
aswa.org

American Woman's Society of Certified Public Accountants (AWSCPA)
136 South Keowee Street
Dayton, OH 45402
awscpa.org

Association of Government Accountants (AGA)
2208 Mount Vernon Avenue
Alexandria, VA 22301-1314
agacgfm.org

Association of Latino Professionals in Finance and Accounting
510 West Sixth Street, Suite 400
Los Angeles, CA 90014
alpfa.org

Information Systems Audit and Control Association (ISACA)
3701 Algonquin Road, Suite 1010
Rolling Meadows, IL 60008
isaca.org

Institute of Internal Auditors, Inc.
247 Maitland Avenue
Altamonte Springs, FL 32701-4201
theiia.org

Institute of Management Accountants
10 Paragon Drive
Montvale, NJ 07645
imanet.org

National Association of Black Accountants (NABA)
7249A Hanover Parkway
Greenbelt, MD 20770
nabainc.org

National Society of Accountants (NSA)
1010 North Fairfax Street
Alexandria, VA 22314-1574
nsacct.org

The NSA offers scholarships to those who have completed their sophomore year.

The American Assembly of Collegiate Schools of Business (AACSB) provides a list of accredited accounting and business programs. To obtain one, contact:

AACSB
600 Emerson Road, Suite 300
St. Louis, MO 63141-6762
aacsb.edu

Each state has a State Society of Certified Public Accountants as well as a State Board of Accountancy. The national association and address is as follows:

National Association of State Boards of Accountancy (NASBA)
150 Fourth Avenue N., Suite 700
Nashville, TN 37219
nasba.org

Sources of Additional Information in Canada

Canadian Academic Accounting Association
12 Donwoods Drive
Toronto, ON M4N 2G1
caaa.ca

Certified General Accountants Association of Canada
800-1188 West Georgia Street
Vancouver, BC V6E 4A2
cga-canada.org

Certified Management Accountants of Canada (CMA Canada)
One Robert Speck Parkway, Suite 1400
Mississauga, ON L4Z 3M3
cma-canada.org

Canadian Comprehensive Auditing Foundation
55 Murray Street, Suite 210
Ottawa, ON K1N 5M3
ccaf-fcvi.com

CAREER DECISION-MAKING MODEL

Now that you have some information on careers in accounting in general, it is time to consider accounting as a possible career for you. Figures 2.2a and 2.2b include the factors in the career decision-making model from Chapter 1. Follow these directions to complete them:

1. Enter the position that interests you most on the line titled "Job."
2. Enter any additional factors used to personalize your model (from Chapter 1) in the blank spaces provided.
3. Enter the weights you assigned to the factors (from Chapter 1) in column WT. (It would be wise to review the explanations of these factors in the description of the model in Chapter 1 before going on to Step 4.)
4. Assign a value from 1 (lowest) to 10 (highest) to each factor, based on the information in this chapter and on your personal self-assessment. (This value is different and separate from the weight.) Enter the value in column V. If you feel that you have a certain aptitude or attribute needed for success in this career area, you should assign a fairly high value. If a certain interest, such as amount of variety, is desirable to you and you feel the area provides the variety you enjoy, again, assign this a fairly high value. If not, assign a low value. Use this technique to assign values to all factors in the model. If you cannot assign a value based on the information in the chapter for some of the factors in the model, either use other sources to acquire the information or leave the space beside the factor blank.
5. Multiply the weight times the value, and enter the score in column S.
6. Add the scores in column S for each group of factors, and enter the number in the space labeled "Total."

You will use this evaluation in Chapter 11, along with the evaluations of each career explored in this book.

WHAT DID YOU LEARN?

In this chapter you learned about careers in accounting. You learned what services accountants provide, where they are employed, what salaries they

Figure 2.2a

Career evaluation for accounting

			Career Evaluation	

Job: _____

Internal factors

WT	×	V	=	S	Factors
					Academic aptitudes and achievement
					Occupational aptitudes and skills
					Social skills
					Communication skills
					Leadership abilities
					_____
					_____
					_____
					_____
					_____

Total: _____ Aptitudes and attributes

WT	×	V	=	S	Factors
					Amount of supervision
					Amount of pressure
					Amount of variety
					Amount of work with data
					Amount of work with people
					_____
					_____
					_____
					_____
					_____

Total: _____ Interests

WT	×	V	=	S	Factors
					Salary
					Status/prestige
					Advancement opportunity
					Growth on the job
					_____
					_____
					_____
					_____
					_____

Total: _____ Values

Figure 2.2b

Career evaluation for accounting

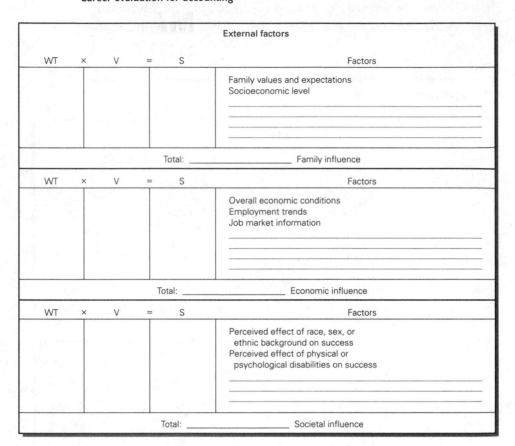

earn, what mobility they have, what trends are currently affecting the profession, what the job outlook is, how to prepare yourself for a career in accounting, and where to find additional information. In Chapter 3, "Careers in Computers and Information Technology," you will gain insights into careers in the dynamic world of high technology.

NOTE

1. National Association of Black Accountants, Inc., nabainc.org/pages/Naba_history.jsp, (accessed March 7, 2005).

CAREERS IN INFORMATION TECHNOLOGY

After reading this chapter, you will be able to:

- Describe the work of information technology professionals in systems analysis; database administration; programming; systems operations, support, and security; networks and communications; web development; e-commerce; and information systems management
- Discuss the impact of trends on information and communications technology
- Diagram career paths for those in information technology professions
- Discuss job opportunities in information fields today
- List the educational preparation and skills needed for positions in these fields
- Evaluate careers in information technology according to your individualized career decision-making model

Most people today can barely remember life or work without computers or the Internet, which was first brought online in 1969 and was followed by e-mail shortly thereafter. The World Wide Web was developed in 1990, and the use of the Internet for commercial purposes followed in 1991, leading to the level of e-commerce we have today. Researchers are now attempting to add an express lane to the information superhighway by developing separate systems paralleling the Internet, so that data-intensive applications won't compete with the abundance of e-mail and e-commerce.[1]

All over the world people are using the Internet to find information and to communicate. Over time, information and communications technology have changed the structure of organizations, the way we do business, the types of jobs we hold, and the nature of work itself throughout all professions. Internet and global telecommunications reforms are creating new business and career opportunities. High-speed computers enable organizations in all industries to process vast quantities of data more quickly than in past years and with fewer people. Organizations are able to offer more services to customers and employees, maintain better records, and obtain the vital information needed by management to make decisions that maximize profits and assure survival in a turbulent and competitive global environment.

This advancing technology is eliminating some jobs and changing others, while creating new positions at the same time. Many routine clerical jobs have been eliminated, creating in their place new, higher-paid positions in information technology fields. On the other hand, advancing technology also enables the outsourcing of jobs overseas, which began a decade ago. Such information technology (IT) jobs as application programming, call center operations, help desk work, and systems maintenance are now moving abroad. Forrester Research projects an increase from 27,171 in 2000 to 472,632 in 2015.[2] In the manufacturing sector, cheaper wages overseas and the increased use of robots in industry has displaced many workers. The jobs of workers in practically every industry have been affected by the expanded use of information technology.

In this chapter you will examine careers in information technology, and it includes the following information:

- What tasks information technology professionals perform
- Current trends
- Job opportunities
- Career development and compensation
- Aptitudes and attributes needed to pursue information technology careers
- Sources of additional information on computers and information processing

INFORMATION TECHNOLOGY (IT)

Information technology permeates all organizations today and IT professionals are employed in virtually every industry. Technology is used at every level in most organizations. Because of information technology, managers in the corporate United States receive timely information needed for making the decisions that keep their companies competitive in a dynamic business environment. From management decision making to simple record keeping, billing, payroll, and inventory-control applications, technology plays a valuable role in businesses. Research labs have made amazing advances using new technologies. Automated equipment is essential in most manufacturing plants. Executives are rarely without a laptop or handheld computer used to call up the information required to make complicated and crucial decisions. In grocery stores and other retail outlets, computerized scanners enable quicker service and better inventory control. And the banking and airline industries have been dependent on technology for almost every aspect of their operations for years.

IT professionals are employed in a variety of positions that fall into the following general categories: systems analysis, database administration, programming, operations, systems support, security, networks and communications, and information systems management. Figure 3.1 is a sample chart of the function of information technology within an organization. IT professionals use a combination of systems including hardware, software, database, and communications to input, process, output, communicate, and manage the information needed to run an organization. These individuals may enter fields with business degrees in information technology, such as information systems majors, or technology-oriented degrees such as computer sciences majors.

Systems Analysis

Many individuals working independently or in teams composed of employees, users, and managers are involved in systems development. Although systems vary in scope and complexity, each one is a collection of people, machines, programs, and procedures organized to perform a certain task. Large systems may include mainframe computers and hundreds of small computers or workstations connected by networks. The work of the sys-

Figure 3.1

Information technology organization chart

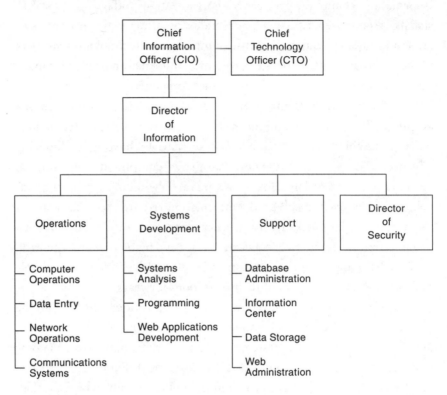

tems analyst is to design new systems or to improve existing ones. Basically a professional problem solver, the systems analyst must first analyze problems or informational needs within the organization, then design efficient patterns of information flow from the data sources to the computer to solve them. The systems analyst also plans the distribution of information, based on how it is to be used within the organization. In order to design and maintain a reliable and efficient system of information flow, the systems analyst works closely with managers, accountants, and other user groups within the organization to determine informational needs or problems. An understanding of how various areas in the organization operate, such as accounting, finance, marketing, and management, and the ability to communicate effectively with coworkers in these areas are crucial to the effectiveness of the systems analyst.

Most systems analysts have some supervisory or management duties such as estimating, scheduling, controlling time, and accepting final responsibility for projects. An important part of the systems analyst's job is to relate the requirements of the system to the capabilities of the computer hardware and prepare specifications for programmers developing the software to make the system work. In some organizations the systems analysts also may do the programming, and hold the job title of analyst/programmer. In other organizations analysts and programmers have separate job titles and areas of responsibility. Software quality assurance analysts determine whether program requirements have been met and diagnose problems and recommend solutions.

Programming

The work of the computer programmer involves coding—that is, writing detailed sets of instructions using a designated programming language according to the problem descriptions and specifications of the systems analysts and software engineers. These programs are made up of a series of logical steps for the machine to follow to process the data into usable information. After writing the code, programmers test and maintain the programs. Programs may be written in a matter of hours or may require more than a year of work; thus programmers may work alone on small projects or in teams on larger ones. Once written, programs must be updated and modified as needed by programmers.

In programming, a strong orientation to detail is important. Something as small as a misplaced comma could cause the program to malfunction. This characteristic becomes crucial as a programmer debugs programs to ensure that they are error free. Debugging usually entails making trial runs on the computer with sample data. Programmers also may be involved in writing documentation or instructions that explain how to use the software. Often technical writers are employed to prepare the documentation according to the programmers' instructions. There are several types of programmers: scientific and business applications programmers, operating systems programmers, and maintenance programmers. The work of scientific or engineering applications programmers is highly mathematical in nature and involves developing programs that solve scientific or engineering problems. Normally an undergraduate degree in engineering, math, or computer science is a minimum requirement.

Business applications programmers are involved in a wide range of tasks, from developing user programs to handling such routine activities as billing customers. They also may develop programs designed to satisfy the complex informational needs of managers. Programming experience pays off in landing desirable jobs if that experience is pertinent to the systems in use within a company. However, the improved quality and quantity of software packages in business applications has somewhat reduced the demand for business applications programmers.

Maintenance programmers are employed to constantly enhance or debug existing programs. Skill in debugging techniques and experience in program development are required for this highly complex job. The maintenance programming staff is usually a combination of seasoned veterans and newly hired programmers who are trained by the most experienced maintenance programmers on the staff.

The work of operating systems programmers is highly technical in nature and can be somewhat difficult for the layperson to understand. Basically, the operating systems programmer writes sets of instructions to make the programming of computers easier; for example, programs that schedule the various components of the computer or that permit the computer to deal with many tasks simultaneously. These sets of instructions, called operating systems, control the operation of the entire computer system. They frequently become a permanent part of the computer's memory so that all of the components and related equipment perform in harmony with one another. Thus, the operating systems programmer must have a good technical knowledge of the various parts of the computer and how each operates. Systems programmers might be involved in developing new languages or adapting existing languages to specific needs. A degree in computer science with a solid background in computer architecture (the way circuits are structured) is required for most positions.

Operations

The manager of operations oversees computer operators who are responsible for setting up the computer and its equipment; mounting and removing tapes, disks, and printer forms; monitoring jobs in progress; and troubleshooting when problems occur. Data entry operators are involved in input—that is, entering data into the computer using keyboards and tape or disks. Production control operators handle output, routing jobs to the proper place upon completion. Most positions in operations require training that may be obtained in high school, vocational school, community college, or on the job. Advancement is somewhat limited, though it is common for employees to advance to supervisory levels within operations. However, the manager of operations usually has more formal education and experience than most operations workers.

Systems Support and Database Administration

The huge increase in computer usage at all levels in organizations has created the need for specialists to assist and train users and help maintain computer systems and networks. Computer support specialists provide technical assistance to users and help solve problems. This might include minor repairs on hardware, software, and peripheral equipment; testing equipment to evaluate performance; working with users to identify the need for system modification; and maintaining records of installation, maintenance, and repairs. Technical support specialists must remain current on the new technologies used within their organizations. Some companies maintain help desks or information centers staffed by technicians who instruct users in more productive ways to use the organization's systems.

A database is a set of related data used by systems analysts and programmers to produce and store the information needed by the organization. Database administrators analyze the company's information requirements, coordinate data collection, organize data into usable databases, store data for efficient access by analysts and programmers, keep databases up-to-date, and establish rules pertaining to the databases and their security. This position has become more important because of the huge amount of data generated by the Internet and electronic e-commerce. Working under the manager to assist in these tasks are database analysts and librarians.

Communications and Networks

Communications involves the use of hardware and software that carry data and information from a sender to a receiver. Telecommunications uses electronic transmissions via cable, microwave, satellite, cellular, and infrared technology to transmit information faster and more freely. Data communications uses telecommunications technology for the electronic collection, processing, and distribution of data among computer system hardware devices, such as to link a computer to remote terminals and other computers.

The communications manager and a number of specialists working under the manager are responsible for analyzing data communications needs, aiding in the design of data communications networks, selecting equipment, installing and operating data links, organizing the use and maintenance of the system, training users, and solving data communications problems. Communications specialists must be knowledgeable in languages, applications, and communications devices. They are responsible for program design, coding, testing, debugging, and documentation, as well as for the implementation of communications software. Their work also involves the evaluation and modification of existing communications hardware and software. They serve as technical advisors to applications programmers.

Advancements in network technology including the widespread use of local area networks (LANs) and wide area networks (WANs), have created new positions in the information field. LAN/WAN managers design and administer the communications networks that connect staff throughout the organization. This includes hardware, software, and all other computing equipment associated with the network. The network engineer designs networks and transmissions systems and conducts traffic studies. Network analysts do specific systems analysis.

The Internet and World Wide Web

The Internet and World Wide Web have added a whole new group of jobs to the information systems career spectrum. The Internet is the international network that allows communications among systems throughout the world, and gives access to information housed in websites throughout the World Wide Web. Intranet technology enables the use of Internet technology within a company. Compiling, entering, and maintaining information in websites is done in-house under the direction of project managers who employ Webmasters, Web developers, intranet network administrators, and

Web user-support consultants. Marketing through the Web has created a host of possibilities. Knowledge of technology such as Java, HTML, and browsers is necessary. Security, such as firewalls that prevent electronic break-ins through networks or telecommunications, must be in place before websites are established. Numerous Internet companies have arisen over the past few years to compile, organize, and prepare information accessed through the Internet. These companies hire managers, analysts, researchers, and others to provide this service. In addition, independent researchers offer services to those who need information from the Internet. These individuals have the necessary skills to locate specific information from the vast sea of information now available.

Security

The increased use and decentralization of database and network technologies has created the need for improved security to assure protection from invasion of privacy, computer viruses, theft, fraud, and waste resulting from greater access by more individuals to computer systems, and a host of other problems including natural disasters such as flood or fire damage. The director of security of an organization oversees security specialists in the protection of data and computer resources. For data security, specialists have programming and systems analysis backgrounds. Some data security specialists may have experience in auditing information systems as well. Disaster recovery specialists usually come from operations with communications expertise. The director may come from either background. Computer security may be conducted by external teams of computer security specialists, sometimes called tiger teams. These teams conduct periodic, often unscheduled, security checks on systems at the request of management to detect existing and potential problems.

Information Systems Management

Throughout all of the areas described above are information systems (IS) managers working at various levels within their departments. The vice president of information, or chief information officer (CIO), is an important executive in corporations today, has a vital role in corporate strategic planning, and is in charge of all information functions. The CIO focuses on business management. Because of rapidly changing technology, some companies feel the need for an executive to focus on it full time. The position of chief technology officer (CTO) was created to define and implement an effective information technology infrastructure throughout the organization utilizing the newest, most innovative technologies. To remain competitive in a dynamic global market requires knowledge of these technologies. The key management positions are shown in Figure 3.1. Information systems (IS) managers must have both technical and managerial skills. The higher the level of management, the more important managerial skills become. The lower the level, the more vital technical expertise is, since it is the systems analysis managers, programming managers, database managers, and communications managers who direct the work of these specialists on the cutting edge of new technology.

Basically, managers at all levels are involved with planning, budgeting, hiring, scheduling, supervising, evaluating performance, and many other tasks. The buck stops with managers who have authority over various operations. Those who successfully move up the ranks to the highest levels of information management must possess excellent decision-making and communication skills, have an understanding of business and the management style of the company, and have the ability to work well with people and to command their respect. IT managers oversee operations in various areas including user services and security. With greater emphasis being placed on management information systems and decision support systems, information managers are rising to top level positions in organizations.

There are numerous ways to organize work in information technology. In many companies today work is organized around projects that are conceived, staffed, completed, then shut down. These projects are then replaced with new ones requiring teams of individuals who have the expertise to complete the project working under a project manager. These projects often are prioritized by steering committees composed of senior management. Project managers have an opportunity to prove themselves while working on a specific project with a smaller group of specialists. The role of project manager is one of communication, conflict-resolution, and coaching. An effective manager can produce a positive result, gain the attention of top management, and learn from the high level of expertise exhibited by team members. In addition to projects, IT managers use "stretch assignments" to challenge and develop staff members, exposing them to the newest technologies or enabling them to work on a team with high-profile end users.[3] Developing and keeping talented workers is one of the most important responsibilities of IT managers.

Assisting information managers are both internal and external consultants, who keep up with the latest technological advances and integrate them into the organization to keep it competitive. You will learn more about a career in consulting in Chapter 10.

CURRENT TRENDS

There have been significant technological breakthroughs in recent years, as well as better use of existing technologies. Mobile computers are now so small that they can be carried around in pockets and provide message centers for e-mail. Network and wireless technologies have contributed to this global connection and placed cell phones in the hands of people of all ages. Web logs ("blogs") are online journals displaying information on public Internet sites where those with shared business or personal interests can meet in cyberspace. One estimate is that 11 percent of Internet users or roughly fifty million people read blogs regularly and about twelve thousand new web logs are created each day.[4] The Internet and World Wide Web have enabled a boom in electronic commerce (e-commerce). Computer-aided software engineering (CASE) and object-oriented programming (OOP) are now widely used tools for people without a high level of technical training. Information technology has had a dramatic effect on our careers and personal lives.

Mobile Computers

Today, the portability and power of mobile computers allow access to information to all types of users wherever they are. Personal digital assistants (PDAs), handheld computers, tablet PCs, and palmtop computers have become indispensable to many people. Work done on such devices can be easily transferred to a personal computer using cables, a docking station, or a wireless connection. Devices such as the iPAQ by Hewlett-Packard function both as PDAs and cell phones. New technology has had a large impact on where and when people are able to work.

Networks

Banks, airlines, retail stores, and other consumer industries use computer terminals for online transaction processing (OLTP). The electronic pathways that connect these terminals with a central or main computer are called a network. More widespread use of LANs and WANs has given users access to vast information sources. Electronic mail (e-mail) is used widely within organizations since it is easier and quicker to send a memo electronically than through the office mail. LANs and WANs provide a more efficient and productive way for company employees to perform their jobs, share information, and communicate throughout the organization without ever leaving their offices. Advances in communications technology provide LANs with the ability to transmit not only print and graphics, but also voice, video, and three-dimensional animated digital graphics as well. Today global area networks (GANs) or WANs that cross international borders are being used to conduct business, but with restrictions because of the laws of some countries.

The Internet

The Internet, the international network that allows communications via computer, continues to expand its offerings. Any type of information imaginable, including historic and scientific facts, politics, current affairs, sports and entertainment news, and job openings, is available on the Internet. State-of-the art software is available that allows users to bypass traditional telephones in making long-distance calls around the world. The use of Internet technology within a company, called intranet, enables employees to access confidential documents using a Web browser.

E-Commerce

Stimulated by the increased use of the Internet, e-commerce has created many new business opportunities and jobs. E-commerce is the way many choose to do business today. Online shoppers find a variety of products and better deals without ever leaving home. Investors monitor and transfer funds, conduct research, and buy and sell stock. Companies conduct business-to-business transactions, which makes purchasing easier. Small companies are able to market and sell their products at a low cost worldwide. Advertising on the Internet earns billions for companies such as Yahoo, MSN, Google, and AOL.

CASE and OOP

Computer-aided software engineering (CASE) tools are software packages used to generate code according to parameters specified by programmers. CASE tools can greatly reduce the time required by programmers to generate new programs and revise old ones. The greatest cost in information systems is in programming because of the time required to write and debug programs. For this reason, many companies began to use independent contractors to develop programs or packaged software. Off-the-shelf software does not always work well for highly specific applications and must still be modified to serve the company's purposes. The new CASE tools enable organizations to once again develop their own software without the tremendous cost and time commitments of the past. Object-oriented programming (OOP) allows programming code or modules to be used in a number of projects, speeding systems development.

JOB OPPORTUNITIES

When the technology bubble burst in 2001, many information and computer professionals found themselves unemployed. Many companies perceived as dot-com stars went out of business, dumping talented workers into the job market. Many had to settle for jobs outside information technology to pay the bills because supply exceeded demand. Today, technology start-ups are experiencing difficulty recruiting managers because of the uncertainty associated with the technology recovery.[5] IT jobs were cut throughout 2001 and 2002, but numbers began to grow in 2003 according to Forrester Research, Inc., and will continue to grow at an annual rate of 3 percent from 2004 to 2008.[6]

Job market figures for IT careers must be carefully considered because demand is not increasing uniformly in all areas: changing technology affects areas of specialization, and the trend toward outsourcing IT jobs to reduce costs continues. A 2004 survey of 450 global CEOs conducted by IBM revealed that 75 percent of respondents felt that poor education and the lack of qualified candidates will have the greatest effect on their businesses over the next three years.[7]

It is important for those who plan to pursue IT careers to keep up with what's happening in their field throughout college, and attempt to project what skills will be most in demand when they graduate. For example, a recent hiring forcast of 1,400 CIOs at companies with over 100 employees conducted by Robert Half Technology indicated that 80 percent need IT employees with Microsoft Windows (NT/2000/XP) administration skills and 51 percent need those with Cisco network administration and Check Point firewall administration skills.[8] However, specific skill requirements will vary over time. The annual workforce study conducted by Information Technology Association of America estimated that most new jobs will be in technical support, security in networking and databases, and programming, with the biggest increases being in the Northeast this year.[9]

According to the Bureau of Labor Statistics, computer systems analysts, database administrators, and computer scientists will be among the fastest growing occupations through 2012. Contributing factors include growth in computer system design and related services, demand for networking, expanding client/server environments, and the perception of these computer specialists as problem solvers. As more organizations adopt increasingly sophisticated technologies, the need increases for personnel who understand how to use them in business environments. The growing need for specialists who can develop and support the integration of Internet and intranet applications such as e-commerce and wireless Internet (WiFi) will continue.

Jobs for computer programmers are expected to have average growth through 2012 with most opportunities occurring in data-processing service firms, software companies, and computer consulting businesses. This growth will be slower than for other computer specialists because of the centralization of systems and applications, packaged software, advances in programming languages and tools, and the existence of sophisticated computer software that enables users to write more of their own programs. Demand will continue for programmers with skills in data communications, e-commerce and the Internet, object-oriented programming (OOP), client/server programming, WiFi applications, multimedia technology, and security. Graduates should have experience and knowledge in a variety of programming languages and tools such as C++, Java, and the latest languages used in networking, database management, and Internet applications. Certifications can help increase job prospects.

Faster-than-average growth through 2012 is projected for computer support specialists due to the expansion of computer system design and services, one of the fastest-growing industries in the economy. Despite the outsourcing of jobs overseas, newer and more complex technologies will create demand for professionals who can help manage and customize systems. Demand for systems administrators will increase much faster than average because of the emphasis on networks and security. The growing use of e-commerce and technology will increase the need for computer support specialists and administrators. However, the need for computer operators will continue to decline through 2012, due in part to automation by improved computer software. Fewer numbers of operators are required to monitor operations with this improved software. Operators must gain greater knowledge in the current software and systems to find opportunities in this field.

Much faster-than-average growth through 2012 is projected for computer and information systems managers. As employment grows for computer specialists because of advancing technology, so grows the need for managers. The best management jobs will go to applicants with management information systems degrees or MBAs with technology emphases. As companies grow more dependent on computer networks for communications and conducting business, managers will be required to keep systems running efficiently, maintain security, create and manage e-commerce opportunities, and adapt to an environment of changing technology to take advantage of the growing opportunities.

There will be a continued emphasis on research and development because new product development is a key growth factor. Every industry will seek out the specialists in networks and database technologies. Systems analysts and applications programmers with expertise in these areas as well as in expert systems, systems integration, and image processing will be very much in demand. Multimedia programmers also will find many opportunities. Network professionals including network managers, network systems integrators, and network consultants will be in high demand by banks, insurance companies, financial service companies, and others. There will also be a great need for client/server designers and computer security experts. And, currently, there is a shortage of computer science and information systems professors.

Opportunities for Women, Minorities, and the Disabled

Because computer programming is an activity that engages the mind rather than the body, it has been a very promising career for the physically disabled. Computer technology has allowed the disabled and homebound to work in a number of other fields as well, such as accounting, bookkeeping, and other areas that permit outside contact using computers. A number of IT companies have been identified in the publication *Careers and the Disabled* as progressive in recruiting, hiring, and promoting those with disabilities, including CACI International Inc., provider of IT and network solutions; EMC Corporation, leader in information storage systems, software, networks, and services; Freedom Scientific, manufacturer of technology-based products and services for the vision-impaired and learning disabled; Internet Security Systems, a leader in information protection solutions and security software; and Sun Microsystems, a leading provider of hardware, software, and services that empower the Internet.[10]

The computer industry has fewer age-related biases than most and allows older workers to continue working longer. This is especially important, given the projected worker shortages in the future. Recent research by the American Association of Retired Persons (AARP) shows that 80 percent of baby boomers intend to work part-time after retiring from full-time jobs and will desire flexible work arrangements and project-based assignments.[11] The IT field offers many such arrangements.

The generation that is growing up with computers is also growing wealthier with them. Young entrepreneurs ages twelve to twenty are turning their command of computer programming skills into sizable profits by writing software. Their imagination and enthusiasm has given them the edge over work-weary, time-constrained adults in the development of games. In past years, talented teens have earned royalties in six-digit figures for developing popular games. The demand for these games has increased every year, making electronic games one of the fastest-growing segments in the computer industry.

Women have been very successful in IT careers, many making it to the top IT position in the corporation. According to three female CIOs in 2004, Barbara Cooper of Toyota America, Anne M. Harten of SIRVA, and Jane Fishkin of the Brookings Institution, who are members of the CIO Executive Council (recently formed to study how to move forward in a complex technological environment), women will continue to advance in computer careers if they have the following abilities: to continually broaden their experiences by taking on new projects, to achieve a mix of technical and business assignments, to influence others, and to be aggressive learners.[12]

Working at Home

Apart from the millions of Americans who work full-time for companies and bring work home from time to time, there are three major categories of those who work at home: entrepreneurs who run small businesses from their homes, home-based employees who are electronically linked to the company office (telecommuters), and independent contractors. The personal computer, with its user-friendly operation, affordable prices, and variety of software, has been the driving force behind this trend. Networks have made vast databases of information available for home workers. Several economic factors contribute to the growth in home-based work. Individuals who have been laid off or retired early often start home-based businesses. Women or men with child-care responsibilities find working at home an alternative to expensive day care centers, and a way to spend more time with their children. Corporations can save money on office space and workplace maintenance using telecommuters and independent contractors.

Sources of information for home-based workers include:

American Home Business Association
4505 South Wasatch Boulevard, Suite 140
Salt Lake City, UT 84124
homebusiness.com

National Association for the Self-Employed
P.O. Box 612067
DFW Airport
Dallas, TX 75261-2067
nase.org

The U.S. Small Business Association offers many publications that can be useful to those considering a home-based business. Publications are available online at sba.gov/library.

Numerous books on home-based businesses are available in your local library, including *The Perfect Business* by Michael LeBoeuf.

Temporary Employment

In addition to working at home, temporary service agencies offer an alternative to full-time permanent positions at offices. Temporary service firms have expanded from offering low-skill workers for emergency fill-in positions to workers with personal computer skills who may be hired routinely to meet business fluctuations or to complete an entire project headed by a temporary manager. Automation skills make up roughly one-fourth of the business requested of temporary service firms. Demand has increased for PC programmers and consultants.

CAREER DEVELOPMENT AND COMPENSATION

Salaries vary considerably among information technology careers. A premium is placed on the kind of knowledge and experience in demand at a particular point in time. The annual salary survey conducted by *Computerworld* in 2004 showed that the highest percentage salary increases went to chief security officers at a 6 percent increase, followed by information security managers and data warehousing managers at 5 percent, then Web developers, information security specialists, and quality assurance specialists at 4 percent. On average, IT salaries increased 3 percent—lower than the 4 percent national average for all workers, as reported by the Bureau of Labor Statistics.[13] Supply and demand plays an important part in career mobility and salary. The more in demand the particular area of specialization, the more mobility an individual has and the higher salary he or she earns. Outsourcing of some IT jobs has substantially increased the supply of workers to fill the available jobs.

Advancement

Computer professionals are employed in a variety of positions in organizations. How these positions are organized or how many specialized positions exist depends on the philosophy and size of the organization, the technological orientation of the company, and the industry norms. More opportunities for employment and advancement rest with the larger organizations. Many have professional training facilities available to entry-level personnel. Some firms have dual-career ladders, which provide training in both management and technical skills. There are more available positions to which you can advance in a larger firm, and many firms promote from within. On the other hand, small firms often offer a wider variety of work experiences in one position, a greater possibility of entering a management position early in one's career, and continued involvement in technical areas even though a move into management is made. This last advantage is worth considering. Jumping too quickly into management and leaving the technical front could render one's knowledge obsolete in a short time because of continuous technological advancement. This poses the greatest dilemma for IS managers, since mobility is greatly limited for those who fail to keep abreast of the changes.

Salaries

A number of factors affect salaries of computer professionals. Salaries vary with company size, industry, and geography. In addition, they may be affected by installation size and level of technological sophistication. As an installation becomes more sophisticated with more online systems, greater use of telecommunications technology, and more complex operating systems, salaries tend to be higher. Usually the larger the information systems budget, the higher the salaries of the computer professionals. Also, the higher the company revenues, the higher the salaries. Two other factors affect the salary picture—industry and geography—but these vary somewhat with each position. Technology-oriented industries usually offer higher salaries to individuals in technical areas. And, geography affects salaries by region. For example, in 2004 IT workers in the South Atlantic region got better pay raises than in other parts of the country, but salaries for each position varied. Compensation studies in Canada show IT manager salaries in the United States are as much as 25 percent higher than for those holding similar positions in Canada, and IT salaries in general are 30 percent higher.[14]

According to the National Association of Colleges and Employers, the average yearly salary offer to bachelor's degree candidates by functional area for all types of employers in 2004 are as follows:

Computer Programming	$46,744 versus $44,547 in 2003
Network Administration	$38,254 versus $39,597 in 2003
Systems Analysis & Design	$47,050 versus $43,626 in 2003
Technical/Computer Support	$40,737 versus $35,638 in 2003
Other Computer Related	$41,106 versus $40,597 in 2003

The survey also showed that overall salaries by academic major for management information systems graduates averaged $41,579, a 2.5 percent increase over 2003 with most offers for systems analysis/design positions averaging $45,543; computer science graduates averaged $49,036, a 4.1 percent increase over 2003; and information sciences and systems graduates averaged $42,235, a 10.7 percent increase over 2003. These figures are useful for those considering entry-level positions.

Other Factors

Salary is not the only factor important to computer professionals. It may not be the most important factor in many cases. Such factors as the challenge of being on the cutting edge, the opportunity to use new technology, a humanistic managerial style, and promotion from within with no barriers all have great appeal. Training and career development are vital to information professionals if they are to stay in touch technically and advance. The 2004 *Computerworld* Salary Survey revealed that a number of IT workers would actually consider a pay cut if some of the following factors were involved: a better work/life balance, more job satisfaction, location, flexibility, or stock options. The top five perks desired by IT workers include additional time off, the option of telecommuting, comp time, flexible scheduling, and a company car.[15]

APTITUDES AND ATTRIBUTES NEEDED FOR SUCCESS

In response to the demand for skilled computer professionals, numerous educational programs are available in every state. Depending on an individual's career goal, the required experience may be gained in a high school, vocational school, data processing school, community college, college, or university. Educational requirements have been discussed as part of the specific job descriptions in this chapter, so this section will focus on where to obtain the needed education and training.

Education

Children today are exposed to computers in preschools as early as two years old. New electronic learning aids help students become very comfortable with the new technology. More elementary and secondary schools are offering computer courses—not only computer literacy courses, but programming and word processing at the high school level. The first programming course is often a good determinant of whether an individual has an aptitude and a strong enough interest to pursue an information processing career. Often performance in a programming course is a better indicator of aptitude and interest than a data processing aptitude test. The earlier the exposure to computers, the better. Since knowing how to use a computer is valuable in any career, it is beneficial for any student who can afford a computer to buy one. There are many manufacturer-sponsored discount programs, often accompanied by free introductory courses in computer use. Early exposure to computers is helpful, but success in educational programs in computer and information fields depends on strong basic skills in language and math.

Vocational and technical schools offer a variety of programs for those interested in data entry, operations, maintenance, service, electronics, programming, and so on. Usually, specialized data processing schools offer programs in these areas as well. At the community college level, one-year or two-year programs in data entry, programming, or computer operations are usually offered. Often these credits can be transferred to a college offering four-year degree programs. And sometimes, employers may pay for the additional education. The majority of the careers discussed in this chapter require college and university degrees and, in some cases, graduate study.

Information majors are usually able to find internships or cooperative education (co-op) positions. Traditionally, internships were three-month summer positions, while co-op programs were six months or longer. Internships usually were arranged by an interested faculty member and a company manager, and the intern was not always paid. Co-ops, on the other hand, were part of an ongoing college program for which students received both credits and pay. These distinctions aren't as clear any more, since companies now want interns for longer periods and pay frequently is offered. Students earn wages and gain valuable experience. Many organizations later hire their brightest interns and co-op students for full-time jobs. Apart from these programs, many students with computer skills find part-time jobs on their own that offer both pay and experience.

Training

Training is the most important ingredient in the success formula for computer professionals. It is the lack of good training and development opportunities that causes individuals to become dead-ended early in their careers. The first question that a job applicant should ask is, "What kind of training and development will the company provide if I accept this position?"

The recent emphasis on training is due in part to the failure of college curricula in computer and information sciences to educate graduates in the high-demand skill areas. Dramatic changes in technology and organizational structure require constant educational program evaluation and modification. Curriculum change occurs too slowly. Along with the companies specializing in training services, major computer vendors such as IBM and Compaq offer seminars and institutes for all technical levels. Training opportunities are also available through professional organizations.

Certification

The Institute for Certification of Computing Professionals (ICCP) is a nonprofit, international organization that tests and certifies professionals in the various fields of computer technology and science. The certification process is a coordinated industrywide effort to establish professional competence. Over fifty thousand professionals have earned the Certified Computing Professional (CCP) designation. To receive the CCP, one must pass the examinations and accept the ICCP codes of ethics, conduct, and good practice. Professionals must be recertified every three years. For specific information concerning certification, write to:

Association of the Institute for Certification of Computing Professionals
2350 East Devon Avenue, Suite 115
Des Plaines, IL 60018-4610
iccp.org

Vendors such as Microsoft, Cisco, Java, Linux, Novell, Oracle, and Unix offer certifications as well. Some require years of experience and training. Of course, holding various certifications can result in higher salaries. According to one survey, the highest-paying IT certifications adding a premium from 11 to 16 percent of base pay are the following: Oracle Certified Professional, Novell Master Certified Network Engineer, Microsoft Certified Solution Developer, Microsoft Certified Database Administrator, Global Information Assurance Certification Security Expert, Citrix Certified Enterprise Administrator, Cisco Certified Internetwork Expert, Certified Information Systems Auditor, Certified Information Systems Security Professional, and Project Management Professional.[16] There are costs in terms of time and money to obtain such certifications, but sometimes employers will pay for this. Leading individuals in information careers and professional associations are those who desire to establish professionalism in their field, as has been done in other professions such as law, medicine, and accounting. They are willing to spend time and energy to develop standards of performance and good practice. Some professional groups concerned with standardizing software development processes and certifying professionals are the Canadian Standards Association, the American National Standards Institute, and the Technical Committee on Software Engineering of the IEEE Computer Society. These groups have set widespread standards for the information industry. The Canadian Information Processing Society (CIPS) and the International Programmers Guild (IPG) certify qualified professionals who adhere to the set standards.

SOURCES OF ADDITIONAL INFORMATION

Numerous resources are available to those interested in computer careers including computer periodicals, journals, and professional organizations. Computer periodicals and journals are excellent sources of general information. A number of them, such as *Computerworld*, post job openings which can give someone considering a career in IT a good idea of what skills are in demand. Hundreds of periodicals are published today in the area of computer technology and its applications. To see this impressive list, one can find *Ulrich's International Periodicals Directory* in the reference section of the library. It is published annually by R. R. Bowker Company, New York and London.

A good many computer periodicals also can be found in public and university libraries and online. The following is a short list of well-known periodicals and the group of computer professionals for whom they are written.

Computer Security Journal—computer security professionals
Computerworld—information technology professionals
Data Communications—computer network professionals
Datamation—information technology professionals
Information Systems Management—managers and consultants
Information Week—information technology professionals
Journal of Systems and Software—systems analysts and programmers
Network Computing Magazine—network professionals
Telecommunications Reports—telecommunications specialists

A tremendous amount of current information is disseminated through professional organizations, which encourage students to participate by offering student memberships at greatly reduced rates. The following list of associations provides sources of information in computer fields for both prospective and established computer professionals over a wide range of interest areas:

American Society for Information Science and Technology
1320 Fenwick Lane, Suite 510
Silver Spring, MD 20910
asis.org

Association for Information and Image Management
1100 Wayne Avenue, Suite 1100
Silver Spring, MD 20910
aiim.org

Association for Information Systems
P.O. Box 2712
Atlanta, GA 30301-2712
aisnet.org

Association of Information Technology Professionals
401 North Michigan Avenue, Suite 2200
Chicago, IL 60611-4267
aitp.org

Association for Women in Computing
41 Sutter Street, Suite 1006
San Francisco, CA 94104
awc-hq.org

Independent Computer Consultants Association
11131 South Towne Square, Suite F
St. Louis, Missouri 63123
icca.org

Information Industry Association/SIIA
1090 Vermont Avenue NW, 6th Floor
Washington, DC 20005-4095
siia.net

Information Technology Association of America
1401 Wilson Boulevard, Suite 1100
Arlington, VA 22209
itaa.org

Society for Information Management
401 North Michigan Avenue
Chicago, IL 60611-4267
siamnet.org

World Organization of Webmasters
9580 Oak Avenue Parkway, Suite 7-177
Folsom, CA 95630
world-webmasters.org

Sources of Additional Information in Canada

Association of Professional Computer Consultants
PO Box 24261, Hazeldean RPO
Kanata, ON K2M 2C3
appconline.com

Canadian Association of Internet Providers
176 Bronson Avenue
Ottawa, ON K1R 6H4
caip.ca

Canadian Community of Computer Educators
15 Lone Oak Avenue
Brampton, ON L6S 5V4
ccce.on.ca

Electronic Commerce Council of Canada
885 Don Mills Road
Toronto, ON M3C 1V9
eccc.org

Information Resource Management Association of Canada
PO Box 5639, Station A
Toronto, ON M5W 1N8
irmac.ca

Information Technology Association of Canada
2800 Skymark Avenue, Suite 402
Mississauga, ON L4W 5A6
itac.ca

Information on computer careers also can be found on numerous Internet sites including dejanews.com and computerjobs.com. Certcities.com offers information on many certifications of interest to IT professionals. In Canada, monster.ca offers not only job opportunities but current technology issues as well, and features articles, events, and salary information.

CAREER DECISION-MAKING MODEL

Using the career decision-making model, find out how a career in computers or information processing rates with you. Figures 3.2a and 3.2b are forms with the factors included in the career decision-making model described in Chapter 1. Follow these directions in completing them.

1. Enter the position that interests you most on the line titled "Job."
2. Enter any additional factors used to personalize your model (from Chapter 1) in the blank spaces provided.
3. Enter the weights that you assigned to the factors (from Chapter 1) in column WT. (It would be wise to review the explanations of these factors in the description of the model in Chapter 1 before going on to step 4.)
4. Assign a value from 1 (lowest) to 10 (highest) to each factor, based on the information in this chapter and on your personal

Figure 3.2a

Career evaluation for computing

Career Evaluation

Job: _____

Internal factors

WT	×	V	=	S	Factors
					Academic aptitudes and achievement
					Occupational aptitudes and skills
					Social skills
					Communication skills
					Leadership abilities
					_____
					_____
					_____

Total: _____ Aptitudes and attributes

WT	×	V	=	S	Factors
					Amount of supervision
					Amount of pressure
					Amount of variety
					Amount of work with data
					Amount of work with people
					_____
					_____
					_____

Total: _____ Interests

WT	×	V	=	S	Factors
					Salary
					Status/prestige
					Advancement opportunity
					Growth on the job
					_____
					_____
					_____
					_____

Total: _____ Values

Figure 3.2b

Career evaluation for computing

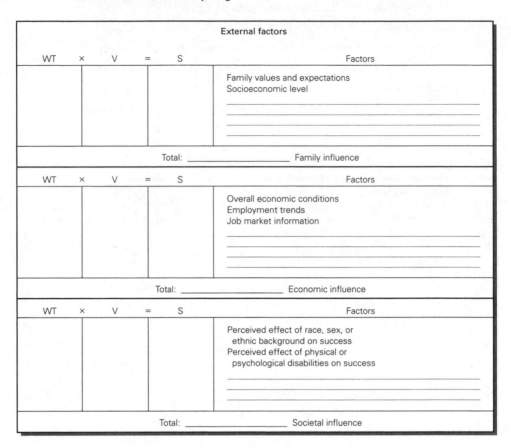

External factors				
WT	× V	= S		Factors
				Family values and expectations
				Socioeconomic level
				_____
				_____
				_____

Total: _____ Family influence

WT	× V	= S		Factors
				Overall economic conditions
				Employment trends
				Job market information
				_____
				_____
				_____

Total: _____ Economic influence

WT	× V	= S		Factors
				Perceived effect of race, sex, or
				ethnic background on success
				Perceived effect of physical or
				psychological disabilities on success
				_____
				_____

Total: _____ Societal influence

self-assessment, and enter the value in column V. If you feel that you have a certain aptitude or attribute needed for success in this career area, you should assign a fairly high value. If a certain interest, such as amount of variety, is desirable to you and you feel the area provides the variety you enjoy, again, assign this a fairly high value. If not, assign a low value. Use this technique to assign values to all factors in the model. If you cannot assign a value based on the information in the chapter for some of the factors in the model, either use other sources to acquire the information or leave the space beside the factor blank.

5. Multiply the weight times the value, and enter the score in column S.

6. Add the scores in column S for each group of factors, and enter the number in the space labeled "Total."

You will use this evaluation in Chapter 11, along with the evaluations of each career explored in this book.

WHAT DID YOU LEARN?

You learned a lot about careers in computers and information processing in this chapter. Now you should know what these professionals do on the job, where they are employed, what salaries they earn, what kind of job mobility they have, what prevalent trends in the computer industry might affect their jobs, what job opportunities will be in the future, how to prepare for a job in computer and information fields, and where to get additional information. You also completed a career evaluation for computer careers. Chapter 4, "Careers in Finance," will give you similar types of information about careers in the interesting areas of banking, securities, and credit.

NOTES

1. Anick Jesdanun, "At 35, Net's Work, Far from Finished," *Rocky Mountain News* (August 30, 2004), 1B, 6B.

2. Stephanie Overby, "The Future of Jobs and Innovation," *CIO* (December 15, 2003/January 1, 2004), 46.

3. Steve Ulfelder, "Stretch Your Talent," *Computerworld* (July 26, 2004), 33.

4. Lauren Gard, "The Business of Blogging," *BusinessWeek* (December 13, 2004), 119.

5. Daniel Nasaw, "Tech Start-Ups Have Trouble Filling Top Jobs," *Wall Street Journal* (August 31, 2004), B1.

6. Kathleen Melymuka, "U.S. IT Staffing Is Up," *Computerworld* (November 1, 2004), 43.

7. Julia King, "Grooming Next-Gen IT Pros," *Computerworld* (August 23, 2004), 32.

8. "Numbers Watch," *Computerworld* (September 13, 2004), 56.

9. Frank Hayes, "IT Jobs Chill," *Computerworld* (September 13, 2004), 66.

10. Barbara Woodworth, "Information Technology Careers Score," *Careers and the Disabled* (Spring 2003), 30.

11. Julia King, "Smart Companies Are Enticing Their Older, Wiser IT Workers to Remain on the Job a Little Bit Longer," *Computerworld* (September 6, 2004), 37.

12. "IT Careers: CIOs Share Career Tips for Women," *Computerworld* (June 7, 2004, advertising supplement), 59.

13. Stacy Collett, "*Computerworld* Salary Survey 2004," *Computerworld* (October 25, 2004), 49–50.

14. Patrick Thibodeau, "Canadian IT Execs Say U.S. Peers Are Overpaid," *Computerworld* (June 7, 2004), 6.

15. Stacy Collett, "*Computerworld* Salary Survey 2004," *Computerworld* (October 25, 2004), 52.

16. "Career Watch," *Computerworld* (May 24, 2004), 44.

C H A P T E R

4

CAREERS IN FINANCE

After reading this chapter, you will be able to:

- Describe the work of financial specialists in the areas of banking, consumer credit, corporate finance, securities, international finance, financial journalism, and investment banking
- Discuss trends and their impact on financial careers
- Diagram typical career paths in financial areas
- Discuss job opportunities in banking, consumer credit, corporate finance, and securities
- List the educational preparation and skills needed to enter financial careers
- Evaluate careers in finance according to your individualized career decision-making model

The road to a position as chief executive officer of a major corporation may well be through the field of financial management. Stephen Bollenbach, CEO of Hilton Hotels Corp., moved into his position from the post of chief financial officer at the Walt Disney Co. after having arranged Disney's $19-billion acquisition of Capital Cities/ABC. Finance, the art of administering and managing money, is crucial to the success of every business enterprise. Financial managers who serve as part of the top management team involved in strategic planning with contacts on Wall Street, in banking, and associated with various other sources of capital, play an integral role in this success.

The field of finance has undergone tremendous change since the deregulation of financial institutions in the early 1980s. A wave of acquisitions, mergers, and divestitures devised by financiers has had a strong impact on the identities of the best-known corporations in the United States. Complex changes both within and between the various financial institutions have occurred. The nature of banking has changed, as a variety of new financial products has been introduced into the marketplace. The line between commercial and investment banking has disintegrated, as both types of institutions now offer similar products including insurance, while insurance companies now sell securities. Huge financial conglomerates offering every type of financial service—banking, brokerage, real estate, and insurance—are the way of the future because of the acquisitions and mergers currently taking place. Changes in the field of finance have many career implications for those entering the ranks.

Financial products such as certificates of deposit (CDs), mutual funds, limited partnerships, bond funds, hedge funds, and variable annuities, as well as life and disability insurance, are especially attractive to middle- and upper-income-level professionals. From parents providing for their children's college expenses to the extremely wealthy, clients flock to estate and financial planners, who use sophisticated computer programs to analyze and evaluate financial alternatives. Baby boomers, forced to think about retirement, also seek the help of financial planners.

In this chapter you will look at a wide variety of careers in the field of finance, and it includes the following information:

- What financial specialists do
- Who employs them
- Salaries and career paths
- Latest trends
- Job opportunities
- Education and skills needed to pursue a career in finance
- Sources of additional information on financial careers

FINANCE

Careers in finance are found in virtually every type of industry. The field includes various categories and specific areas in which finance professionals may choose to work. Some broad areas are described in the following sections.

Banking

The past emphasis on operational efficiency has given way to selling the bank's services, which today are many and varied. Competition from other banks, brokerage firms, and insurance companies has posed new challenges for bankers. The securities industry now offers such products as cash management and ready asset accounts that compete directly with bank products. Banks in turn are able to underwrite commercial paper, municipal revenue bonds, and other securities.

Large banks hire new college graduates as bank trainees to work in specific areas, including corporate finance (leveraged buyouts and mergers and acquisitions), sales and trading, retail banking, credit cards, mortgages, branch management, fee-based services, operations and systems, and audit. Trainees are rotated through product and industry specialties within these areas. Managers determine the best permanent place for each individual after completing the training program. Many college graduates "move to the line" after training, which is bank jargon meaning to become bank officers.

Loan officer. Customers applying for loans provide information on applications with the help of loan officers. These officers then analyze and verify this information and make recommendations on whether credit should be extended to the applicant. Generally, a loan officer specializes in commercial, consumer, or mortgage loans.

A commercial loan officer is responsible for deciding whether the bank will finance business or corporate ventures. These ventures include acquisitions of other companies, new product development, plant expansion, farm production, equipment leasing, short-term loans, and community improvements. Big banks lend to corporations and governments all over the world, including the U.S. government. Commercial loan officers usually further specialize, for example, in local companies or major corporations. The commercial loan officer faces continuous change in the economy, a fast pace, and considerable risk taking. The size of loans that an officer is authorized to make determines his or her influence and promotability in the bank.

Working closely with the loan officer are the credit investigators and analysts who compile the financial data on loan applicants. It is this information that forms the basis of the loan officer's decision of whether or not to approve a loan. Often an employee might begin as a credit investigator or analyst, then move into a position as a commercial loan officer.

A consumer loan officer works with customers who apply for personal, automobile, or home equity loans. Collateral is often used to lower the interest rate and reduce the bank's risk on these loans. Explaining the terms of the loan and assisting applicants with the forms are part of the job. Loan officers also offer financial counseling for clients who are inexperienced in loan matters.

Mortgage loan officers specialize in home loans. Banks offer a variety of mortgage products that must be explained to applicants. These officers help clients qualify for mortgage loans by reviewing applications and locating government programs that might help individuals procure loans. Normally, mortgage loan officers may take on as many clients as they can handle. Their work may involve visiting clients at home and viewing their prospective purchases. They can also take application information by telephone, making it easier for customers to purchase homes in other states.

Consumer bank officer. Working with individual customers on a personal basis is very important because consumer transactions make up a large part of the banking business. The consumer bank officer sells as many of the bank's services as possible to the customer—asset, savings, and checking accounts; loans; certificates of deposit; travelers' checks; and safe deposit boxes, to name the major ones.

Trust administrator. The trust administrator has a constructive and humanly rewarding position in the bank. Responsible for helping individuals and corporations manage their financial assets, the trust administrator is knowledgeable in how to use trust techniques to minimize the negative effects of inflation and taxes. Trust administrators may work with a number of different types of financial instruments and trusts, including living trusts, which enable people to better manage their assets while they are alive; Individual Retirement Accounts (IRAs) to shelter income from taxes; various estate planning trusts to plan how assets will be distributed among heirs and/or charities after death while minimizing taxes; life insurance trusts; corporate pension and profit-sharing funds; trusts holding politicians' assets during their period of government service; and property management for income-producing real estate.

International banking officer. Most large- and medium-size banks have accounts located throughout the world. The international banking officer is responsible for maintaining these accounts and determining the foreign exchange position. International banking sometimes involves figuring at what price currency can be purchased or sold by reading financial reports and money market quotations. An international banking officer may also sell foreign exchange drafts and determine what proceeds of the sale will go to the bank. World banking is common in our increasingly global economy, and international banking expertise will be in high demand in the future.

Bank manager. There are several levels of managers in big banks. In addition to management positions in all of the areas previously discussed, there are management positions in operations. The operations department is the largest in the bank, primarily composed of clerical employees— tellers, bookkeepers, data entry and computer operators, customer service representatives, and others. A bank manager in the operations department supervises these employees and keeps the bank running smoothly on a day-to-day basis. Along with electronic banking, knowledge of computers, telecommunications, and other high-technology equipment is essential for managing various facets of operations.

Managerial positions such as branch bank manager are open to bank officers with promise. After an executive training program providing experience in a variety of banking activities, an employee may be assigned to a bank branch as manager. The branch manager usually works under pleasant, fairly autonomous conditions, reporting only to upper-level executives of the main bank. Responsibilities include supervision of branch employees, final decisions on loans, and ideas for new services, procedures, or security to improve the efficiency of the bank. To be effective, the branch manager must be aware of local business, as well as economic and social conditions.

Bank officers and managers may aspire to such executive levels as assistant vice president, vice president, or even bank president. Why not? Promotion from within and general conservatism in banks suggest that career service pays off.

Opportunities with the Federal Reserve System. The Federal Reserve System is the country's central bank. Twelve reserve banks located throughout the United States are overseen by a seven-member Board of Governors that is nominated by the president and confirmed by the senate. In addition to the positions found throughout the Federal Reserve banks and their branches, the Federal Reserve System (the Fed) offers a variety of career opportunities for professionals in several areas of business.

Financial analysts who work in the Division of Banking Supervision and Regulation review applications for bank formation or expansion, monitor state member banks and bank holding companies, develop supervisory policy and inspection practices, and design and implement corrective action regarding supervised institutions.

Analysts in the Division of Reserve Bank Operations and Payment Systems oversee Reserve Bank financial services; fiscal agency services; and Reserve Bank support functions, such as accounting, human resources, information technology, and internal audit. They review operations and monitor Reserve Bank expenditures, financial planning, and information technology initiatives.

The Division of Consumer and Community Affairs employs analysts and examiners to protect consumer rights and to implement laws to help communities meet their financial needs, such as the Truth in Lending, Equal Credit Opportunity, and Community Reinvestment Acts. Their responsibilities include training examiners and reviewing the results of examinations of banks that are subject to the Board's credit regulations.

The Fed also offers several opportunities for students. Research assistants are hired to work at the Board of Governors. Positions typically last about two years before individuals enter graduate programs or careers in economics, business, or related fields. Research assistants are hired in the divisions of economic research, consumer and community affairs, and reserve bank operations and payment systems. Applicants must submit college transcripts, three letters of recommendation, a résumé, and a cover letter.

Internships are available for undergraduate and graduate students who are interested in careers in finance, economics, and computer science. The divisions that regularly offer internships are Banking Supervision and Regulation, Economic Research, Information Technology, and Reserve Bank Operations and Payment Systems.

The Cooperative Education Program provides experience for undergraduate and graduate students in finance and accounting, economics, information systems, and the law. Candidates are selected based on scholastic achievement, recommendations, and completed course work in relevant areas of study. One-year assignments and summer-only positions are typically available. In some cases undergraduate students are invited back during their graduate studies.

Consumer Credit

The rapidly growing career area of consumer credit deserves special attention. Because it is the American way to buy on credit, now more than ever before, credit itself has become a field that is rich in job opportunities. Most forms of consumer credit fall into one of two types. The first type—non-installment credit—involves a bill that is paid in one payment. It includes single-payment cash loans, thirty-day charge accounts, and such service credit as medical, telephone, and utilities.

The second type of credit—installment credit—involves bills that are paid in two or more installments. Most job opportunities in consumer credit are related to installment cash credit and installment sales credit. Consumer finance companies extend installment cash credit in the form of cash to consumers to be spent according to their needs. Sales finance companies offer installment sales credit to enable consumers to "buy on time" whatever merchandise or services they need, such as an automobile or a membership in a health club. A special kind of credit, mortgage credit, is used to purchase a home. Consumer finance and sales finance companies compete with banks, savings and loan companies, department stores, and credit unions. Also, large corporations provide credit to consumers as an incentive to purchase their company's goods and services.

Positions in consumer credit are similar in most institutions. Consumer credit counselors interview customers to gather credit information, explain arrangements for making payments, and complete supporting papers. They work with customers to help them decide whether they can afford the credit they are seeking. The decision to extend credit is made by a credit officer. Employees in the collections department monitor payments. The credit manager may be in charge of a credit department of a store, of a credit union, of the loan department of a savings and loan, of the consumer loan department of a bank, or of a specialized area in a consumer finance or a sales finance company.

Consumer credit, then, is a specialized area of finance offering many opportunities for employment and advancement. As in all areas of finance, it is becoming more sophisticated and complex. For example, students interested in consumer credit today will enroll in such courses as computer applications to credit, financial decision making, managerial psychology, international credit and finance, and modern marketing strategy keyed to financial and manufacturing policy.

Three professional designations are sponsored by the National Association of Credit Management (NACM). The Credit Business Associate (CBA) is an academic designation indicating mastery over basic financial accounting, credit and collection principles, and introductory financial analysis. The Credit Business Fellow (CBF) designation indicates that a credit professional has both received the CBA and has completed additional course work. The highest professional designation, the Certified Credit Executive (CCE), indicates that the achiever is able to manage the credit function at an executive level.

Corporate Finance

Corporate financial managers direct investment activities, implement cash management strategies, and oversee the preparation of financial reports. Their jobs are vital to an organization's success.

Chief financial officer. The top position in corporate finance is the chief financial officer (CFO), usually titled vice president of finance. This executive is in line for the position of chief executive officer (CEO) of the company. In fact, the largest percentage of the CEOs of major corporations today have risen through the finance or accounting ranks. Responsibilities include participation with other key executives in developing company policy and implementation of financial policy within the organization.

Promotion to this position used to be from within the organization and based on length of service and dedication to the company. This is no longer always true. More companies are hiring professional managers with strong credentials and experience in finance who, rather than moving up in a single corporate hierarchy, have moved laterally from one position of financial management to another, even across industries.

Treasurer and controller. The key elements of effective financial management are those performed or supervised by the chief financial officer, the treasurer, and the controller. The treasurer has two major responsibilities—the acquisition of funds and the administration and protection of funds. The controller manages accounting and other financial information systems, conducts financial planning and performance evaluation, and complies with the requirements of the Internal Revenue Service and other regulatory agencies.

The controller and treasurer may have educational backgrounds in either accounting or finance. Entry-level employees work in either the controller's or treasurer's domain, depending on background and interest. A person with an M.B.A. might be hired as a financial analyst, a position established primarily to speed the entry into a line position in a large corporation. Responsibilities include the analysis of overall financial operations, policies, or problems of the company, and the preparation of reports making specific recommendations to management.

Pension fund manager. Another opportunity for employment within most large corporations is in the position of pension fund manager. The responsibilities of this position depend on how the fund is managed. The balanced fund manager treats the fund as a total portfolio that is actively managed by the corporation itself. The trend today, however, is away from this and toward dividing the fund among professional money managers, who are usually industry specialists working for money management firms. This reduces the extent of responsibility and status of the pension fund manager, who may find the job to be potentially a dead end. For example, a growing number of pension funds allocate assets to hedge funds. Hedge fund managers are highly specialized, working to hedge against downturns in the market.

Positions in financial public relations. An area in corporate finance in growing demand is financial public relations. Responsibilities associated with a position in financial public relations include financial publicity, stockholder correspondence, stockholder surveys, preparation of annual financial reports or quarterly earnings statements, and financial and educational advertising. Financial public relations personnel also may be involved in planning annual stockholders' meetings and working with security analysts.

Securities

The securities industry is involved in the buying and selling of stocks, bonds, government issues, shares in mutual funds, or other types of financial instruments. Thousands of security firms of all sizes work to serve the financial and investment needs of organizations and individuals. The four basic functional areas are sales, trading, underwriting, and research. Sales and trading personnel must meet state licensing requirements, which normally require passing an examination and sometimes posting a personal bond. The National Association of Securities Dealers (NASD) administers the General Securities Representative Examination, also called the Series 7 exam, which is required of beginners wishing to become registered sales representatives. Passing this exam qualifies one to purchase, sell, and solicit all securities products, including corporate and municipal stocks, investment company products, and municipal fund securities, among others. In addition to passing the exam, applicants must be employees of a registered firm for at least four months. Passing a second examination, the Uniform Securities Agents State Law Examination (Series 63), is required by most states as well. This exam qualifies candidates as securities agents.

Sales. Both individual investors and organizations with millions to invest work through securities sales representatives, also called registered representatives or stockbrokers. Over 600,000 are registered with the NASD. These securities sales representatives provide numerous services to their customers, including financial counseling; advice on the purchase or sale of a particular security; development of a financial portfolio including securities, life insurance, and other investments according to the needs of the individual customer; the latest stock and bond quotations on any security that interests the investor; information on activities and the financial positions of companies; and the sale of securities for a commission. Securities sales representatives may specialize by customer (small individual investors, large institutional investors, or pension fund managers) and by the type of security (stocks, corporate bonds, municipal bonds, federal government or agency bonds and notes, stock options, commodity futures, mutual funds, or annuities).

Financial planning. New investment opportunities and confusing tax laws make financial planning an area in great demand today. Financial planners, also called money managers or investment counselors, provide services to individuals or to organizations such as banks, corporations, brokerage houses, insurance companies, and savings and loan associations. Clients may be provided with a complete money management strategy—that is, a workable budget, adequate insurance, an investment program, a will, and an estate plan or trust. Financial planners may specialize by industry rather than provide a wide range of services. In this case, they would sell a client on investing a sizable portion of available investment funds in a particular industry. Financial planners may work for large or small financial services firms, banks, or insurance companies, or they may be self-employed.

The Certified Financial Planner credential, or CFP, is conferred by the Certified Financial Planner Board of Standards, Inc. This designation indicates that a planner has extensive training and competency. It requires relevant experience, the completion of certain education requirements, passing a comprehensive examination, and adherence to a code of ethics. Personal financial advisors may also obtain the Chartered Financial Consultant (ChFC) designation, issued by the American College in Bryn Mawr, Pennsylvania, which requires experience and the completion of an eight-course program of study. Both designations have a continuing education requirement.

Although a license is not required to work as a personal financial advisor, those advisors who sell stocks, bonds, mutual funds, insurance, or real estate may need licenses to perform these additional services. Also, if legal advice is provided, a license to practice law may be required. Financial advisors who do not provide these additional services often refer clients to those qualified to provide them.

Trading. Traders work for an investment firm as opposed to dealing directly with investors. Floor brokers spend their entire working day on the trading floor at the New York or American Stock Exchanges, filling their own investment firm's buy-and-sell orders or developing an inventory of particular securities. Traders may also trade securities with other firms. They specialize by type of security, as do security sales representatives.

Traders who deal in commodity futures spend their days at the Chicago Board of Trade, buying and selling such things as mortgages and soybeans for a given price at a future time, as much as eighteen months into the future. Traders must have a high level of expertise and be able to make quick judgments.

Technology has had an impact on stock trading in recent years, giving rise to alternative trading systems known as Electronic Communications Networks (ECNs), and making it possible for more brokers to trade securities in the after-hours market. ECNs provide investors with more flexibility and lower trading costs. In addition, they provide alternatives to established securities exchanges and to the Nasdaq stock market. According to the Securities and Exchange Commission (SEC), ECNs account for approximately 30 percent of the total share volume and 40 percent of the dollar volume traded in Nasdaq securities, as well as about 3 percent of total share and dollar volume in listed securities.[1]

At the Chicago Board of Trade (CBOT), volume in the financial future pits (floor trading) fell 11 percent in the first half of 2004, while volume in electronic trading rose 50 percent.[2] Ninety percent of U.S. Treasury futures volume is electronic, as is 60 percent of CBOT's overall volume. With ECNs, traders can work from anywhere, creating a wider marketplace.[3]

Research. Securities research and analysis is crucial to the sales, trading, and underwriting of securities. Securities analysts provide investment advice for sales reps, brokerage firms, institutions, agencies, and the investment community in general. Most analysts specialize by industry in summarizing statistical data, describing short-term and long-term trends in investment risks, and defining measurable economic influences on various investments.

Two specialty areas other than specialization by industry are money market analysis and technical analysis. Money market analysts closely watch the activities of the Federal Reserve System and collect information on the money supply both in the United States and abroad. Technical analysts work with computers to gain timely information for quick trading.

The growing number of companies offering financial services to consumers has created demand for securities researchers and analysts. Professionals working in this area employ methodologies based on strict criteria, and use various software applications and other resources to evaluate securities in order to present the most profitable options to customers.

The Chartered Financial Analyst (CFA) designation is conferred by the CFA Institute. Candidates must pass a rigorous three-part examination and be sponsored by accepted professionals. The CFA certification is becoming an industry standard, and preparation courses for the exam are becoming more widely available. The CFA Institute offers sample exam questions and preparation textbooks. Test preparation services such as Kaplan offer preparatory courses. Certain schools, such as the Freeman School of Tulane University and Queens College of the City University of New York, also offer programs designed to prepare students for the CFA exam.

Other opportunities in the securities industry. The National Association of Securities Dealers (NASD) is the nonprofit trade organization for the securities industry. Its members function on the floors of exchanges and participate in corporate and public finance departments. NASD retains a paid staff, with additional volunteers from the brokerage community, who enforce the rules of conduct for the securities industry by examining firms once every three years; by reviewing the backgrounds of the registered representatives; by observing, reporting, and analyzing excessive price changes in securities; and by taking disciplinary action when professional standards are not strictly adhered to. Paid employees of NASD include accountants, lawyers, investigators, and financial analysts.

The Securities and Exchange Commission (SEC) of the federal government also investigates the securities industry. Opportunities with the SEC range from investigator trainee through senior investigator. The senior investigator trains the entry-level worker, who performs such tasks as examining books and records of registered reps, traders, and investment counselors for possible violations of federal securities laws. The SEC monitors all stock offerings to the public to ensure that corporations and investment bankers are providing full and accurate information to potential investors.

International Finance

Opportunities for work in international finance occur in a number of areas. Through investment banking firms that specialize in international operations, a foreign enterprise or government can issue securities to be sold in the United States or can raise capital in other countries. Some American financial institutions are exclusively international in scope, raising capital only for U.S. firms with overseas operations, or are involved in financing the many multinational corporations. Many graduate programs offer specialization in international finance or international affairs and numerous banks, corporations, and government agencies provide training in this area. Corporations, banks, and other financial organizations pay premium salaries to M.B.A.s who have specialized in international finance.

Financial Journalism

Financial journalism is still another area in which researchers and analysts who are trained in finance, economics, and statistics may find jobs. Financial journalists write for such statistical publications as *Standard & Poor's* and *Dun & Bradstreet* or for news publications such as the *Wall Street Journal*, *Forbes*, or *BusinessWeek*. Television news channels such as CNN and MSNBC also employ financial journalists.

Financial journalism is perhaps the only area of financial careers that has a very tight job market. Because of limited opportunities, those who seek positions as financial journalists must plan a very aggressive job search and often accept a position with a very low entry salary. However, once a journalist is established, salary becomes comparable to those in the securities industry in general. A person seeking to enter this field should have not only a good background in finance and business, but also strong writing and communication skills. Computer experience is necessary.

Investment Banking

An industry that has grown in importance over years of mergers, acquisitions, and divestitures is investment banking. Financial officers use investment banking firms in a number of ways. Investment bankers assist companies in creating stock, bond, and other types of security offerings to be sold to the public. Essentially, the investment banker underwrites or finances the sale of a corporation's securities to the public by purchasing the securities and then selling them on the open market. In recent years, the role has expanded to include structuring joint ventures as well as providing assistance in lease financing, interest rate and currency hedging, and acquisition advising. Investment bankers also may create new financial instruments. Areas of specialization within investment banking include corporate finance, mergers and acquisitions, real estate, and sales and trading.

Because of the enormous amount of capital involved, this is one of the riskiest, most challenging, and exciting areas of finance. If the stock sells, handsome profits can be made. If it doesn't, the investment banker suffers the loss of prestige as well as money. Only top-level professionals are employed as investment bankers, and success is crucial to maintaining their status.

CURRENT TRENDS

The fields of finance and banking will see intense competition as banks, financial service firms, and insurance companies vie for the same customers. The continuing shift from national to global markets will lead to further changes in the financial field. Improved communications and deregulation of barriers provide access to these markets. Multinational corporations contend with shifting dollar values. Large brokerage firms are participating in foreign exchanges in London, Tokyo, and Sydney. The need now is to have financial analysts who are fluent in foreign languages and who understand foreign customs, cultures, and politics.

New Technologies

New technologies permit rapid exchanges of dollars and information. The growing use of electronic funds transfer and expanded network systems require financial officers with technical backgrounds. A study by the American Banking Association and Boston-based Dove Consulting indicated that in 2003 Americans made more electronic payments than payments by check or cash. Fewer banks return canceled checks to customers. Under the Check Clearing for the 21st Century Act, called Check 21, banks can send a digital image of a check to the payer's financial institution rather than sending the paper check, which means that checks can clear in a matter of hours as opposed to days.[4]

Diversified Products

Financial firms have diversified with new products, multiple types of accounts, and investment services. The financial needs of baby boomers will lead to an increase in investment. Saving for retirement has been made much easier by the government, which continues to offer a number of tax-favorable pension plans, such as the 401(k) and the Roth IRA. As the public and businesses become more sophisticated about investing, they are venturing into the options and futures markets. Brokers are needed to buy or sell these products, which are not traded online. Markets for investment are expanding with the increase in global trading of stocks and bonds. The New York Stock Exchange (NYSE) has extended its trading hours to accommodate trading in foreign stocks and to compete with foreign exchanges.

Bank mergers and acquisitions are likely to continue along with diversification of offerings. Easing restrictions on bank offerings will allow banks to offer mutual funds, annuities, securities underwriting, and numerous other fee-based areas that heretofore have been the domain of financial services.

Banks are reorganizing their services, identifying niche markets, and tapping into new technologies to implement more cost-effective operations. These changes are necessary to compete with financial services firms and insurance companies that now offer products once exclusively offered by banks. Technological advances have made it possible for consumers to trade directly, using websites designed specifically for the nonprofessional trader. Companies such as Ameritrade allow customers to trade directly on the Internet, either independently or with the assistance of a broker. These are only a few of the trends in the ever-changing finance and banking communities. Trends in job opportunities will be discussed in the next section.

JOB OPPORTUNITIES

Opportunities in banking are impacted by various factors. The following points should be considered by anyone contemplating a career in banking.

Demand

The consolidation that resulted from bank mergers contributed significantly to employment declines throughout much of the past decade. Merger activity is expected to continue, but at a slower pace, thus slowing overall employment growth. A renewed focus on bank branches as a vital means of serving customers will lead many banks to open more branch offices. However, because of widespread automation of many banking services, fewer employees will be hired to staff new branches than in the past.

Technology, deregulation, mergers, and population growth will continue to affect total employment growth and the mix of occupations in the banking industry. Overall declines in office and administrative support occupations will be offset by growth in professional, managerial, and sales occupations.

Advances in technology should continue to have the most significant effect on employment in the banking industry. Demand for computer specialists will grow as more banks make their services available electronically and eliminate much of the paperwork involved in many banking transactions.

Deregulation allows banks to offer a variety of financial and insurance products that they were once prohibited from selling. The need to develop, analyze, and sell these new services will add to the demand for securities and financial services sales representatives, financial analysts, and personal financial advisors.

However, banks will face continued competition in lending from non-banking establishments, such as consumer credit companies and mortgage brokers. Companies and individuals now are able to raise money by obtaining loans or credit through a variety of means other than bank loans; therefore, certain loan officers will be replaced by financial services sales representatives, who sell loans along with other bank services.

The number of households in the United States with more than $10 million in net worth has increased over 50 percent since 1998. This upward surge in assets has led to the niche field of wealth management for financial planners who specialize in very wealthy clients.[5] Demand for wealth managers to advise and manage the assets of wealthy clients is expected to grow. The financial needs of the aging baby-boom generation will also contribute to the demand for financial planners.

Employment in the securities industry is dependent on the state of Wall Street. Generally, however, the number of securities sales workers is expected to increase between 10 and 20 percent through 2012. Although increased Internet trading will reduce the need for brokers for many transactions, employment of brokers overall should increase due to the increase in investment. With the strong economy today, the retirement planning of the huge mass of baby boomers, and the growth in the number of institutional investors, the financial services field will require many new workers. Beginners must work hard to develop a client base but, once established, they are rewarded by even more clients and high earnings.

Competition for positions in corporate finance will be strong over the next several years. Employment is expected to increase by as much as 20 percent through 2012, but the number of individuals seeking jobs is likely to be higher than the number of available positions. Those candidates with the best education credentials as well as knowledge of international finance and changing federal and state laws will have the best opportunities for employment.

Equal Opportunities

Although most bank employees are women, the great majority are in low-level clerical and teller jobs. Banking is a conservative, tradition-bound field. While successful sex discrimination suits against big banks have helped the advancement of women into management positions, many female managers are locked into lower- and middle-management jobs because they lack the required educational background or end up in operations, personnel, or branch banks. Most top bank managers come up through the money-making side of banking—the trust department or commercial loans, which in the past were not open to women. Today banks have instituted affirmative action programs to give special commercial loan training to female officers.

The last few years have seen women on Wall Street fight for equality in the securities industry. Only 10.6 percent of the corporate officers on Wall Street are women, compared with 15.7 percent for other industries on average. Sexual discrimination suits have been filed against major corporations, and internal lobbying among female employees is common.[6] There is an evident cultural divide as well. A 2004 study by the research organization Catalyst indicates that 65 percent of the women on Wall Street believe they have to work harder than men for the same rewards, but only 13 percent of men agree. In addition, only 8 percent of men polled agree with the 51 percent of women who say they are paid less than men for doing similar work.[7]

Minorities are also underrepresented on Wall Street. Investment banker Harold Doley was the first African American to own a seat on the New York Stock Exchange. To date he remains the only one.[8] In 2002 Roel C. Campos became the first Hispanic to serve as a commissioner on the SEC. Commissioner Campos observes that while minorities have the education and talent to be successful, their opportunities are limited because they do not have enough predecessors in the industry to act as mentors. This points to the need for diversity to make the securities industry more accessible to the qualified individuals who would be an asset to the field.[9]

In a move toward greater diversity, members of racial and ethnic minorities are being actively recruited by the banking industry these days. For job referrals, contact:

Bank Administration Institute
1 North Franklin, Suite 1000
Chicago, IL 60606
bai.org

Financial Women International
1027 West Roselawn Avenue
Roseville, MN 55113
fwi.org

Education and training options that will help you achieve a successful career in finance are discussed in this section.

Education

The best way to tap into the many job opportunities in finance is to get a good education. Although people with a variety of college majors may enter the field of banking, it is probably apparent from what you have just learned about mobility that those who successfully move up in bank professions have a solid background in the field of finance. In banking, the best "in" is an educational background in banking, finance, economics, accounting, marketing, or general business. Banks hire people with bachelor's and master's degrees in equal numbers, but an M.B.A. will increase your starting salary by several thousand dollars. In consumer credit, college graduates with business majors in finance, accounting, economics, statistics, and business law have the best opportunities. An M.B.A. is good but not necessary. Many companies will finance graduate education.

Although a bachelor's degree in finance, accounting, math, statistics, or economics will gain an entry-level position in the sphere of the treasurer or controller of a corporation, M.B.A.s with technical undergraduate degrees may have an easier time finding employment. A background in computer science or information systems is particularly advantageous for undergraduates. Opportunities for advancement are good once you get into the mainstream of the corporate financial operation, but competition gets tougher the higher up you go, so it's wise to keep graduate school in mind. Credentials as well as experience will influence your career path in finance.

Educational requirements for entry into the securities industry are about the same as for corporate finance, which in part explains the mobility between them. However, personality characteristics may differ somewhat between Wall Street and corporate professionals. For example, consider the move from a position as a security analyst into a corporation. The brokerage world tolerates the headstrong, independent thinker very well, but in corporations, individuals are more accountable for their actions and must have the cooperative and diplomatic personality required to play the corporate game.

In careers in banking, consumer credit, and the securities industry, human relations and communication skills are very important. For example, in banking and consumer credit such things as tact, enthusiasm, a sincere desire to be of service to others, and an ability to be friendly but businesslike, are very important. In all finance-related fields, such characteristics as personal integrity, precision and accuracy, an ability to analyze facts and make intelligent decisions, an aptitude for math, an ability to work well under pressure, and an ability to handle heavy responsibility are all necessary for success.

Training

Getting the proper training is essential for success in all careers in finance. Your first job should be carefully selected, with consideration given to the kind of in-house training offered to you by the company, as well as any outside training programs that will be made available to you through your job. The banking industry, consumer credit, and securities industries offer institutes, workshops, and training programs for all levels of employees, sponsored by industry firms and associations. For example, the New York Institute of Finance is the primary source of training for those in the securities industry. In banking, courses are offered to member banks by the Bank Administration Institute and the American Bankers Association. Successful people in the field of finance stress the importance of training.

Certification in those professions where it is available demonstrates commitment to the field and is a big plus in the job market.

CAREER DEVELOPMENT AND COMPENSATION

Impressive success stories abound in the financial community, and advancement can be rapid for those with desirable attributes and educational background. For example, Howard Marks rose from trainee to vice president at Citibank in five years. He majored in accounting and finance at Wharton with master's work in accounting and marketing at the University of Chicago. While completing his master's degree, he became a summer trainee at Citibank where his specialty was trust banking. A sample bank organizational chart can be seen in Figure 4.1. Positions vary somewhat from bank to bank.

Some general career paths for careers in consumer credit, securities, and corporate finance are simply depicted in Figure 4.2. Considerable mobility exists between corporate America and the securities industry. If upward mobility in a corporation seems questionable, brokerage houses and investment firms offer salaries close to the treasurer range for well-qualified individuals. On the other hand, Wall Street has its own type of career crisis. Many financial planners peak early and feel a lack of opportunity for career

Figure 4.1

Bank positions and mobility

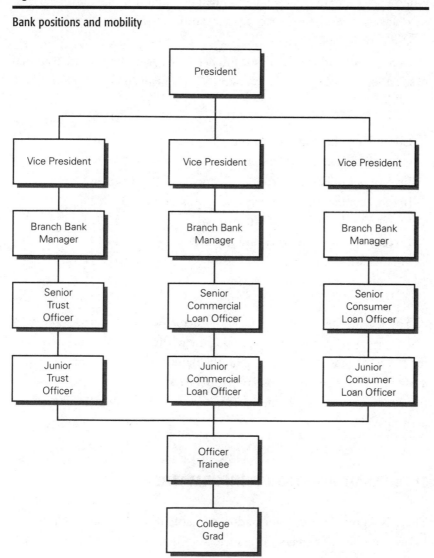

growth and higher salary. Fund managers have exceptionally stressful jobs in that there is pressure to maintain or surpass a fund's performance despite fluctuations in the stock market.

Remember that it is no longer unusual for corporations to recruit outside the corporation for key financial executives. An important consideration in any move to a corporation from Wall Street is whether or not entry into the mainstream or the company's long-range financial planning and acquisition programs is likely. Some analysts have taken a detour that has proved to be somewhat of a dead end into an investor relations position. It is harder to move into a key management position from investor relations. Also, investor relations salaries are substantially less than the salaries successful security analysts get.

Average beginning salaries for finance fields according to the National Association of Colleges and Employers (NACE) Fall 2004 Salary Survey are as follows:

Commercial banking (consumer)	$32,965
Commercial banking (lending)	$34,773
Investment banking (corporate finance)	$46,662
Investment banking (mergers and acquisitions)	$53,929
Investment banking (real estate)	$41,519
Investment banking (sales and trading)	$44,165
Financial/treasury analysis	$42,921
Portfolio management/brokerage	$37,841

The salary range for bank positions is dependent on the size of the bank and varies widely. Also, salaries within each individual bank may vary for the same job title depending on the bank officer's amount of lending authority or scope of responsibility. Salaries vary greatly in the securities industry, too, as personal effectiveness and sales ability determine earnings.

SOURCES OF ADDITIONAL INFORMATION

There is a great deal of information available to you if you would like to know more about careers in finance. Such periodicals as *Fortune, Busi-*

Figure 4.2

91
Careers in
Finance

Positions and mobility in consumer credit, securities, and corporate finance

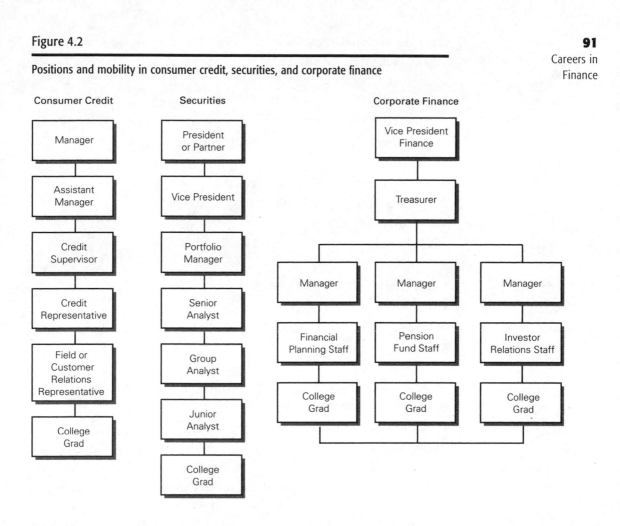

ness Week, *Forbes*, *American Banker*, *Canadian Banker*, *Trust and Estates*, *Money*, *Business Finance*, the *Journal of Portfolio Management*, and, of course, the *Wall Street Journal* are just a few of the periodicals from which you can learn a tremendous amount about the field of finance. Contact the sources below for more information.

For information on banking, contact:

American Bankers Association
1120 Connecticut Avenue, NW
Washington, DC 20036
aba.com

Bank Administration Institute
1 North Franklin, Suite 1000
Chicago, IL 60606
bai.org

For information on consumer credit, contact:

American Financial Services Association
919 18th Street, NW, Suite 300
Washington, DC 20006
afsaonline.org

Credit Union National Association
P.O. Box 431
Madison, WI 53701
cuna.org

National Association of Credit Management
8840 Columbia 100 Parkway
Columbia, MD 21045
nacm.org

For information on the securities industry, contact:

American Stock Exchange
86 Trinity Place
New York, NY 10006
amex.com

CFA Institute (Chartered Financial Analyst)
560 Ray C. Hunt Dr.
Charlottesville, VA 22903
cfainstitute.org

Financial Planning Association
1615 L Street NW, Suite 650
Washington, DC 20036
fpanet.org

International Association of Registered Financial Planners
The Financial Planning Building
P.O. Box 42506
Middletown, OH 45042
iarfp.org

Investment Company Institute
1401 H Street NW
Washington, DC 20005
ici.org

National Association of Personal Financial Advisors
3250 North Arlington Heights Road, Suite 109
Arlington Heights, IL 60004
napfa.org

National Association of Securities Dealers
One Liberty Plaza
New York, NY 10006
nasd.com

New York Stock Exchange
11 Wall Street
New York, NY 10005
nyse.com

Securities Industry Association
120 Broadway, 35th Floor
New York, NY 10271
sia.com

Be sure to check your college career information center. You will find many additional sources of information there.

Sources of Additional Information in Canada

Canadian Association of Financial Planners
439 University Avenue, Suite 1710
Toronto, ON M5G 1Y8
cafp.org

Canadian Bankers Association
Commerce Court West, 30th Floor
P.O. Box 348
199 Bay Street
Toronto, ON M5L 1G2
cba.ca

Canadian Institute of Financial Planning
151 Yonge Street, 5th Floor
Toronto, ON M5C 2W7
cifp.ca

Canadian Investor Relations Institute
1470 Hurontario Street, Suite 201
Mississauga, ON L5G 3H4
ciri.org

Canadian Securities Institute
121 King Street, #1550
P.O. Box 113
Toronto, ON M5H 3T9
csi.ca

Financial Executives International Canada
141 Adelaide Street West, #1701
Toronto, ON M5H 3L5
feicanada.org

Institute of Canadian Bankers
Tour Scotia
1002 rue Sherbrooke ouest, #1000
Montreal, QC H3A 3M5
icb.org

Treasury Management Association of Canada
8 King Street East, #1010
Toronto, ON M5C 1B5
tmac.ca

Women in Capital Markets
595 Bay Street, #300
Toronto, ON M5G 2C2
wcm.ca

95
Careers in
Finance

CAREER DECISION-MAKING MODEL

At this point you should seriously consider the various careers in finance as career possibilities for you. The forms in Figures 4.3a and 4.3b show the factors included in the career decision-making model described in Chapter 1. Using the career decision-making model, complete the following forms according to the directions below. When entering the position that interests you most, try to focus on the one area in which you would most likely want to work from among banking, consumer credit, corporate finance, and securities.

1. Enter the position that interests you most on the line titled "Job."
2. Enter any additional factors used to personalize your model (from Chapter 1) in the blank spaces provided.
3. Enter the weights that you assigned to the factors (from Chapter 1) in column WT. (It would be wise to review the explanations of these factors in the description of the model in Chapter 1 before going on to step 4.)
4. Assign a value from 1 (lowest) to 10 (highest) to each factor, based on the information in this chapter and on your personal self-assessment and enter the value in column V. If you feel that you have a certain aptitude or attribute needed for success in this career area, you should assign a fairly high value. If a certain interest, such as amount of variety, is desirable to you and you feel the area provides the variety you enjoy, again, assign a fairly high value. If not, assign a low value. Use this technique to assign values to all factors in the model. If you cannot assign a value based on the information in the chapter for some of the factors in the model, either use other sources to acquire the information or leave the space beside the factor blank.

5. Multiply the weight times the value and enter the score in column S.
6. Add the scores in column S for each group of factors and enter the number in the space labeled "Total."

You will use this evaluation in Chapter 11, along with the evaluations of each career explored in this book.

Figure 4.3a

Career evaluation for finance

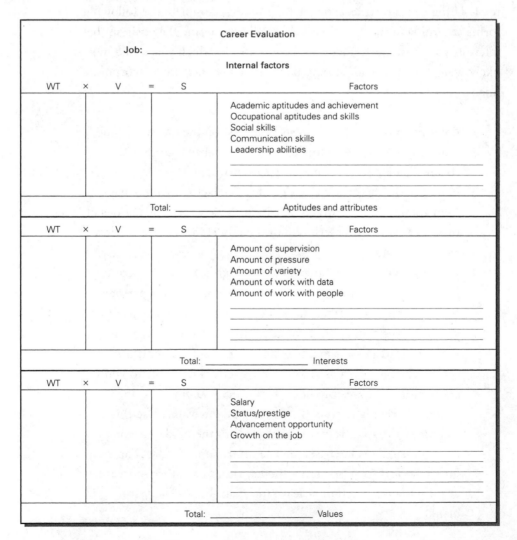

Figure 4.3b

97

Careers in
Finance

Career evaluation for finance

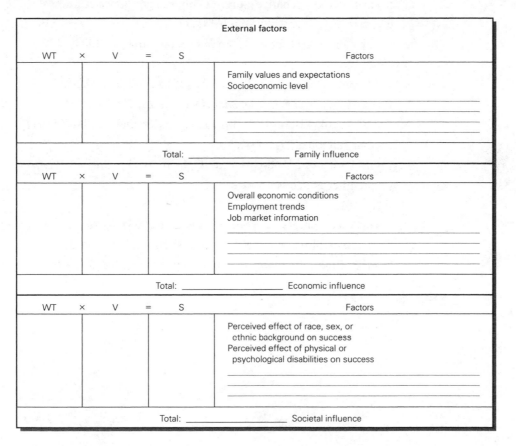

WHAT DID YOU LEARN?

You have just learned a great deal about careers in finance. Four areas of possible employment—banking, consumer credit, corporate finance, and securities—were described. Now you know what kind of work finance professionals do, what kinds of salaries they earn, the career paths that many of them follow, what the job outlook is, what trends are affecting it, how to prepare yourself for a career in finance, and where to find additional information. You then completed an evaluation for a career in finance.

In Chapter 5, "Careers in Insurance and Real Estate," you will add to your knowledge of careers in business by exploring two fields that are among the highest in income potential.

NOTES

1. Securities and Exchange Commission, sec.gov/news/studies/ecnafter.htm, (accessed March 14, 2005).

2. Emily Lambert, "Last Call," *Forbes* (September 20, 2004), 122.

3. Ibid., 126.

4. Robin Sidel, "Banks, Customers Adapt to Paperless Check Processing," *Wall Street Journal* (October 28, 2004), B1.

5. Robert Frank, "Is Your Wealth Manager Certifiable?" *Wall Street Journal* (October 27, 2004), D4.

6. Emily Thornton, "Fed Up—And Fighting Back," *BusinessWeek* (September 20, 2004), 100.

7. Ibid., 101.

8. "Why Race Matters," *Fortune* (December 2003), fortune.com/fortune/smallbusiness/articles, (accessed March 14, 2005).

9. "Money Rules," *Hispanic Business* (September 2004), 35–36.

C H A P T E R

5

CAREERS IN INSURANCE AND REAL ESTATE

After reading this chapter, you will be able to:

- Describe the work of insurance and real estate professionals
- Discuss trends in the insurance and real estate industries and their impact on careers in general
- Diagram career paths for professionals in insurance and real estate fields
- Discuss job opportunities in insurance and real estate
- List the educational preparation and skills needed to enter these fields
- Evaluate careers in insurance and real estate according to your individualized career decision-making model

A major milestone was reached in March 2004, when the membership of the National Association of Realtors reached one million, making it the largest trade association in the United States. Of the 290 million people in this country, 68.6 percent own homes.[1]

The last few years have seen a rise in the popularity of real estate. This is evidenced by the number of television shows with real estate themes that have been introduced lately. *The Apprentice* and its colorful host Donald Trump captivated the public along with a number of shows offered by Home & Garden Television (HGTV). Available in over eighty million homes, programs that deal with buying, selling, and renovating homes include *House Hunters*, *Building Character*, *Curb Appeal*, *Dream Builders*, and *This Old House Classics*, reruns of the innovative show *This Old House* that aired on Public Broadcasting Station (PBS).[2] Still more real estate shows are being aired on a number of other network and cable stations.

Low interest rates have enabled many first-time homeowners to enter the market. And a fluctuating stock market has caused investors to focus on real estate investments. Real estate purchases must be insured when financed, thus creating business for the insurance industry, which offers more products and services than ever before.

Real estate and insurance are two fields that offer incredible opportunities for outstanding salespeople. Both of these industries have changed considerably in recent years. Today, an individual can buy property, insure it, and even arrange the financing all in the same place. The same changes affecting financial institutions also have influenced the insurance and real estate industries. Expanding information technology and an increased interest in real estate investments and financial products offered by insurance companies have expanded opportunities in these two career fields.

Historically, insurance and real estate have shared common characteristics as career options. Many people regard sales careers in these areas as offering freedom and unlimited earning potential. However, both fields offer a variety of options beyond sales. Real estate also offers careers in real estate appraisal, property management, land development, urban planning, real estate securities and syndication, counseling, research, mortgage financing, and title examination.

In addition to the traditional insurance careers in sales, investments, underwriting, and claims adjusting, insurers are becoming involved in a growing number of activities including rehabilitation of injured persons, product safety, industrial hygiene, research, training of commercial drivers, accident prevention, and consumer education.

Education and training requirements for insurance and real estate careers have not been as clear-cut as in other areas of business. Many people entering these fields hold college degrees with majors in insurance and real estate; however, others with a variety of backgrounds study and successfully complete exams for licenses. While on-the-job training positions still exist, recent changes require employees to have more technical knowledge as well as financial backgrounds. To meet the demands, most two- and four-year colleges offer programs in these fields. Careers in both insurance and real estate offer opportunities for autonomy, flexible work schedules, geographic mobility, excellent training, and high income potential.

Careers in insurance and real estate are worthy of consideration because of the variety of positions available. This chapter will give you a comprehensive look at both fields, and it includes the following information:

- The work performed by insurance and real estate professionals
- Current trends
- Job opportunities
- Career paths and compensation
- What is needed for success in a career in insurance or real estate
- Sources of additional information on insurance and real estate opportunities

INSURANCE

The trillion-dollar insurance industry has been redefined through major changes, including deregulation as well as mergers and acquisitions into full-service financial services companies. These companies hire millions of people and offer, in addition to traditional products, investment management, annuities, mutual funds, securities, health care management, employee benefits and administration, real estate brokerage, and even consumer banking. The insurance industry hires those with the financial backgrounds discussed in Chapter 4 to fill some positions. This section will emphasize careers for insurance majors and others who focus on the traditional areas such as life insurance, health insurance, and property and casualty insurance.

Actuaries

Insurance premiums are calculated by the amount of risk that a particular policy holder represents. Actuaries estimate probabilities of occurrences and costs associated with these occurrences by collecting and analyzing data. Combining strong mathematical abilities with knowledge of business, finance, and statistics, they design insurance policies, pension plans, and financial arrangements that minimize risk and maximize returns to the company. Actuaries play an integral part in determining company policies and practices, assure that the financial reserves of the company are sufficient to pay all claims and expenses, and work with investment analysts to calculate the probabilities of loss. Many actuaries specialize in property-casualty or life-health insurance.

Basically, property-casualty actuaries are responsible for analyzing the frequency of catastrophes or chance occurrences such as fires, thefts, and accidents; tabulating the damage done or the injuries caused; calculating the mathematical probability or risk associated with recurrences; and then recommending the price or premium that should be charged for insurance against these risks. They construct probability tables that show the likelihood and amounts of claims. For example, they consider factors such as age, gender, driving history, and type of vehicle in determining the cost of automobile insurance policies, and construction materials, location, and market value of real estate in home insurance policies. Actuaries must establish premiums for these policies that are consistent with competing companies but are sufficient to cover claims in the event of loss.

In life and health insurance policies, actuaries analyze mortality factors such as age, family health history, environmental hazards, and job hazards in order to establish insurance premiums. These premiums must be competitive with those of other insurance companies. Long-term health care is becoming more necessary as the population ages, and actuaries are involved in developing the policies to extend health care for the elderly. Annuity policies are part of the investment plan of many individuals.

Other actuaries work in financial services industries and play a role in designing pension plans, managing credit, pricing corporate securities, and developing other investment tools. Actuaries may be employed by companies to evaluate pension plans, develop plans to enter new markets, and help reduce insurance costs by reducing risk levels within the company. Some become consulting actuaries and work on a contractual basis with clients, sometimes testifying in court cases regarding legislation, claims, and other areas requiring their expertise.

Agents and Brokers

Once the premiums for policies are established by the actuary, it is up to the agents and brokers to sell the policies. Insurance sales is basically a three-step process involving prospecting, interviewing, and providing service. Prospecting includes identifying and soliciting potential buyers of insurance. The successful agent will make roughly forty calls per week and will conduct ten selling interviews to make two sales. Interviews determine the financial needs of individual clients or groups. Services provided by agents and brokers include billing clients, issuing policies, keeping detailed records, responding to client questions and assisting in settling claims. This is a crucial aspect of the job because good service leads to more clients.

Agents can work for an insurance company or operate as brokers, selling insurance for one company or for a number of companies. Brokers represent their clients and place insurance policies with the company that offers the best rate and coverage. Often an agent or broker will select target groups such as clients in a certain geographical area or profession, students, or other groups and sell them specific types of insurance. Much life insurance is sold to groups, so group specialists are visible throughout the insurance industry. The group specialist works with business firms, unions, or associations rather than with individual policyholders.

Insurance sales agents or producers sell one or more of a variety of types of insurance. Property and casualty insurance protects individuals from financial loss due to fire, theft, storms, accidents, and other events that cause damage. Residential policies are designed for homeowners. Commercial policies are for businesses and include items such as workers' compensation, product liability, and medical malpractice. Life insurance agents sell policies that provide for beneficiaries in the event of the death of the policyholder. Various life insurance policies have been designed to meet a variety of needs. Whole life, term, lump sum, second-to-die, and other types of insurance offer numerous products for agents to sell. Health insurance policies provide coverage for medical care, long-term health care, and loss of income due to illness or injury. Today, many insurance sales agents offer financial planning services such as estate planning, retirement planning, and pension planning. Some are licensed to sell securities such as stocks, bonds, mutual funds, and variable annuities.

Field Representatives

Field representatives are the liaisons between the insurance companies and the insurance agents and brokers who sell the companies' policies. These company reps do not sell insurance themselves but rather keep agents and brokers informed of the company's policies and practices, and assist them in making sales and servicing customers. The field representative must be poised, diplomatic, and willing to travel, as the position often requires speeches before civic organizations and involvement in public service activities such as fire prevention, traffic control, and safety surveys.

Insurance Underwriters

After a policy has been described and offered for sale by the agent or broker, an application for insurance is made by the client. Because insurance companies assume billions of dollars in risk, underwriters are employed to determine whether the candidate is a good or bad risk. This is done by analyzing information in insurance applications, in reports of safety engineers, and in actuarial studies. The underwriter in most cases has the final word on whether a policy will be issued. The ability to make personal judgments and the willingness to accept considerable responsibility are essentials of the job. If the underwriter rejects too many risks, the company will lose business to competitors. However, if the underwriter accepts a large number of poor risks, the company may have to pay too many claims.

Underwriters sometimes specialize by the type of risk involved, such as fire, auto, or workers' compensation. Some may handle only business insurance. Usually underwriters work with "packages" that include various types of risks insured under a single policy. No matter how effective an underwriter is in determining which policies should be issued, accidents and catastrophes happen and claims are filed.

Claims Adjusters and Examiners

Both claims examiners and claims adjusters are responsible for determining if a loss is covered by the terms of the insurance policy, if the policy is still in force, if the claim is valid, the value of the loss, and the company's obligation. The claims adjuster uses reports, testimony of witnesses, and physical evidence when investigating a claim. The work involves settling valid claims with speed and efficiency, while guarding against inflated and false claims. Adjusters may be called to the site of an accident, fire, or burglary at any hour during the day or night. Some adjusters handle several types of claims, while others specialize in one area such as auto accident claims or claims by business firms.

Claims examiners work in the home office settling small claims and reviewing the work of claims adjusters before final settlement with the claimant is made. The work of the claims examiner involves much correspondence, maintenance of records, and preparation of reports to be submitted to the data processing department. Since examiners may be called upon to testify in court on contested claims, they must be thoroughly knowledgeable about their company's settlement procedures and basic policy provisions. Many claims examiners specialize in life, medical, or disability claims.

Somewhat related to these private industry positions is the civil service position of social security claims adjudicator, who explains to people the government benefits to which they are entitled and how to receive them.

Risk Managers

The risk manager is a loss prevention and insurance specialist usually employed by corporations or firms outside the insurance industry. The risk manager is concerned with such risks as property damage, legal liability for faulty products or injuries, fraud, and business interruption. Major responsibilities include estimating the cost of losses in light of these risks, determining the amount of insurance required to cover these losses, and choosing from which company or companies insurance is to be purchased.

The function of the risk manager is highly sophisticated and requires a thorough knowledge of all types of insurance as well as a broad business background with emphasis in finance, accounting, and loss control. Risk managers may be involved in employee benefit programs, pension plans, and workers' compensation programs, thus working closely with the human resources department. In multinational companies, the risk manager must take on the additional responsibility of educating people overseas in loss prevention and must study how workers of different nationalities might react under conditions of potential loss.

Because of the company-wide influence of the risk manager and the required broad educational background, the individual holding this position is an important member of the management team and is involved in major decisions on many complex issues. Most risk managers report directly to a key company executive and may, in fact, be in line for an executive position.

REAL ESTATE

Real estate has some unique advantages over most careers in business. It is one of the few areas in which you can start your own business with a small financial investment and make a great deal of money, or affiliate with someone else without entirely losing your independence and still make a great deal of money. Real estate offers the kind of flexibility that enables individuals to control their own lifestyles—you can work part-time or round-the-clock, you can enter a career in real estate at any age, you can earn enough money to retire early or continue to work until well past age sixty-five, and you can live in any geographical area of the country and change areas without total career disruption.

This section describes the many specialty areas in which people may be employed. Real estate agents include both brokers and salespersons. Brokers, often called realtors, are generally in business for themselves, although a few work for large firms where they specialize in managing or selling a particular type of property. Brokers who manage their own firms may be involved in selling, renting, managing, and appraising properties. They must be aware of economic trends, business trends, zoning and other laws, and types of loans and financing.

Brokers employ salespersons, also called agents, who sell and rent real estate for and to clients. Selling real estate involves securing property listings, writing descriptive ads, making preliminary appraisals to determine fair market value and establish price, writing purchase agreements, obtaining seller acceptances, helping buyers arrange financing, and working with title companies or escrow agencies until transactions are completed. In smaller agencies, the broker is involved in selling. In larger agencies, the broker functions entirely in a management position, hiring and training salespersons and managing office activities.

Residential Brokerage and Sales

The largest single area of real estate activity is residential brokerage; that is, helping people buy and sell homes. In smaller communities, most of the homes sold are single-family houses. In urban areas, many clients purchase duplexes, triplexes, and other multifamily dwellings as well as cooperative apartments and condominiums. To succeed as a residential broker or salesperson, one must have a broad knowledge of neighborhoods and their stores, schools, and public transportation; tax and utility rates; building and zoning restrictions; and street and highway plans. An ability to work well with people in gaining an understanding of their tastes, lifestyles, and what they are able to afford is essential.

Commercial Brokerage and Sales

A commercial broker specializes in income-producing properties, such as apartments, office buildings, retail stores, and warehouses. Since commercial property transactions usually involve large sums of money, a commercial broker often may assist the buyer in arranging financing. Successful commercial brokers can understand and explain why properties are good investments in terms of location, tax regulations, and advantageous purchasing arrangements.

Opportunities are big for the industrial broker, who specializes in developing, selling, or leasing properties for industry or manufacturing. Industrial clients will want such information from brokers as availability of transportation, raw materials, water, power, and labor supplies; local building, zoning, and tax laws; schools, housing, and recreational activities, and cultural facilities for their employees. The broker, therefore, must have in-depth knowledge of the community.

The farm broker needs some agricultural training to estimate the income potential of farmland for prospective buyers. A working knowledge of local soils and the crops best suited for them, planting seasons, water supply, draining, erosion, farm market centers, transportation facilities, current farm production costs, and the latest developments in agricultural technology is essential. Farm brokers also may be involved in farm management for absentee owners. The sale of rural land for urban expansion is another aspect of the farm and land broker's job.

Real Estate Appraisal

Although some appraising knowledge is needed for any real estate work, the real pros are the real estate appraisers. Appraisers are employed not only by large real estate firms, but also by insurance companies, banks and other lending agencies, government agencies, and tax assessors. Many are self-employed. The work of the appraiser involves gathering and evaluating all facts affecting the value of a property and rendering an opinion of that value—assessed value for tax purposes, investment value, rental value, insured value, and so on. Appraisers usually have backgrounds in real estate plus mathematics, finance, accounting, and economics. These professionals are well respected in the real estate field.

There is a demand in the marketplace for nonappraisal analyst services to include such areas as site selection studies, competitive property studies, demand studies for space, real estate market studies, environmental impact studies, and land use analyses. Reports are prepared by real estate analysts who may also, but not necessarily, be appraisers. Analysts are employed by firms in design and consulting service industries such as architecture, engineering, planning, legal, and real estate counseling firms. Entry into this field requires a strong background in business, specifically market research, since a major part of the analyst's job is the application of quantitative market research techniques to real estate.

Property Management

The property manager is often the key to a successful or unsuccessful investment property. Responsible for supervising every aspect of the property's operation, the property manager is involved in leasing the property, collecting rent, maintaining tenant relations, building maintenance and repair, record keeping, and advertising. Property managers usually work for real estate firms but also may find employment in the real estate departments of banks and trust companies or corporations. Property managers may be self-employed and manage properties for numerous owners. Large apartment complexes hire resident property managers who live on-site. Both commercial and residential properties offer opportunities for professional property managers.

Land Development and Urban Planning

Land development is turning raw land into marketable subdivisions, shopping centers, industrial parks, and other residential, commercial, or industrial enterprises. A land developer selects sites, analyzes costs, secures financing, contracts for buildings, supervises construction, and promotes and sells the development to prospective investors. To succeed in this profitable, challenging, and high-risk area requires business experience and some background in engineering, construction, real estate, and finance.

The urban planner is responsible for proposing productive, economical ways of using land and water resources for urban development and renewal. Working with local governments and civic groups to anticipate a city's future growth is a critical part of this planning. A degree in urban planning is required for this job.

Real Estate Securities and Syndication

A new area increasing in importance is real estate securities and syndication. The real estate securities and syndication specialist develops and offers limited partnerships in real estate investments to individuals with limited funds to invest. This service is valuable both to the real estate industry and the individual investor. It generates capital for expanding the industry and allows individuals to invest in large properties without becoming involved in the management of them or being exposed to unlimited liability for the investment.

Real Estate Research

Trained real estate researchers and economists are not plentiful because of the extensive technical training in business and economics required to do the job. Research is done in two major areas: physical—how to improve buildings and structures—and economic—compiling such data as demand for new homes, changes in financing and interest rates, and the effects of urban growth, for future planning. Precise information on land use, urban environmental patterns, and market trends is much needed by business and government, and many government opportunities exist in real estate research today.

Mortgage Financing

The work of the mortgage financing specialist is to bring together borrowers and lenders. Finding sources of investment money such as insurance companies, banks, and other financial institutions for borrowers is half of the service that mortgage financing specialists provide. The other half is finding good investment properties for lenders and providing them with detailed information about the properties.

A mortgage broker's only job is to place the loan; a mortgage banker both places and services loans, collects payments, and sees that taxes and insurance are paid and the property is maintained. Real estate financing specialists find a variety of employment opportunities with both lending institutions and real estate firms.

CURRENT TRENDS

Competition and reorganization characterize both the insurance and real estate industries. Huge financial conglomerates offering every type of financial service—banking, brokerage, real estate, and insurance—are the way of the future.

Technology has improved the efficiency of insurance agencies, enabling them to link their computers directly to insurance providers, using the Internet to obtain price quotes, process applications, and stay up-to-date on new product offerings. Prospective clients can access company websites, review policies, and comparison shop before choosing insurance. This makes referrals and servicing accounts to keep clients satisfied especially important to agents because customers have so much more access to information. Call centers addressing customer matters twenty-four hours a day, seven days a week, are becoming more common. Customer service representatives can handle routine inquiries, enabling agents to spend more time marketing products and selling policies.

Given new packaging schemes, the role of the corporate real estate professional is expanding to include more complex property management functions. On the other hand, many small, local brokers are affiliating with franchise firms and large corporate structures because they feel a need for national identification. National identity is growing more important because of the increasing number of Americans who move between cities each year. This movement has given birth to a new industry—the relocation business. The relocation industry uses a network of affiliated brokers who buy and sell homes for transferred employees. These brokers pay a fee to the relocation firm—a percentage of the commission.

New Technologies

The real estate industry is seeing the emergence of the "smart" building and new marketing techniques. Multitenant megastructures offer computerized operating and monitoring systems, shared telecommunications systems, and sophisticated environments designed to maximize productivity and comfort. Video marketing via telecommunications systems allows clients to view properties without traveling.

Technology has changed the insurance agent's marketing strategies as well. Agents use portable computers instead of rate books to analyze actuarial data, provide instant illustrations, and produce printed output. Computers have allowed the agent to be even more detached from the office.

Diversified Products

Throughout the insurance industry, changes in both the type and number of product offerings can be seen. The increase in the number of older Americans is creating a demand for more home care plans, retirement home options, and cooperative arrangements between government and insurance companies. Long-term health care policies offer additional coverage when benefits from regular health insurance end. Insurers operating managed-care networks are best positioned to take advantage of this situation. Another factor affecting both health and life insurance is rising health costs at a time when cancer and AIDS cases are increasing.

In the property/casualty area, new insurance policies are being written to protect against skyjacking, inept securities brokers, and other areas not clearly covered by traditional policies. To compete in the financial services market, insurance companies are offering more tax-related products such as single-premium life insurance and second-to-die life insurance to enable heirs to pay estate taxes. They are offering more services such as financial counseling and estate planning. With this diversification of products and services come many new job opportunities.

JOB OPPORTUNITIES

In general, the insurance industry is relatively stable, fairly immune to the ups and downs of the economic cycle. Most people regard insurance as a necessity. Agents with expertise in a wide range of insurance products and financial services are likely to find the most opportunities.

The insurance industry is the largest employer of actuaries. Employment opportunities are predicted to grow from 10 to 20 percent through 2012. Some growth will be attributed to the growth of interest in annuities and some will result from continuing medical reform and the effort to contain health care costs.

Unlike the insurance industry, the real estate industry is inextricably linked to the U.S. economy, which runs in cycles from weak to peak periods. Like the insurance industry, there is both high turnover and failure among beginning salespeople. Generally, women and minorities have been widely involved in the real estate industry. Various industry studies have shown that neither sex, age, nor race have any bearing on job performance. Some aptitudes and attributes that do have an effect on job performance in both insurance and real estate are explored in the following section.

CAREER DEVELOPMENT AND COMPENSATION

A premium is placed on experience in the insurance industry. Figure 5.1 shows some typical employment positions and their relationships in an insurance company. Some generalizations can be made about the insurance industry relative to salaries. Generally, the larger the company, the higher the salary. Also, specialists in one area of insurance tend to make higher salaries than do generalists. Executives employed by large, nationwide companies with tremendous resources, many agents, and vast portfolios of holdings offer top dollar to key executives. Small companies offer much less. Movement from small companies after experience has been acquired is very common. Normally, the higher up on the organizational chart, the higher the salary, with the exception of sales.

The National Association of Colleges and Employers (NACE) 2004 Salary Survey shows beginning offers for insurance underwriters as $35,391, insurance claims adjusters as $33,049, and actuaries as $46,046 for all types of employers. Insurance companies and consulting firms give merit increases to actuaries as they gain experience and pass examinations. Some companies also offer cash bonuses for each professional designation achieved. A 2003 survey by Life Office Management Association, Inc., one

Figure 5.1

Insurance positions and mobility

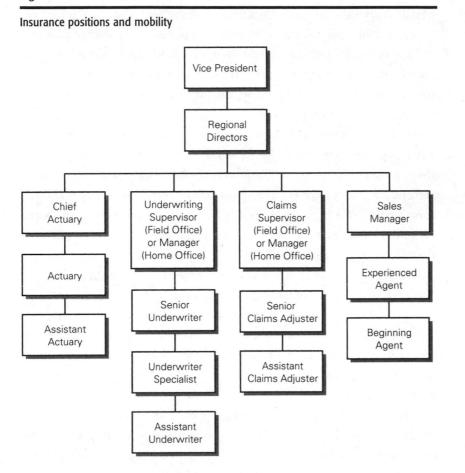

of the largest U.S. insurance and financial services companies indicated that the average base salary for an entry-level actuary was $46,991.

Successful sales agents can earn more than top company executives. It is difficult to talk about salaries of brokers and agents because they work primarily on a commission basis. Salary is contingent upon the size of the commission, which is determined by the type of insurance, the amount sold, and whether the policy is a new one or a renewal. Beginners often receive a minimum salary or advances on their commissions. For those who own agencies, expenses such as office rent, utilities, and clerical wages must be paid. Even so, owners of independent agencies stand to make huge profits if they are successful.

The insurance industry is a competitive field for beginners, and many who attempt insurance sales eventually leave the field. The agent must have a great deal of initiative and self-confidence to make it. The high potential of large monetary rewards and the great independence of the job provide the incentives for many to give it a try. The Million Dollar Round Table is a prestigious association honoring members who sell $1 million of life insurance in a year, and many do.

Real estate is a unique industry in that titles are relatively unimportant. Status is governed primarily by the number and amount of sales. There is also a Million Dollar Round Table in real estate sales. Brokers pay salespersons a percentage of the selling price, and keep a percentage. A salesperson may earn 6 to 10 percent of the selling price of a property. Therefore, the greater the cost of the property, the higher the commission agents and brokers earn.

Commissions may be divided among several agents and brokers. The broker or agent who obtained the listing usually shares the commission when the property is sold with the broker or agent who made the sale, and also with the firm that employs them. Although an agent's share varies greatly from one firm to another, often it is about half of the total amount received by the firm. Agents who both list and sell a property maximize their commissions.

Income usually increases as an agent gains experience, but individual ability, economic conditions, and the type and location of the property also affect earnings. Sales workers who are active in community organizations and in local real estate associations can broaden their contacts and increase their earnings. A beginner's earnings often are irregular, because a few weeks or even months may go by without a sale. Although some brokers allow an agent to draw against future earnings from a special account, the practice is not common with new employees. The beginner, therefore, should have enough money to live on for about six months or until commissions increase.

Recessions pose risks to the financial rewards and career development of real estate professionals. When housing starts are down, sales are affected. Although there are some large national real estate firms, the majority of firms in the real estate industry are small local firms that face the risk of going under during recessionary periods.

Salaries for real estate appraisers vary depending on experience, certification, type of employer, and geographic location. Their code of ethics prohibits professional appraisers from accepting any commissions. Property managers usually are paid a percentage of the rents they collect, although they may also receive shares or an interest in the investment. Apartment managers in residence may receive a rent-free apartment as part or all of their compensation. On average, property managers earn about $36,880.

APTITUDES AND ATTRIBUTES NEEDED FOR SUCCESS

In this section, we will examine the aptitudes and attributes requred for careers in both insurance and real estate.

Insurance

A solid educational background is the best preparation for a career in insurance.

Education. Although a college degree is not strictly required for employment in the insurance industry, it is preferred by many companies and is essential for promotion to positions of greater responsibility. Many colleges and universities offer courses in insurance, and a few schools offer a bachelor's degree in the field.

College courses in finance, mathematics, accounting, economics, business law, marketing, and business administration enable insurance sales agents to understand how social and economic conditions relate to the insurance industry. Courses in psychology, sociology, and public speaking can prove useful in improving sales techniques. In addition, because computers provide instantaneous information on a wide variety of financial products and greatly improve agents' efficiency, familiarity with computers and popular software packages has become very important.

Most companies prefer to hire college graduates for claims adjuster and examiner positions. No specific college major is required, although most workers in these positions have a business, accounting, engineering, legal, or medical background.

For entry-level underwriting jobs, most large insurance companies prefer college graduates who have a degree in business administration or finance, with courses or experience in accounting. However, a bachelor's degree in almost any field—plus courses in business law and accounting—

provides a good general background and may be sufficient to qualify. Because computers are an integral part of most underwriters' jobs, computer skills are essential.

Actuaries need a strong background in mathematics and general business. Applicants for beginning actuarial jobs usually have a bachelor's degree in mathematics, actuarial science, statistics, or a business-related discipline, such as economics, finance, or accounting. About 100 colleges and universities offer an actuarial science program, and most offer a degree in mathematics, statistics, economics, or finance.

Risk management is another area to consider when examining insurance careers. Many universities offer a risk management major at undergraduate and sometimes graduate levels. Many organizations offer internships to risk management students both inside and outside the insurance industry. A student might land an internship with a large corporation, a group of risk management consultants, the government, or an insurance company, all of which are promising employers after graduation.

Licensing. To pass the actuarial exams needed for licensing, candidates must be proficient in mathematics and statistics as well as have specific knowledge in areas of insurance. The Society of Actuaries (SOA) conducts a series of examinations covering life insurance, health benefits systems, retirement systems, and finance and investments. The Casualty Actuarial Society (CAS) gives examinations pertinent to the property and casualty insurance field including fire, accident, medical malpractice, workers' compensation, and personal injury liability.

Successful completion of the series of examinations results first at the associate level, awarding the applicant the ASA or ACAS designation. Successful completion of the next series results at the fellowship level, awarding the applicant the FSA or FCAS designation. These examinations require months of preparation and years to complete. Many employers pay hundreds of dollars for study materials and examination fees and some allow time off to study.

Claims adjusters, agents, and brokers must be licensed in the states in which they practice. Sales agents apply for licenses in either life and health insurance or property and casualty insurance and must successfully complete courses and pass written exams on insurance fundamentals and state insurance laws. Most licensing authorities require continuing education that keeps agents up-to-date on insurance laws, consumer protection, and other essential information. The Gramm-Leach-Bliley Act of 1999 established uniform licensing standards and reciprocal licensing that make it easier to obtain a license from one state to the next after successfully completing the required courses and examinations.

As the demand for financial products and financial planning increases, many insurance agents are choosing to gain the proper licensing and certification to sell securities and other financial products. Doing so, however, requires substantial study and passing an additional examination—either the Series 6 or Series 7 licensing exam, both of which are administered by the National Association of Securities Dealers (NASD). The Series 6 exam is for individuals who wish to sell only mutual funds and variable annuities, whereas the Series 7 exam is the main NASD series license that qualifies agents as general securities sales representatives. In addition, to further demonstrate competency in the area of financial planning, many agents find it worthwhile to earn the designation "Certified Financial Planner" (CFP) or "Chartered Financial Consultant" (ChFC).

Training. Many insurance companies will pay all or part of tuition costs for additional education. Most large companies have excellent on-the-job training programs, which may include rotation among various departments to allow new employees to get an overall look at the company and to choose an area in which to work. It is very important to determine what educational and training opportunities a company offers before accepting employment.

Real Estate

People enter the real estate field from diverse backgrounds. However, there are some basic requirements that must be met by agents and brokers.

Education. Although a college degree is not a requirement for entrance into the field, real estate transactions have become more legally complex, and many firms have turned to college graduates to fill positions. A large number of agents and brokers have some college training. Many universities and community colleges offer courses in real estate. Some offer associate, bachelor, and even graduate degrees with a major in real estate. College courses in real estate, finance, business administration, statistics, economics, law, and English are helpful. For those who intend to start their own company, business courses such as marketing and accounting are as important as those in real estate or finance. Local real estate associations that are members of the National Association of Realtors sponsor courses in real estate fundamentals, legal issues, appraisal, mortgage financing, property development, property management, and other real estate topics.

Licensing. Real estate brokers and sales agents must be licensed by the state in which they work. Prospective agents must be high school graduates, at least eighteen years old, and pass a written test. The examination, which is more comprehensive for brokers than for agents, includes questions on basic real estate transactions and laws affecting the sale of property. Most states require candidates for the general sales license to complete between thirty and ninety hours of classroom instruction. Licensed brokers need between sixty and ninety hours of training and from one to three years of selling experience. Some states waive the experience requirements for the broker's license for applicants who have a bachelor's degree in real estate.

State licenses typically must be renewed every one or two years. While testing is usually not required for renewal, many states require continuing education. Prospective agents and brokers should contact the real estate licensing commission of the state in which they wish to work in order to verify exact licensing requirements. Many firms and real estate boards offer formal training for agents and brokers as preparation for obtaining a state license.

Personal attributes. Many studies have been conducted to attempt to pinpoint the qualities needed for success in this field. Findings show that successful real estate pros are:

- Able to work alone
- Emotionally stable
- Tolerant of stress
- Full of drive and energy
- Trusting of people
- Persuasive
- Warm and friendly
- Results-oriented
- Organized
- Objective

SOURCES OF ADDITIONAL INFORMATION

There are numerous sources of additional information on careers in insurance and real estate. For information on careers in insurance, contact:

Association for Advanced Life Underwriting
2901 Telestar Court
Falls Church, VA 22042
aalu.org

Casualty Actuarial Society
1100 North Glebe Road, Suite 600
Arlington, VA 22201
casact.org

Chartered Property and Casualty Underwriters Society
720 Providence Road
Malvern, PA 19355
cpcusociety.org

Independent Insurance Agents and Brokers of America
127 South Peyton Street
Alexandria, VA 22314
iiaa.org

Insurance Information Institute
110 William Street
New York, NY 10038
iii.org

Life Insurance Marketing and Research Association International
  (LIMRA)
300 Day Hill Road
Windsor, CT 06095
limra.com

Million Dollar Round Table
325 West Touhy Avenue
Park Ridge, IL 60068
mdrt.org

National Association of Insurance Women International
6528 East 101st Street
PMB #750
Tulsa, OK 74133
naiw.org

National Association of Health Underwriters
2000 North 14th Street, Suite 450
Arlington, VA 22201
nahu.org

Property Casualty Insurers Association of America
2600 South River Road
Des Plaines, IL 60018-3286
www.pciaa.net

Society of Actuaries
475 North Martingale Road, Suite 600
Schaumburg, IL 60173
soa.org

For information on real estate careers, plus online courses in various aspects of real estate, contact:

National Association of Real Estate Brokers
9831 Greenbelt Road
Lanham, MD 20706
nareb.com

Information on other aspects of the real estate industry can be obtained from the following organizations:

National Association of Independent Real Estate Brokers
7102 Mardyke Lane
Indianapolis, IN 46226
nationalrealestatebrokers.org

National Association of Realtors
30700 Russell Ranch Road
Westlake Village, CA 91362
realtor.com

National Society of Real Estate Appraisers
9831 Greenbelt Road
Lanham, MD 20706
nsrea.org

Sources of Additional Information in Canada

Insurance

Association of Canadian Insurers
155 Queen Street, #808
Ottawa, ON K1P 6L1

Canadian Association of Insurance Women
caiw-acfa.com

Canadian Institute of Actuaries
800-150 Metcalfe
Ottawa, ON K2P 1P1
actuaries.ca

Insurance Institute of Canada
18 King Street East, 6th Floor
Toronto, ON M5C 1C4
iic-iac.org

Life Insurance Marketing and Research Association International
  (LIMRA) Canada
350 Bloor Street East, 2nd Floor
Toronto, ON M4W3W8
limra.com

Real Estate

Appraisal Institute of Canada
203-150 Isabella Street
Ottawa, ON K1S 1V7
aicanada.ca

Canadian Real Estate Association
344 Slater Street, Suite 1600
Ottawa, ON K1R 7Y3
crea.ca

Independent Real Estate Brokers Association of Canada
447 Locust Street
Burlington, ON L7S 1T9
ireba.ca

CAREER DECISION-MAKING MODEL

It is now time to consider whether a career in insurance or real estate is a possibility for you. Using the career decision-making model, complete the following forms according to the directions. The forms in Figures 5.2a and 5.2b include the factors in the career decision-making model described in Chapter 1. Follow these directions in completing them.

1. Enter the position that interests you most on the line titled Job.
2. Enter any additional factors used to personalize your model (from Chapter 1) in the blank spaces provided.
3. Enter the weights that you assigned to the factors (from Chapter 1) in column WT. (It would be wise to review the explanations of

these factors in the description of the model in Chapter 1 before going on to step 4.)

4. Assign a value from 1 (lowest) to 10 (highest) to each factor, based on the information in this chapter and on your personal self-assessment, and enter the value in column V. If you feel that you have a certain aptitude or attribute needed for success in this

Figure 5.2a

Career evaluation for insurance and real estate

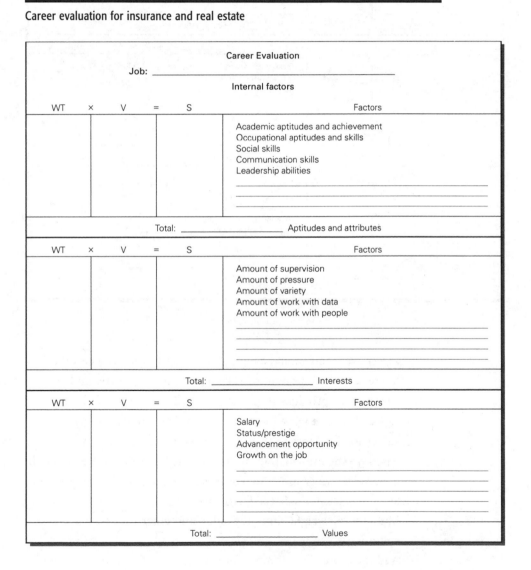

| Career Evaluation |
| Job: _____ |

Internal factors

WT	×	V	=	S	Factors
					Academic aptitudes and achievement
					Occupational aptitudes and skills
					Social skills
					Communication skills
					Leadership abilities
					_____
					_____
					_____

Total: _____ Aptitudes and attributes

WT	×	V	=	S	Factors
					Amount of supervision
					Amount of pressure
					Amount of variety
					Amount of work with data
					Amount of work with people
					_____
					_____
					_____
					_____

Total: _____ Interests

WT	×	V	=	S	Factors
					Salary
					Status/prestige
					Advancement opportunity
					Growth on the job
					_____
					_____
					_____
					_____

Total: _____ Values

Figure 5.2b

Career evaluation for insurance and real estate

			External factors		

WT × V = S   Factors

Family values and expectations
Socioeconomic level

_____
_____
_____
_____

Total: _____ Family influence

WT × V = S   Factors

Overall economic conditions
Employment trends
Job market information

_____
_____
_____
_____

Total: _____ Economic influence

WT × V = S   Factors

Perceived effect of race, sex, or
  ethnic background on success
Perceived effect of physical or
  psychological disabilities on success

_____
_____
_____
_____

Total: _____ Societal influence

career area, you should assign a fairly high value. If a certain
interest, such as amount of variety, is desirable to you and you
feel the area provides the variety you enjoy, assign a fairly high
value. If not, assign a low value. Use this technique to assign
values to all factors in the model. If you cannot assign a value
based on the information in the chapter for some of the factors in
the model, either use other sources to acquire the information or
leave the space beside the factor blank.

5. Multiply the weight times the value and enter the score in
   column S.
6. Add the scores in column S for each group of factors and enter
   the number in the space labeled "Total."

You will use this evaluation in Chapter 11 along with the evaluations of each career explored in this book.

WHAT DID YOU LEARN?

You have now learned about the various careers in insurance and real estate. Information about the nature of the work, areas of specialization, salaries, career paths, current trends, job opportunities, educational requirements, and attributes needed for success was included in the chapter. The career evaluation form you completed reflects this knowledge of insurance and real estate careers and how it relates to you.

Chapter 6, "Careers in Marketing," will introduce you to such popular careers as advertising, sales, marketing research, public relations, and international marketing.

NOTES

1. Frederik Heller, "The Power of One Million," *Realtor Magazine* (May 2004), 41.
2. Robert Sharoff, "A Star Is Born," *Realtor Magazine* (January 2004), 26.

CHAPTER 6

CAREERS IN MARKETING

After reading this chapter, you will be able to:

- Describe the work of marketing professionals in the areas of marketing research; product development; advertising; sales promotion; public relations; wholesale, industrial, retail, and direct selling; and international marketing
- Discuss trends in marketing and their impact on the careers in general
- Diagram career paths in the field of marketing
- Discuss job opportunities in marketing careers
- List the educational preparation and skills needed to enter each of the marketing career areas
- Evaluate careers in marketing according to your individualized career decision-making model

Companies of all sizes offer goods and services to today's consumers. For this reason, the field of marketing offers more variety in career choices than any other area of business. Marketers face the challenge of a fluctuating economy, changing consumer tastes and values, emerging and disappearing brands, and numerous other factors when making decisions about what products to offer and how to advertise and sell them. Marketing has grown from the peddler's annual visit to rural settlements to complex telemarketing systems that provide at-home shopping to consumers.

The American Marketing Association defines marketing as "an organizational function and a set of processes for creating, communicating, and delivering value to customers and for managing customer relationships in ways that benefit the organization and its stakeholders."[1] As the definition suggests, the primary emphasis of marketing is not necessarily selling already planned and produced goods or services, but rather identifying customer wants and planning products to satisfy those wants.

The "marketing concept" is basically a philosophy that focuses on customer wants and identified markets. Companies have found that they can create the desire in potential customers for certain types of products. Thus marketing has grown into a complex and sophisticated field needing a large number of highly trained professionals to perform its many specialized functions.

The many facets of marketing are interesting to consider along with the many career opportunities those facets provide such as marketing research, product management, advertising, sales promotion, wholesale and industrial sales, retailing, international marketing, and public relations. This chapter includes the following information:

- What marketing pros do
- Who employs them
- Salaries and career paths
- Latest trends
- Job opportunities
- Education and skills needed to pursue a career in marketing
- Sources of additional information on marketing careers

MARKETING

Marketing is an incredibly broad field that covers the life span of a given product or service from the time it is conceived until after it is sold, including service and maintenance. Professionals are employed in such fields as marketing research, product development, promotion, advertising, selling, and public relations. Industrial, wholesale, retail, and direct selling provide numerous job opportunities for moving products into the marketplace through different channels of distribution. The growth in international marketing has also created new possibilities for marketing professionals.

The variety of marketing careers and the growing demand for marketing professionals suggest that this field has much to offer. An investigation of careers in marketing will point out not only specific areas of opportunity, such as those outlined above, but the broader nature of marketing as a whole. Numerous opportunities for growth and change exist within marketing careers. Marketing itself is so diverse that most individuals with the right training and qualifications can find jobs well suited to their skills and interests.

Marketing Research

Marketing research is the first step on the ladder of promoting a new product. In this initial phase of marketing, researchers compile and assess information that is used to determine the need for a potential product or service, and the potential sales that it will generate. These professionals identify potential consumer groups, describe them in detail, find out what these consumers want, detail these wants in terms of specific products, determine if such products exist and which competing companies supply them, forecast what products consumers are likely to want in the future, and which competitors are likely to produce them. And that's only part of it!

Marketing researchers often obtain the information they need by conducting surveys that are designed according to the specific product and consumer base in question. They might use telephone, mail, or Internet surveys to gather information. Some surveys are conducted as personal interviews by leading focus group discussions, or by setting up booths in public places such as shopping malls. In either case, the surveys are conducted by trained interviewers working under the supervision of the market research analyst.

Marketing research analysts evaluate the collected data and make recommendations based on their findings. From the information they gather, they can provide management with the information needed to make decisions on the promotion, distribution, design, and pricing of products or services. Researchers might also contribute to the development of advertising materials, sales plans, and product promotions such as rebates and giveaways.

The marketing research department of a company includes the marketing research director, research analysts, and trainees, who hold the position of junior marketing research analysts. In addition, a field service director hires and supervises interviewers and coders. Marketing research professionals engage in such activities as identifying market trends, developing customer profiles, monitoring competition, measuring market share, evaluating brand images, designing products and packages, planning distribution channels, assisting in advertising and promotion campaigns, analyzing audience characteristics, and evaluating the impact of advertising and promotion.

Marketing researchers generally have degrees in marketing with strong backgrounds in statistics and psychology. These professionals are employed by manufacturers of both goods and services, nonprofit organizations, marketing research firms, or as independent consultants. Marketing research is not limited to consumer products but is also conducted in such areas as environmental concerns, business decisions, political campaigns, and association images, among others.

Recent college graduates are hired as junior or associate analysts who are usually assigned such responsibilities as editing questionnaires, handling correspondence, and collecting data from libraries, company files, or trade journals.

Field service directors, who may have been promoted from junior analysts, hire and supervise field service and tabulation personnel who conduct interviews, enter numbers into computer systems, or run standard types of programs. Sometimes the field service director contracts with field service firms to perform these activities. Field service and tabulation workers do not need college degrees, often work for minimum wage, and do not normally advance to other positions in marketing research. The field service director however, is an integral member of the marketing research team.

Experienced analysts develop proposals for research projects, design questionnaires, analyze data, organize studies, and write reports. Advancement to the position of senior analyst and ultimately to the position of research director or head of the marketing research department involves more and more administrative and supervisory tasks such as preparing budgets, overseeing projects, and reporting to higher-level marketing management. In marketing research firms, senior analysts are also involved in obtaining new clients.

Product Management

Hundreds of millions of dollars are spent each year to develop and market new products. Despite this huge investment, a high percentage of these products fail. Perhaps insufficient or inaccurate answers to the following questions may be the cause:

- Should the product be made?
- Who is expected to buy it?
- What characteristics do consumers want in this type of product?
- What are consumers willing to pay for such a product?
- What competing products are already on the market?
- How is the proposed product better than the existing ones?
- What are the best ways to distribute the product?
- How should the product be promoted?

Using information compiled by marketing researchers, companies decide whether or not to introduce new products into the marketplace. Once a firm makes a commitment to develop a specific product, a product manager is assigned or hired to spearhead the project. This person is often called a brand manager in firms producing consumer products. Product managers may be assigned to products from initial development throughout the length of their life cycle. Sometimes, however, new-product development managers are assigned for a product's initial development and test marketing, and then a product manager is assigned who will take over and remain in charge of the product throughout its life cycle. Special product recall managers are sometimes assigned when products posing threats to consumers must be recalled.

Normally, the product manager assembles a development team whose members work with other units of the marketing department to develop a new product or service. The product manager and his or her staff interact with the marketing researchers to define the characteristics of the product; with the engineers who design the product; and with the production staff on the actual creation of the product. The production team also works with those involved in physical distribution, packaging, finance, sales, advertising, and sales promotion. It is the product manager who is responsible for coordinating the interaction of these various specialists. Given the degree of exposure that product managers have to the different aspects of marketing, this can be an excellent avenue of advancement to other positions within the organization once a project is completed.

The general responsibilities of product managers, assistant product managers, and their teams are as follows:

1. Evaluate product testing and recommend whether to terminate development, modify the product, or begin the campaign.
2. Plan the introduction and scheduling of the packaging and final product with the production department.
3. Provide information and recommendations on the price for the product.
4. Develop marketing budgets and sales and profitability forecasts with the finance department.
5. Analyze statistics and recommendations from marketing research to allocate funding for advertising and promotion campaigns.
6. Identify channels of distribution, such as wholesalers, retailers, and/or direct selling.
7. Work with marketing research and advertising to create a product image in the minds of consumers as having the attributes they want in that product.
8. Coordinate the production and promotion of the product.
9. Monitor and evaluate consumer reaction to the product.

In a way, product management is similar to running a small business. Most companies look for entrepreneurial types with a broad knowledge of business and a degree in marketing. Some firms give preference to M.B.A. holders for the entry-level position in product management—assistant product manager. Smaller manufacturers consider outstanding undergraduate degree holders for entry-level positions. In either case, the possibility of advancement may be to the position of product manager. Some companies offering dozens of brands in various categories promote exceptional product managers to the position of category manager or group product manager. Advancement to middle and top-level marketing management is possible from product and category management positions.

Direct Marketing

Direct marketing, or nonstore retailing, is growing at a faster rate than in-store selling. Every imaginable type of product is sold through direct marketing today—apparel, plants, high-tech items, portraits, home improvements, gourmet food items, communications and financial services, and the list goes on and on. Direct marketers use such methods as Internet sales; direct selling (door-to-door); direct-response retailing, in which items are advertised in catalogs and other periodicals and on radio and television with toll-free telephone numbers for placing orders; and database marketing, which offers lists of prospective customers to organizations, direct mail firms, and telemarketing agencies who contact potential consumers by phone.

Two types of firms engage in direct marketing: those that sell their own products directly to the public, and those that sell the products of other companies. Direct mail firms and telemarketing agencies are employed by both large and small manufacturers. Many companies employ a telemarketing director and telesales representatives to offer their products for sale over the telephone or to set up appointments for visits by company sales representatives. A variety of career opportunities exist in direct marketing—some require no formal education and pay roughly minimum wage and perhaps bonuses, and others in management require college degrees in business, marketing, or related areas.

Since excessive telemarketing is considered an annoyance, the government has taken action on behalf of consumers to protect them against unwanted calls. In 2003 the Federal Trade Commission (FTC) amended its Telemarketing Sales Rule (TSR), which implements the Telemarketing and Consumer Fraud and Abuse Prevention Act. While the amended TSR comprises many stipulations intended to protect consumers, perhaps the most widely known is the prohibition of telemarketing calls to consumers who have listed their telephone numbers with the National Do Not Call Registry.

Similarly to the FTC, the Canadian Radio-televison and Telecommunications Commission (CRTC) in 2004 announced new rules governing telemarketing calls. Although Canada does not at this time have a national do not call registry, the new regulations offer consumers the opportunity to add their telephone numbers to individual do not call lists.

International Marketing

The field of international marketing holds much fascination for those with an interest in travel and foreign countries. Opportunities exist in international marketing research, product management, and promotion. The growing import and export business and the global economy resulting from such free trade agreements as the General Agreement on Tariffs and Trade (GATT) and the North American Free Trade Agreement (NAFTA), have changed the nature of the global marketplace and created many opportunities in this field. As more businesses become involved in international marketing by establishing foreign operations or entering joint ventures with foreign companies, more positions become available. Other ways in which companies enter foreign markets are by exporting their products or by foreign licensing arrangements through which a company allows a foreign company to produce and market its product in exchange for royalties.

The growth in international marketing due to changes abroad will create more positions based in the United States for individuals interested in this field. Travel and assignments abroad are usually associated with high-level managers, managers or owners of advertising agencies with operations abroad, owners of export/import businesses, sales representatives of industrial or pharmaceutical companies, and fashion coordinators and buyers. Usually companies hire foreign nationals for most positions in foreign branches. Although positions abroad for recent college graduates are less common, even for those with an M.B.A. and knowledge of the language, this is beginning to change with the current growth level of international business.

Individuals interested in international marketing should become proficient in a language and systematically collect information on the countries and industries of interest. Before being assigned a position abroad, marketing professionals are usually required to have a thorough knowledge of their firm's domestic marketing operations.

Advertising, Sales Promotion, and Public Relations

Perhaps the most competitive areas for entry-level positions within marketing are advertising, sales promotion, and public relations. Whether employed by a company or an agency, these professionals must work in a highly charged atmosphere with extreme pressure to produce.

Advertising. In addition to dedicated departments within companies, there are 47,000 advertising and public relations companies in the United States, a figure that indicates the importance of advertising in our economy. Working on behalf of their customers, these agencies write copy and prepare artwork, graphics, and other creative work, and then place the resulting ads on television, radio, or the Internet or in periodicals, newspapers, or other advertising media. Many of the largest agencies are international, with a substantial proportion of their revenue coming from abroad. Since many advertising campaigns are temporary, some companies do not maintain their own staff, but rather solicit bids from ad agencies to develop advertising for them.

In companies that do handle their own advertising, a manager generally oversees the advertising and promotion staffs. In larger firms, advertising managers are responsible for the in-house account, and the creative and media services departments. The account executive manages the account services department, assesses the need for advertising and, in agencies, maintains the accounts of clients. The creative services department develops the subject matter and presentation of advertising. The creative director oversees the copy chief, art director, and associated staff. The media director is responsible for organizing the planning groups that select the media in which the ads will be placed.

Within advertising agencies, the account management department links the agency with the client. Account management brings business to the agency and ultimately is responsible for the quality of the advertisement or public relations campaign. Once account management has brought the agency an idea from a client, the creative department works to bring that idea to life. As the idea takes shape, copywriters and their assistants write the words of the ads, and art directors and their staffs develop the visual concepts and designs to accompany the words.

Graphic designers use a variety of print, electronic, and film media to create designs that meet clients' commercial needs. Using computer software, they develop the overall layout and design of print ads for magazines, newspapers, journals, corporate reports, and other publications. They also produce promotional displays and marketing brochures for products and services, as well as design logos for products and businesses. An increasing number of graphic designers develop material to appear on the Internet.

Research analysts perform similar functions to those of market researchers, studying consumers' perceptions of products and advertising effectiveness, and interacting with creative and media personnel both in the production of ads and modification of ad campaigns. Corporate advertising managers must decide for each product whether to conduct the ad campaign completely in-house or whether to hire an advertising agency for certain ad campaigns.

Media planners gather information on the public's viewing and reading habits, and evaluate editorial content and programming to determine the potential use of media such as newspapers, magazines, radio, television, or the Internet in an ad campaign. Media buyers track the media space and times available for purchase, negotiate and purchase time and space for ads, and make sure ads appear as scheduled. They also calculate rates, usage, and budgets. Advertising sales agents, who generally work in firms representing radio stations, television stations, and publications, sell air time on radio and television, and page space in print media.

Product promoters try to persuade retail stores to sell particular products. Demonstrators promote sales of a product to consumers, often in shopping malls or department stores. Product demonstration is an effective technique that can be employed to introduce new products or promote sales of existing products because it allows face-to-face interaction with potential customers.

Sales promotion. Closely linked to advertising, sales promotion is geared toward individual consumers rather than large groups. Sales promotion falls into three categories: consumer promotion including samples, coupons, rebates, games, and contests; trade promotion for intermediaries including cooperative ads, free goods, and dealer sales contests; and sales-force promotion including incentives such as sales meetings, contests for prizes, and bonuses.

Specialists in sales promotion have previous sales or advertising experience. These professionals may be employed by companies or sales promotion firms, which play a role similar to advertising agencies. Sales promotion specialists plan promotion campaigns for products working with information from marketing research, a product concept, and a specified budget. They direct a creative team, including artists and copywriters, in designing materials such as coupons, free goods, and packages to accomplish the campaign objectives. Coming up with promotion ideas such as contests, games, and rebates is also part of the job. While advertising is ongoing throughout the life of a product, sales promotion campaigns generally accompany the introduction of new or improved products. Sales promotion specialists must have research abilities, administrative skills, and creativity to function well in their positions.

Public relations. Both sales promotion and advertising focus on a product. The sale of all products in a company may be improved through the creation of goodwill. This is the job of the public relations department, whose objective is to build and maintain a positive image of the company in the eyes of the public. Large companies have public relations departments with staffs of specialists working under a director of public relations.

Smaller companies may hire one individual to conduct public relations activities. Some companies contract out work with public relations firms that function in the same manner as advertising agencies or sales promotion houses.

Public relations is important to all types of organizations, from retail stores to health care facilities. Public relations firms help secure favorable public exposure for their clients and design strategies to help them attain a certain public image. Public relations professionals, often called public relations officers or PR reps, create publicity to provide information about the organization to the general public, stockholders, and government agencies, among others. They analyze public opinion about clients; establish relationships with the media; write speeches and coach clients for interviews; issue press releases; and organize client-sponsored publicity events, such as contests, concerts, exhibits, and charity events.

Most entry-level public relations work involves acquiring information from a variety of sources, and maintaining files. With experience, PR professionals begin to write press releases, executives' speeches, and articles for both internal and external publications. Other duties include working with media contacts, arranging speaking engagements for company officials, planning special events, and making travel arrangements for prominent people. In PR agencies, entry-level workers begin as assistants and advance to account executives, where they work with clients to plan a public relations campaign strategy and see that it is carried out.

Public relations professionals are employed by businesses, nonprofit organizations, trade associations, government agencies, colleges, prominent individuals, large advertising agencies with PR departments, and public relations firms that serve a wide range of clients. Since these professionals tend to come from a wide variety of backgrounds, a degree in marketing is not a prerequisite to entering the field. Regardless of their background, however, PR reps are involved in selling—selling organizations or individuals to the public. For this reason, public relations easily fits into the range of marketing careers. Although the marketing concept is the philosophy of business management, it has been effectively employed by nonbusiness groups such as charities, the arts, educational institutions, federal and local governments, and others. Whether an organization is soliciting funds or promoting ideas, it functions in much the same way as a business selling goods or services.

Sales and Merchandising

Consumers are made aware of a company's products through the efforts of advertising, sales promotion, and public relations professionals. The producer then must choose how to move the product from the warehouse to these consumers. This process, called distribution, may be accomplished through various channels. Options include the sale of the product to wholesalers, retailers, or directly to the consumer.

Since sales and customer service are the keys to running a successful business, professional sales people are the backbone of any company. Without an effective sales force, a company could not survive in a competitive environment. With so many similar products available to consumers, it is the sales force that makes the difference.

Many marketing graduates start their careers in sales, which is a perfect area for beginners to learn their company's business and to show what they can do. It is a position in which hard work really does pay off, both in increased earnings and in recognition.

The general field of sales is divided into different categories. Retail sales representatives offer products to end consumers in stores of all sizes. Wholesale or industrial sales representatives sell both finished products and materials to retailers and manufacturers. Industrial sales representatives are company-employed by manufacturers; however, they are not the only ones selling the company's products. Manufacturers' representatives are independent businesspeople who may sell one or more companies' products to many different customers. Wholesale dealers are self-employed sellers who find needed products for client companies.

Sales representatives perform numerous activities, including some of the following:

- Setting goals, planning, and making schedules
- Identifying and contacting prospective customers
- Maintaining contacts with current customers and anticipating their needs
- Planning and making sales presentations
- Reviewing sales orders, scheduling delivery dates, and handling special details
- Maintaining up-to-date records and reports
- Handling complaints and problems
- Monitoring the competition

- Learning new product information and marketing strategies
- Evaluating price trends and advising customers

Time management is crucial to successful selling. Sales reps must carefully allocate their time among the above activities. High-tech items such as laptop computers and cellular phones enable sales reps to be more efficient. Organization, initiative, and communication skills are vital to successful selling.

Retail sales. Retailing is a combination of activities involved in selling goods and services directly to consumers for personal or household use. Retail sales differs from wholesale and industrial sales in that the customer usually comes to the salesperson. Retail professions fall basically into two groups: those involved in merchandising, including merchandise managers, buyers, and assistant buyers who purchase the goods offered for sale; and those involved in selling goods to the public, including department, regional, and national sales managers, and sales representatives.

Recent college graduates enter merchandising as assistant buyers. They work under buyers in dealing with manufacturers, placing orders for merchandise, inspecting new merchandise, supervising the distribution of merchandise, and managing inventory. Experienced buyers work under merchandise managers in analyzing customer needs and choosing products to meet them. Merchandise managers supervise buying activities, allocate budgets, and perform primarily administrative tasks. They work closely with sales managers, who supervise selling activities.

Sales management trainees are recruited from sales positions or from the pool of recent college graduates. These trainees assist the manager in staff scheduling, record keeping, and handling customer complaints. The largest number of opportunities in retailing is in sales, with service sales positions creating the most new opportunities.

Whether selling shoes, computer equipment, or automobiles, retail salespersons assist customers in finding what they are looking for and try to interest them in buying the merchandise. They describe a product's features, demonstrate its use, or show various models and colors. For some sales jobs, particularly those involving expensive and complex items, retail salespersons need special knowledge or skills. For example, salespersons who sell automobiles must be able to explain the features of various models, information about warranties, the meaning of manufacturers' specifications, and the types of options and financing available; those selling electronic equipment must be able to compare models and explain all of the products' features.

To effectively do their job, retail sales representatives must have good communication skills, an understanding of their customers' needs, knowledge of the competition, and a positive attitude. Sales is hard but rewarding work for those with the temperament and initiative to do it well.

Wholesale and manufacturing sales. Sales representatives are an important part of manufacturers' and wholesalers' success. Regardless of the type of product they sell, their primary duties are to interest wholesale and retail buyers and purchasing agents in their merchandise, and to address any of the client's questions or concerns. They also advise clients on methods to reduce costs, use their products, and increase sales. Sales representatives market the company's products to manufacturers, wholesale and retail establishments, construction contractors, government agencies, and other potential users.

Those assuming entry-level positions in this field often accompany experienced representatives on sales calls. As they gain familiarity with the firm's products and clients, new employees are given increasing responsibility until they are eventually assigned their own territory. Some representatives travel frequently; a large territory can sometimes cover several states.

Promotion often means assignment to a larger account or territory where commissions are likely to be greater. Experienced sales representatives may move into jobs as sales trainers, who instruct new employees on selling techniques and company policies and procedures. Those with good sales records and leadership ability may advance to higher-level positions such as sales supervisor, district manager, or vice president of sales. In addition to advancement opportunities within a firm, some manufacturers' agents go into business for themselves. Others find opportunities in purchasing, advertising, or marketing research.

CURRENT TRENDS

Major transformations in the American economy have had a great impact on marketing careers. The shift to a service economy, the globalization of business, the restructuring of corporations, the impact of technology, the diversification of the workforce, and the changing lifestyles of American families have affected the types of products offered and the nature of marketing jobs.

These various changes in American business have created opportunities for entrepreneurs who found market niches or small groups of consumers with unfilled needs for specific goods or services. New small businesses were created to meet these needs in record numbers. The 1990s gave rise to sales and marketing online, opening up a wealth of additional career options for those interested in this vast field.

Retail Trends

The large number of mergers and acquisitions has affected the retail industry by reshaping many large department stores. Although many of these stores have continued to maintain their various departments, they have enlarged their inventory of clothing, which is their real strength. To compete with discount and specialty stores, department stores have added both budget and designer departments.

More price-conscious consumers are shopping for bargains in the increasing number of discount stores, warehouse clubs, and outlet malls. Thus, changing lifestyles and values have made a dramatic impact on markets and products.

The popularity of specialty shops is attributed to the large number of working women who want the convenience of quick shopping with no lines. For example, Gap Inc., is making the most of this trend by preparing to test specialty clothing stores aimed at women over age 35. The retailer plans to open ten stores that target an entire demographic group of nearly 40 million American women, a group with major spending power.[2]

If changing lifestyles have impacted the way Americans shop, then they must also impact the way marketers try to sell us products. Following baby boomers as a desirable demographic, "millenials" are highly sought after by marketers. Born between 1979 and 1994, millenials comprise 60 million young people whose expectations are vastly different from those of previous generations. Members of this age group are the most comfortable with technology, thereby presenting a challenge to advertisers. They are less receptive to standard television advertising, because they spend so much time multi-tasking with various electronics. It is not uncommon for a young person to simultaneously watch television, surf the Internet, send instant messages, and talk on a cell phone. All of these media present new challenges for advertisers, who are constantly looking for ways to insert ads wherever they will be seen.[3]

Another growing trend in marketing is product placement, in which specific brands are highly visible in movies or television shows. Increasingly popular with advertisers as a result of consumers' ability to skip commercials, product placement makes sure the brand is seen during the program itself. Many television series, and in particular reality shows, use a great deal of product placement. In the reality show *The Apprentice*, contestants hoping to win a job in Donald Trump's corporation work for a variety of actual companies, including Mattel Inc., Levi Strauss & Co., and Pepsico.[4]

Name brands are also seen in feature films. In the movie *Shrek 2*, characters drive through a town with a Baskin-Robbins store. In reality, Baskin-Robbins created three ice cream flavors named for characters in the film. The company supported the movie with two ads and in-store promotions for the new flavors.[5]

New Technologies

The tremendous advances in technology over the last decade have also changed how marketers promote products. Digital video recorders make it possible for viewers to watch television without ever seeing an ad. Although only 5 percent of U.S. households currently own digital video recorders, that number is expected to increase to 22 percent by 2008; 90 percent of current users say they skip commercials. To combat this loss of advertising viewers, the industry is using new technologies that allow precise targeting. With targeting, advertisers can pitch commercials for products relevant to individual viewers.[6]

These technological advances are making mass marketing less effective in product promotion. In the 1960s an advertiser could reach 80 percent of women in the United States with a commercial that aired simultaneously on the three major networks, CBS, NBC, and ABC. Today, an ad would have to run on one hundred channels to reach the same number of viewers.[7] Many large corporations are making the move to micromarketing—running ads that target specific groups. For example, McDonald's pitches to young men by advertising on Foot Locker, Inc.'s in-store video network; it reaches mothers through ads in women's magazines such as *O, The Oprah Magazine* and websites such as iVillage. The organization also pays for closed-circuit sports programming piped into Hispanic bars, as well as for ads in *Upscale*, a custom-published magazine distributed to black barber shops.[8]

One of the fastest-growing media for advertising is the Internet. Major companies are advertising on the Web, where they can take advantage of a unique form of micromarketing called "paid search." When a consumer uses a search engine to locate information, the search results are accompanied by a column of paid advertisements. The interactive quality of the Internet makes this advertising especially appealing to marketers, who can use input from consumers to fine-tune their ads.[9] A recent report predicts that the amount of money spent on online advertising will match that spent on magazine advertising by 2007, and will surpass it in 2008.[10]

Consumers' ability to make an actual purchase has also been impacted by technology. Online retailing has grown substantially, since it offers convenience and a wide variety of selections. In addition to specialty online retailers, department store chains and major retailers such as Wal-Mart are also making online shopping available to consumers. A 2004 report by Smith Barney predicts that online sales will grow 10 to 15 percent over the next five to ten years.[11]

Global Marketing

Global marketing is another growing trend that stems from the emergence of China, Singapore, Mexico, Argentina, Malaysia, India, Russia, and Eastern Europe as consumer markets and trading partners. American firms are responding to the invasion of imports with aggressive selling in foreign markets now that many trade barriers have been relaxed. As consumers in Asia enter the middle class, they want to buy cars, computers, and appliances. In Eastern Europe millions of consumers need clothes, appliances, and the most basic items. As American business moves abroad, the need in all areas of marketing for individuals who are familiar with foreign languages and cultures will grow substantially. Both business and nonbusiness organizations such as charities, religious organizations, and universities will be involved in global marketing.

Because of the rapid growth of the Hispanic population in the United States, opportunities are now emerging in Latin American markets for U.S. M.B.A.s with the right training and skills. Some major companies, such as Microsoft, Kraft Foods, Home Depot, and Sony Pictures Entertainment are seeking experienced U.S.-trained M.B.A.s who have the language skills and cultural awareness to work in a challenging environment.[12] While experience is the norm, there are growing opportunities for recent M.B.A. graduates in U.S. companies with divisions centering on Latin America. Those with more experience, however, are more likely to receive assignments in Latin America or overseas.[13]

Cause Marketing

Environmental concerns have also impacted the marketing industry. Preserving the environment has affected product development, manufacturing processes, and packaging. Products now are advertised to emphasize nonpollutants, and recyclable or recycled materials are commonly used in products and their containers. Many plastic bags are now biodegradable, and most plastic products now carry a code number for the recycling process. Concerns for endangered species and rain forests have become international environmental issues. Even the pencil—widely made from jelutong, a wood that grows in the rain forests of Indonesia and Malaysia—is part of a global controversy. Groups such as Rainforest Action Network and performers such as Sting urge preservation of the rain forests in the ongoing fight to reduce deterioration of the ozone layer.

A move to highlight the environmental safety message resulted in green labeling of products that are "friendly" to the environment, including those that are biodegradable, manufactured without polluting, or made with recyclable packaging. Although this type of labeling is often confusing to consumers, more and more companies are modifying products and their containers, rather than risking boycotts of their products by consumer groups.

JOB OPPORTUNITIES

According to the American Marketing Association, there are over 750,000 marketing professionals employed throughout the United States and Canada.[14] The U.S. Bureau of Labor Statistics forecasts employment growth in marketing of up to 35 percent through 2012. Marketing professionals are employed throughout the country by manufacturers, retailers, advertising agencies, consulting and public relations firms, product testing laboratories, business services firms, and others.

Demand

Demand for new college graduates varies from position to position and industry to industry. Employment of market researchers is expected to increase up to 35 percent by 2012. The same increase is anticipated for marketing, advertising, and public relations managers. Sales representative positions in both retail and wholesale and manufacturing are expected to increase by 20 percent. Most areas of marketing will have available job openings; however, because of intense domestic and global competition, graduates seeking jobs in such areas as advertising, sales promotion, and public relations will meet stiff competition.

APTITUDES AND ATTRIBUTES NEEDED FOR SUCCESS

The spectrum of marketing careers provides diverse opportunities for individuals with a range of different educational backgrounds, skills, aptitudes, and interests. More than any other area of business, marketing offers jobs for artistic, communicative, quantitative, and entrepreneurial types. It is important to understand, however, the unique requirements for success in each area and to know in which areas competition for jobs will be particularly fierce. In these areas, experience as well as talent and educational background will play an important part in landing a good job.

Marketing Research and Marketing Management

Marketing research and marketing management are areas in which both undergraduate degrees in marketing or management and sometimes graduate-level business degrees are essential. Undergraduate degrees in marketing, statistics, or economics are the usual entry-level requirements. In addition, an M.B.A. is preferred by many employers because of the broad knowledge of business that it provides, especially in product management. Unlike most other marketing areas, formal education plays a large part in marketing research careers. Courses in psychology provide the background for motivational research and courses in sociology provide information on how social influences affect the buying practices of consumers. Knowledge in both areas is essential, along with the ability to use computers and statistical methods to conduct research and strong organizational and writing skills to write proposals and reports.

Helpful attributes include logical thought processes, curiosity, problem-solving abilities, and interviewing skills. If you have the impression that the marketing researcher who ultimately becomes the research director must be good in all areas, you are exactly right. That's what makes getting ahead in this area a real challenge. For those who aspire to management positions, outstanding performance in the marketing area of their choice along with graduate work in business and marketing are essential. Let your education help you succeed.

International Marketing

Universities are beginning to orient courses toward global marketing and are sponsoring more study abroad. The Institute of International Education (IIE) publishes *Academic Year Abroad* and *Short-Term Study Abroad*, annual directories that list over six thousand worldwide programs that combine travel and study. This publication can be found in libraries or ordered from IIE Books at iiebooks.org.

Advertising, Sales Promotion, and Public Relations

Advertising, sales promotion, and public relations are also areas in which personal attributes and special abilities play the most important role in success. A good background in marketing or communications is certainly helpful, but it will not guarantee you the job you want. Competition for the sought-after positions in these areas comes from majors in English, psychology, sociology, as well as a variety of other areas.

Your educational background will provide you with a knowledge of major concepts of the field, a familiarity with sources of information, the habit of reading and keeping up-to-date, and the ability to make better decisions, but that's only part of it. Creativity, artistic ability, excellent communications skills, insights into people, and willingness to take risks by putting your ideas on the line are essential for success.

For creative jobs, portfolios with samples of work are usually required. One of the best ways to gain experience and to test your abilities for work in advertising, sales promotion, and public relations is through internships and part-time jobs.

Aside from the creative department, beginners in advertising generally start in the account management or media department. Occasionally, entry-level positions are available in the market research or creative departments of an agency, but these positions usually require some experience. Completing an advertising-related internship while in school provides an advantage when applying for an entry-level position; in fact, internships are becoming a necessary step to obtaining permanent employment. In addition to an internship, courses in marketing, psychology, accounting, statistics, and creative design can help prepare potential entrants for careers in this field.

Assistant account executive, the entry-level account management position in most firms, requires a bachelor's degree in marketing or advertising. Some agencies require a master's degree in business administration. Other entry level positions are assistant media planner and assistant media buyer, which both require a bachelor's degree, preferably with a major in marketing or advertising. Requirements for support services and administrative positions depend on the job and vary from firm to firm.

In public relations, most employers look for applicants with degrees in communications, journalism, English, or business. Some four-year colleges and universities have begun to offer a concentration in public relations. Given the strong competition for entry-level public relations jobs, experience gained through internships and co-op programs is most valuable. Entry-level workers often start as research or account assistants and may be promoted to account executive, account supervisor, vice president, and executive vice president.

Employees in advertising and public relations services should have good people skills, common sense, creativity, communication skills, and problem-solving ability. Foreign language skills have always been important for those wanting to work abroad for domestic firms or to represent foreign firms domestically. However, these skills are increasingly vital to reach linguistic minorities in U.S. cities such as Los Angeles, New York, Miami, Houston, and Phoenix.

Many young advertising professionals launch their careers through participation in the InterAd competition. Sponsored by the International Advertising Association, InterAd is an annual competition open to advertising students around the world. Student teams create complete marketing and advertising campaigns for launching real products into international markets. Corporate sponsors make donations to cover research costs and production materials. These sponsors often incorporate InterAd campaign elements into their international marketing plans.

The competition is judged by advertising agency and marketing executives. Some entrants gain experience in international marketing that is invaluable because this arena will afford many new opportunities to advertising professionals in the future.

Retail Sales

A high school diploma is adequate for finding a position in retail sales. Indeed, many students still in high school work in part-time sales positions. The successful retail salesperson needs an ability to communicate well with customers and a knowledge of the products in the department. Knowledge of a second language can be helpful in multiethnic areas.

As salespersons gain experience and seniority, they usually move into positions of greater responsibility and may be given their choice of departments in which to work. This often means moving to areas with potentially higher earnings and commissions. Although the highest earnings potential is usually associated with selling big-ticket items, such a position requires highly detailed knowledge of the product and talent for persuasion.

Traditionally, capable salespersons without college degrees could advance to management positions. Today, however, large retail businesses usually prefer to hire college graduates as management trainees, making a college education increasingly important. Despite this trend, motivated and capable employees without college degrees still may advance to administrative or supervisory positions in large establishments.

Wholesale and Industrial Sales

The background needed for sales jobs varies by product line and market. Many employers hire individuals with previous sales experience who do not have a college degree, but often prefer those with some college education. More employers look for a bachelor's degree as job requirements have become more technical and analytical and competition is strong in the field.

Many sales representatives attend seminars in sales techniques or take courses in marketing, economics, communication, or even a foreign language to provide the extra edge needed to make sales. Companies also offer formal training programs for beginning sales representatives.

Those who want to become sales representatives should be goal-oriented and persuasive, and should work well both independently and as part of a team. A pleasant personality and appearance, the ability to communicate well with people, and good problem-solving skills are highly valued. Furthermore, completing a sale can take several months and thus requires patience and perseverance.

Sales personnel are often promoted to a larger account or territory where commissions are likely to be greater. Experienced sales representatives may move into jobs as sales trainers, who instruct new employees on selling techniques and company policies and procedures. Those with good sales records and leadership ability may advance to positions such as sales supervisor, district manager, or vice president of sales. In addition to advancement opportunities within a firm, some manufacturers' agents go into business for themselves. Others find opportunities in purchasing, advertising, or marketing research.

CAREER DEVELOPMENT AND COMPENSATION

An understanding of the variety and quantity of different careers in marketing can be gleaned from the breadth of the marketing function itself. Figure 6.1 shows how marketing positions in a fairly large organization relate to one another and to job mobility. Corporate sales, where many marketing graduates begin, is an excellent position from which to begin a career path that could lead right to the top of the organization.

Salaries differ from industry to industry in accordance with industry norms. For new graduates in marketing, average annual salaries for the same job may differ depending on location. The cost of living may vary accordingly, explaining in part the salary differences. Compensation packages contain more than salary alone. In response to employee demands, companies are now offering better and more varied benefit packages that differ in value. Fringe benefits may include health insurance, life insurance, disability compensation, vacation time, sick and maternity leave, paid holidays, bonuses, pension plans, employee stock ownership and/or stock purchase plans, and profit-sharing plans. Job applicants must evaluate these benefits to compute total compensation.

Figure 6.1

Marketing positions and mobility

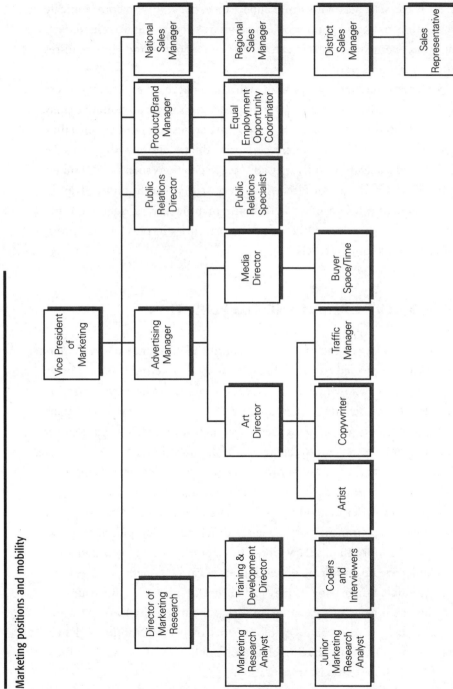

For top marketing executives in major national corporations, six-digit salaries are not unusual. Executive benefit packages are likely to include all of the above plus chauffeur-driven limousines, country club memberships, and a range of personal and professional services. Most managers and supervisors receive profit-sharing benefits as additional incentives. Sales representatives can earn six-digit figures as well when bonuses are added to one's salary and commissions.

For professionals in advertising, sales promotion, and public relations firms, entry salaries are usually lower than for comparable positions in large organizations, but as they advance in these firms, salaries are relatively higher.

Average annual salaries in marketing and communications for recent graduates reported by the National Association of Colleges and Employers (NACE) Fall 2004 salary survey are listed below for all types of employers:

Advertising	$29,543	Purchasing	$41,220
Brand/product management	$39,772	Sales	$34,597
Buyer/merchandising	$38,372	Design/graphic arts	$30,093
Customer service	$29,147	Media planning	$28,044
Distribution	$38,689	Communications/ production	$28,092
Market research	$35,670	Public relations	$28,961

SOURCES OF ADDITIONAL INFORMATION

University career centers and libraries can provide a wealth of information on careers in marketing. General timely information on marketing fields can be found in such periodicals as *Journal of Marketing*, *Journal of Marketing Research*, *Journal of Public Relations Research*, *Advertising Age*, *Adweek*, and *Marketing Week*, and dozens of others. Many are available online as well as in print.

For specific career information, you can contact professional marketing associations. The American Marketing Association offers a wealth of information and sources, including a job search feature and career advice. The American Advertising Federation provides a list of colleges that offer programs in advertising. The addresses of these and other associations are listed here.

Advertising Club of New York
235 Park Avenue S., 6th Floor
New York, NY 10003
theadvertisingclub.org

The Advertising Club has a Young Professionals Division for individuals under thirty.

American Advertising Federation (AAF)
1101 Vermont Avenue NW
Washington, DC 20005
aaf.org

AAF is an excellent source of advertising internships offered by many of its members.

American Association of Advertising Agencies
405 Lexington Avenue, 18th floor
New York, NY 10174
aaaa.org

American Marketing Association
311 South Wacker Drive, Suite 5800
Chicago, IL 60606
ama.org

American Telemarketing Association
3815 River Crossing Parkway, Suite 20
Indianapolis, IN 46210
ataconnect.org

Direct Marketing Association
1120 Avenue of the Americas
New York, NY 10036
the-dma.org

Manufacturers' Agents National Association
P.O. Box 3467
23016 Mill Creek Road
Laguna Hills, CA 92654
manaonline.org

Marketing Agencies Association Worldwide
750 Summer Street
Stamford, CT 06901
maaw.org

Marketing Research Association
1344 Silas Deane Highway, Suite 306
Rocky Hill, CT 06067
mra-net.org

National Association of Wholesaler-Distributors
1725 K Street, NW
Washington, DC 20006
naw.org

National Retail Federation
375 7th Street NW, Suite 1000
Washington, DC 20004
nrf.com

Pi Sigma Epsilon
259 South Broadway Avenue
CBA, Room 115
Akron, OH 44325
pseakron.com

Students may obtain career and scholarship information from this sales
fraternity associated with Sales and Marketing Executives International
(SMEI).

Product Development and Management Association
15000 Commerce Parkway, Suite C
Mount Laurel, NJ 08054
pdma.org

Promotion Marketing Association, Inc.
257 Park Avenue South, Suite 1102
New York, NY 10010
pmalink.org

Public Relations Society of America
33 Maiden Lane, 3rd floor
New York, NY 10038
prsa.org

This organization has a student branch, Public Relations Student Society
of America. Visit the website at prssa.org.

Sales and Marketing Executives International
P.O. Box 1390
Sumas, WA 98295
smei.org

Sources of Additional Information in Canada
Association of Canadian Advertisers, Inc.
175 Bloor Street East
South Tower, Suite 307
Toronto, ON M4W 3R8
aca-online.com

Canadian Marketing Association
1 Concorde Gate, Suite 607
Don Mills, ON M3C 3N6
the-cma.org

Canadian Professional Sales Association
145 Wellington Street West, Suite 610
Toronto, ON M5J 1H8
cpsa.com

Direct Sellers Association of Canada
180 Attwell Drive, Suite 250
Toronto, ON M9W 6A9
dsa.ca

Promotional Products Association of Canada
4920 de Maisonneuve West, Suite 305
Westmount, QC H3Z 1N1
promocan.com

Retail Council of Canada
1255 Bay Street, Suite 800
Toronto, ON M5R 2A9
retailcouncil.org

CAREER DECISION-MAKING MODEL

It is now time to consider a career in marketing. Figures 6.2a and 6.2b are forms with the factors included in the career decision-making model in Chapter 1. Follow these directions in completing them.

1. Enter the position that interests you most on the line titled Job.
2. Enter any additional factors used to personalize your model in the blank spaces provided (from Chapter 1).
3. Enter the weights that you assigned to the factors (from Chapter 1) in the column WT. (It would be wise to review the explanations of these factors in the description of the model in Chapter 1 before going on to step 4.)
4. Assign a value from 1 (lowest) to 10 (highest) to each factor based on the information in this chapter and on your personal self-assessment, entering the value in column V. If you feel that you have a certain aptitude or attribute needed for success in this career area, you should assign a fairly high value. If a certain interest such as amount of variety is desirable to you and you feel the area provides the variety you enjoy, assign a fairly high value. If not, assign a low value. Use this technique to assign values to all factors in the model. If you cannot assign a value based on the

information in the chapter for some of the factors in the model, either use other sources to acquire the information or leave the space beside the factor blank.

5. Multiply the weight times the value, entering the score in column S.

6. Add the scores in column S for each group of factors, entering the number in the space labeled Total.

Figure 6.2a

Career evaluation for marketing

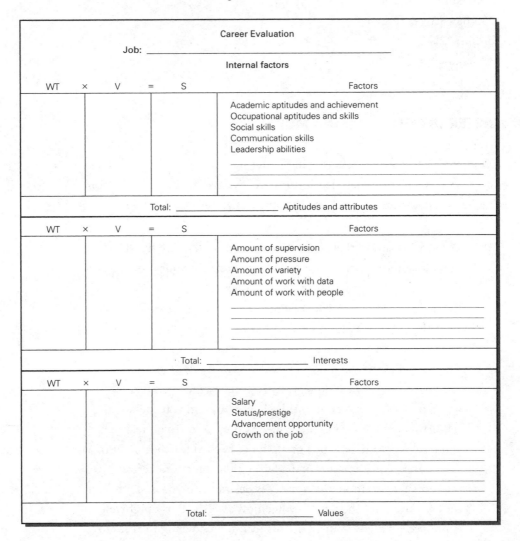

Career Evaluation

Job: _____

Internal factors

WT × V = S — Factors

- Academic aptitudes and achievement
- Occupational aptitudes and skills
- Social skills
- Communication skills
- Leadership abilities

Total: _____ Aptitudes and attributes

WT × V = S — Factors

- Amount of supervision
- Amount of pressure
- Amount of variety
- Amount of work with data
- Amount of work with people

Total: _____ Interests

WT × V = S — Factors

- Salary
- Status/prestige
- Advancement opportunity
- Growth on the job

Total: _____ Values

Figure 6.2b

157

Careers in
Marketing

Career evaluation for marketing

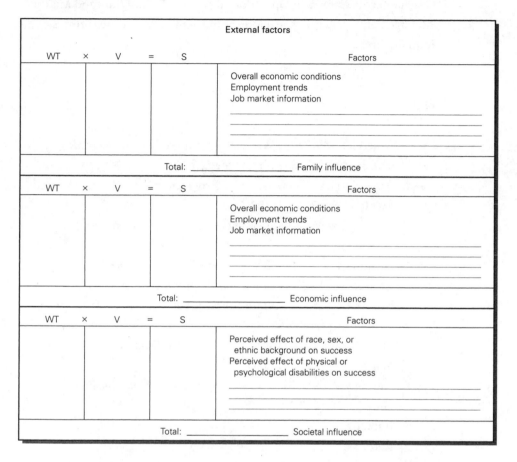

You will use this evaluation in Chapter 11 in combination with evaluations of each career explored in this book.

WHAT DID YOU LEARN?

This chapter included a great deal of information on careers in marketing. Now you know what kind of work marketing professionals do, who employs them, what kinds of salaries they earn, the career paths that many of them follow, what the job outlook is, what trends are affecting it, how to prepare yourself for a marketing career, and where to find additional information. You also completed a career evaluation for marketing.

Chapter 7, "Careers in Operations Research, Production, and Materials Management," will give you a look at the behind-the-scenes professionals in many firms.

NOTES

1. American Marketing Association, marketingpower.com/mg-dictionary-view1862.php, (accessed March 7, 2005).
2. Amy Merrick, "Gap's Greatest Generation?", *Wall Street Journal* (September 15, 2004), B1.
3. Stephen Baker, "Channeling the Future," *BusinessWeek* (July 12, 2004), 70.
4. Suzanne Vranica and Brian Steinberg, "The Robot Wore Converses," *Wall Street Journal* (September 2, 2004), B1.
5. Brooks Barnes, "Trump to Brands: 'You're Hired,'" *Wall Street Journal* (September 2, 2004), B1.
6. Ellen Sheng, "Advertisers Sharpen Their Targeting," *Wall Street Journal* (October 27, 2004), B2D.
7. Anthony Bianco, "The Vanishing Mass Market," *BusinessWeek* (July 12, 2004), 62.
8. Ibid., 61.
9. Ibid., 65.
10. Brian Steinberg, "Online Ad Dollars Set to Match, Then Go Ahead of Magazines," *Wall Street Journal* (July 27, 2004), B7.
11. Conrad DeAenlle, "Is Online Retailing a Victim of Its Own Success?" *New York Times* (February 6, 2005), BU8.
12. James J. Owens, "Opportunities to the South," *Minority MBA* (Spring 2004), 27.
13. Ibid., 30.
14. American Marketing Association, marketingpower.com/content407.php, (accessed March 8, 2005).

CHAPTER

7

CAREERS IN OPERATIONS RESEARCH, PRODUCTION, AND MATERIALS MANAGEMENT

After reading this chapter, you will be able to:

- Describe the work of production managers, line supervisors, manufacturing managers, production planners, quality assurance managers, operations research analysts, material managers, purchasing managers, purchasing agents, buyers, expediters, traffic managers, and inventory managers
- Discuss trends in operations, production, and materials management and their impact on careers
- Diagram career paths for workers in operations, production, and materials management
- Discuss job opportunities in the fields of operations research, production, and materials management today
- List the educational preparation and skills needed for positions in operations, production, and materials management
- Evaluate careers in operations, production, and materials management according to your individualized career decision-making model

Operation and production decisions made by managers are usually justified by numbers. On the basis of quantitative analysis, decisions must be made regarding the amount of demand for a company's products, how much inventory to keep on hand to fill orders, how to best schedule workers and equipment for the greatest productivity, and how much raw material is needed for the manufacturing process. Through computer simulations, mathematical models, and other quantitative techniques, operations research analysts, production managers, and materials managers gain valuable information to assist them in making decisions that keep the company profitable in a competitive environment.

American manufacturing has been greatly impacted by the movement of American business from the industrial to the information age, global business, and the international outsourcing of jobs. Although the service-producing sector expanded rapidly, the manufacturing sector had to work hard to try to maintain and grow. Continued competition from foreign manufacturing firms at home and abroad, expanded use of technology, and increased demand for better-quality products have created other changes in what, how, and where American manufacturing is done.

Production is the area within manufacturing that is least glamorized but most essential. It involves procuring materials to produce a product and planning and controlling the manufacturing process. Materials management is concerned with all activities in the procurement and distribution of materials needed to manufacture a product. After the materials are obtained, the production begins and after production, distribution of the product. The term "operations management" is widely used to include managing the production of goods and services. Such concepts as job design, facility location, capacity planning, workforce management, inventory, and scheduling fall into this category.

The organizational structure and operations of each industry and firm vary as it produces its products. The objective is to work effectively and efficiently to assure high-quality goods and services. This chapter will give you a look at operations and production careers, and it includes the following information:

- What jobs production personnel perform
- Who employs these professionals
- Salaries and career paths
- Latest trends
- Job opportunities
- Education and skills needed to pursue production careers
- Sources of additional information

OPERATIONS RESEARCH

An important position in today's companies is that of the operations research (OR) analyst, sometimes called management scientist. The OR analyst is a specialist who uses mathematical tools and computer technology to analyze business operations, methods, and products, and provides that information to the managers who must make sound decisions.

Improving productivity is a primary goal of OR analysts. These professionals work in the complex area of managing large organizations that require the effective use of money, materials, equipment, and people. Operations research analysts help determine better ways to coordinate these elements by applying analytical methods from mathematics, science, and engineering. They solve problems and propose alternative solutions to management, which then chooses the course of action that best meets the organization's goals. In general, OR analysts may be concerned with diverse issues such as top-level strategy, planning, forecasting, resource allocation, performance measurement, scheduling, the design of production facilities and systems, supply chain management, pricing, transportation and distribution, and the analysis of large databases.

The operations research analyst generally reports to executives fairly high up in the company and deals with solutions to large, complex problems. An analyst might be responsible for planning a production schedule that keeps the cost of production and inventory low and eliminates the piling up of unfilled orders. Many college management programs offer courses in operations and production that combine operations research techniques with production knowledge. However, the work of operations research analysts is performed in all large organizations and in all functional areas, not only in production.

PRODUCTION MANAGEMENT

Millions of goods are produced each year in the United States; the coordination of this production is the responsibility of production managers. The vice president of operations and production, the regional managers, and the individual plant managers are all production managers working at different levels of responsibility. These managers are involved with production planning and control for the company nationwide, for a certain region, or for an individual plant, respectively. Their primary responsibility is planning the production schedule within budgetary limitations and time constraints. They do this by analyzing the plant's personnel and capital resources to select the best way of meeting the production quota. Industrial production managers determine, often using mathematical formulas, which machines will be used, whether new machines need to be purchased, whether overtime or extra shifts are necessary, and what the sequence of production will be. They monitor the production run to make sure that it stays on schedule, and correct any problems that may arise.

An entry-level production job for a college graduate is the line supervisor, whose responsibility is to oversee the workers who run the machines. Many line supervisors are responsible for scheduling production runs, designing budgets, and maintaining employee relations. An individual may be moved a number of times to varied positions before advancing to manufacturing manager, head of the entire manufacturing operation.

Upwardly mobile production management candidates might hold the position of production planner, whose responsibilities include preparing production schedules for manufacturing industrial and commercial products. They also may be responsible for planning new plant layouts, projecting inventory levels, and calculating long-term expenditures for facilities and equipment.

A staff production job to which a beginner might be assigned is assistant quality assurance manager. This assistant works closely with the quality assurance manager, assuming some of the responsibility for preventing product deficiencies by detecting and correcting any that do exist.

The quality assurance manager and staff review a product's design requirements and often participate in the selection of materials and supplies. The manager directs sampling, inspecting, and testing operations and sets standards for the rejection of defective parts. Engineers, technicians, and inspectors work as part of the quality assurance staff.

MATERIALS MANAGEMENT

The materials manager has an important function in the production process. Basically, materials management involves having the right item, at the right place, at the right time, at a reasonable cost. This is true for manufacturers of both goods and services. The emphasis in service firms is ordering, receiving, storing, and distributing within the firm the supplies required to perform the service. In manufacturing firms, the materials management function is extended to include not only management of materials needed to produce the product, but also storing the product throughout all phases of production and in its finished form; moving the product to the shipping department; and transporting the product to distribution centers, warehouses, or directly to customers.

Materials managers must be industry specialists, responsible in many organizations for the procurement, storage, and movement of materials within the company. They keep a production manager informed of the industry's current capabilities, emerging technology, and individual suppliers and their products. The major task of materials managers is the identification of suppliers breaking significant new ground in materials and production technology. Materials and purchasing managers interact regularly with engineering and quality control professionals.

Working under the materials manager is a group of purchasing professionals. The primary purchasing functions are establishing sources of supply, ordering the needed items, setting prices and delivery dates, and dealing with shortages. Purchasing, though sometimes underrated, is extremely important. There are two aspects of profit—making money and reducing costs. Shrewd buying at good prices has established the purchasing manager as an integral part of the management team. The purchasing manager is responsible for establishing and enforcing purchasing department policies, forecasting supply and price trends, seeking new ideas and sources of materials, recommending that specific materials and components be used in production, and participating in new product development with respect to projected cost.

Purchasing agents work under the supervision of the purchasing manager. Usually purchasing agents are involved both in buying personally and in supervising the buying activities of assistant purchasing agents and buyers. Depending on the size of the purchasing department, senior purchasing agents may do more or less buying and supervising. For example, in a large department a purchasing agent may do less buying and more training, development, and supervision of subordinates.

The responsibilities of the buyer include placing orders with suppliers, checking the progress of overdue orders, conducting interviews with industrial salespersons to consider new materials, and keeping in close contact with suppliers through correspondence, phone calls, and plant visits. The buyer must be good at cost/price analysis—that is, able to judge the fairness of a supplier's quoted price by judging what the supplier's costs are. The successful buyer maintains a varied number of sources and always has a backup supplier for necessary items. Some companies certify or qualify suppliers. To be able to take advantage of opportunities to stock up on items that may run short or that are offered at a good price, the buyer must always be aware of market conditions. Building long-term supplier relationships often assures good prices and on-time deliveries. These relationships measure the success of the buyer.

Many buyers specialize, depending on the company or industry in which they work. Such specialty areas include raw materials or commodity buying; production material or component buying; construction buying, which may involve negotiations, tools, spare parts, and operating supplies buying; and general-purpose buying of a wide range of materials generally of low value. Construction buying and general-purpose buying are typical initial assignments and do not require the technical expertise of the other two areas.

Many careers in purchasing start with the position of expediter. The responsibility of the expediter is to see that delivery commitments made by suppliers are kept or, if delays occur, to attempt to speed the deliveries. This job, although clerical in nature, has expanded as companies are seeking to reduce time between order and delivery of materials. As expediter, a beginner has an opportunity to become familiar with most items purchased as well as who supplies them—the necessary background for advancing to an assistant buyer position.

After materials are purchased, the traffic function comes into play. The traffic manager deals mainly with securing delivery of purchased materials, including backup delivery options. Responsibilities for overall supervision of traffic operations are handled by the traffic manager. This might include quoting freight rates to buyers, procuring special cars and equipment for transporting materials, handling claims and adjustments for damaged shipments, routing and tracing inbound shipments, and approving transportation bills. In larger companies, the traffic manager heads a separate department; in smaller companies, the traffic manager may be part of the purchasing department.

A final aspect of the materials management picture is inventory control. The inventory manager is responsible for maintaining the levels of inventory necessary for the production process. Working closely with the purchasing and traffic managers, the inventory manager has an important role in seeing that materials scheduled for use are available in inventory.

CURRENT TRENDS

The global economy has significantly affected American manufacturing firms, which are competing with low-cost, high-quality imports from other countries. American firms are opening plants abroad, improving quality control operations, and shortening the time materials remain in inventory to compete effectively in both the national and international markets. Hiring nationals in foreign operations has reduced labor costs substantially. The outsourcing of jobs is a widely debated political and economic issue today.

Exports

An increasing demand for exports has helped elevate U.S. manufacturing output, which had fallen in recent years. According to the U.S. Commerce Department, exports have risen in scientific instruments, aerospace equipment, car parts, toys, and industrial machinery. However, the pace of export growth has begun to slow down, and high energy prices are seen as likely to slow global economic growth and thereby lessen foreign demand for U.S. goods.[1]

One area in which U.S. goods remain in high demand is the Hispanic export market, which in 2004 reported an increase of 17.5 percent in total export revenues from the previous year. Half of the companies that comprise the 2004 Hispanic Business Top 50 Exporters are based in Florida. Given Florida's location and local culture, it allows exporters to quickly ship goods to Latin America and the Caribbean. Some European companies have begun to use Florida-based companies to handle their Latin American business. Also, multinational corporations have moved international divisions to Florida, finding advantages in the state's communications systems, transportation, and labor pool.[2]

New Technologies

Technology has both eliminated and created industries and careers in manufacturing. Many manufacturing workers have been replaced by robots, and the robotics industry itself now produces many jobs along with the fiber optics, laser, and telecommunications industries. However, the new jobs created by these industries require higher technical levels of training than the old assembly line jobs.

The use of robots with computer technology has created computer-aided manufacturing (CAM) and computer-aided design (CAD). Some organizations have integrated some of the production processes with computers, termed computer-integrated manufacturing (CIM), while in other organizations the entire manufacturing process is controlled and performed by computers (Flexible Manufacturing Systems).

Taking the use of computer technology one step further, some companies have begun using product life-cycle management, or PLM. This new software allows a company to manage a product through every stage of its lifespan, from creation through development, manufacturing, testing, and then maintenance in the field. The PLM technology even cycles back to the product's concept and production phases for redesign or updates.[3] At this time, PLM is still relatively new and therefore not widely used. However, the 55 companies of the 650 leading manufacturers in the United States and Europe that do use PLM reported profits that were 73 percent higher than those of the rest of the group. A recent study estimates that the Fortune 1,000 manufacturers that do not install PLM by 2007 will struggle to remain competitive.[4]

Computerization has also changed the nature of purchasing occupations. With less paperwork, purchasing agents and managers can spend more time on buying decisions using technology such as electronic data interchange (EDI). Computers facilitate accessing up-to-date product and price listings, maintaining desired inventory levels, processing orders, and determining when to place orders. Limited-source contracting, in which purchasing agents deal with fewer suppliers (having identified those who offer the overall best quality, service, and price), saves time and resources. Implications of these technological changes are that the nature of jobs in production and materials management will continue to change and employees will be required to develop new skills.

Reengineering and Continuous Improvement

Reengineering or process design involves investigating and changing both the tasks and activities performed by the organization, and the information systems used to support these tasks. Objectives such as reducing delivery time, increasing product and service quality, enhancing customer satisfaction, and increasing revenues and profitability are all necessary to remain competitive in today's business environment. The notion of continuous improvement of processes to add value to products and services is now fundamental to planning. Continuous improvement and reengineering has resulted in small changes within the corporation to major restructuring of departments that would have a large impact on employees.

Total Quality Management

Total quality management is an approach that makes a commitment to quality throughout the organization. While traditional quality control programs reacted only to problems that reached a certain significant level, newer management techniques and programs emphasize continuous quality improvement. If the problem relates to the quality of work performed in the plant, the manager may implement better training programs or reorganize the manufacturing process, often based upon the suggestions of employee teams. If the cause is substandard materials or parts from outside suppliers, companies may work with their suppliers to improve quality.

The International Organization for Standardization (ISO) has developed quality standards, called ISO 9000 and ISO 14,000, that have been adopted by organizations around the world committed to buying high-quality materials and producing high-quality products and services. ISO 9000 is an international reference for quality management in business dealings; ISO 14,000 is intended to enable organizations to meet environmental challenges.[5]

JOB OPPORTUNITIES

Employment of production and purchasing specialists will be affected by various trends in coming years. Advanced technologies that result in downsizing of production departments, outsourcing of operations, and limited-source contracting or reducing the number of suppliers, will reduce demand for workers in production and purchasing. However, advances in technology could create demand for operations research analysts, whose expertise will be needed to determine how best to utilize the new technology.

Opportunities for operations research analysts exist in almost every industry, but they should be especially good in highly competitive industries, such as manufacturing, transportation, telecommunications, and finance. As businesses and government agencies continue to contract out jobs to cut costs, many operations research analysts will find opportunities as consultants, either working for a consulting firm or setting up their own practice. Opportunities will also exist in the military, but will depend on the size of future military budgets. In this area, operations research analysts will be needed to test and evaluate the accuracy and effectiveness of new weapons systems and strategies.

Nearly half of the opportunities for purchasing positions exist in manufacturing industries, with the remainder in government agencies, hospitals, and educational institutions. Overall employment of buyers, purchasing managers, and purchasing agents is expected to increase only 9 percent through the year 2012. Demand for purchasing workers will be limited by the growing number of electronic purchases and improved software that eliminates extensive paperwork. The wealth of information available on the Internet has increased the productivity of purchasing managers.

The increasing use of computers for scheduling, planning, and coordination will lead to greater productivity among managers. According to the Bureau of Labor Statistics, increases in productivity among industrial production managers and the workers they supervise will limit growth in employment of these managers in the next several years. Increased productivity among workers will limit both the number of employees in factories and the need for supervision. In addition, more emphasis on quality in the production process has redistributed some of the production manager's oversight responsibilities to supervisors and workers on the production line. Because production managers are so essential to the efficient operation of a plant, they have not been greatly affected by recent efforts to flatten management structures. Nevertheless, this trend has led production managers to assume more responsibilities and has limited the creation of more employment opportunities.

APTITUDES AND ATTRIBUTES NEEDED FOR SUCCESS

The areas of operations research, production, and materials management are highly technical in nature and require strong backgrounds in mathematics and computer science. Most employers require a degree in business or engineering with expertise in the latest technologies. Information systems including organization analysis and planning, work measurement and standards, and work simplification are desirable.

Operations Research

In operations research, most employers require at least a master's degree in operations research or a closely related field, such as computer science, engineering, business, mathematics, information systems, or management science. Dual graduate degrees in operations research and computer science are becoming more attractive to employers. Good communication skills are also important, since OR analysts must be able to think logically and work well with people.

Many organizations provide training for experienced personnel, helping them to keep up with new developments in OR techniques and computer science. Some companies pay for OR analysts to attend advanced university classes. Computers are the most important tools for performing in-depth analysis, so training and experience in programming are required for success. OR analysts typically need to be proficient in database collection and management, programming, and the development and use of sophisticated software packages.

Production

As production operations become more sophisticated, more employers seek candidates with graduate degrees in industrial management or business administration. Either of these degrees is considered very good preparation, especially when combined with an undergraduate degree in engineering. Managers who do not have graduate degrees often take courses in decision sciences, where they learn techniques and mathematical formulas that can be used to maximize efficiency and improve quality. Because the job requires the ability to compromise, persuade, and negotiate, successful production managers must be well-rounded and have excellent communication skills.

Most employees who enter the field directly after graduation spend their first few months in the company's training program, where they become familiar with the production process, company policies, and requirements of the job. In larger companies, training may also include assignments to other departments, such as purchasing and accounting. A number of companies hire college graduates as first-line supervisors and later promote them.

Some industrial production managers have worked their way up through the ranks, perhaps after having worked as first-line supervisors. While these employees already have a sound knowledge of the production process and the firm's organization, they will need a college degree to be promoted.

Materials Management

Educational requirements for purchasing specialists vary with the size of the organization. Large wholesale and retail employers generally prefer applicants who have a bachelor's degree with a business emphasis. Many manufacturing firms stress formal training, preferring applicants with a bachelor's or master's degree in engineering, business, economics, or one of the applied sciences. A master's degree is essential for advancement to many top-level purchasing manager jobs.

In manufacturing, new purchasing employees are often enrolled in company training programs to learn about the firm's operations and purchasing practices. They work with experienced purchasers to learn about commodities, prices, suppliers, and markets. In addition, they may be assigned to the production planning department to learn about the material requirements system and the inventory system that keeps production and replenishment functions working smoothly.

Purchasing managers must know how to use word processing and spreadsheet software, as well as the Internet. Other important qualities include the ability to analyze technical data in suppliers' proposals; good communication, negotiation, and mathematical skills; knowledge of supply-chain management; and the ability to perform financial analyses.

Purchasing managers, agents, and buyers spend huge amounts of their companies' money each year. Because of this economic power, they are often under pressure to bend the rules for kickbacks or other favors. In light of this, purchasing professionals must have a high degree of ethics. In general, effective purchasing pros tend to have a more positive self-image, excellent communication abilities, strong professional interests, and a pref-

erence for jobs providing opportunities for variety, challenge, and professional growth.

Certification. Certification by a recognized association is an important step
for advancement in purchasing. In private industry, the Accredited Purchasing Practitioner (APP) and Certified Purchasing Manager (CPM) designations are conferred by the Institute for Supply Management (ISM). The
Certified Purchasing Professional (CPP) and Certified Professional Purchasing Manager (CPPM) designations are conferred by the American Purchasing Society (APS). In federal, state, and local government, the
certifications for professional competence are Certified Professional Public
Buyer (CPPB) and Certified Public Purchasing Officer (CPPO), conferred
by the National Institute of Governmental Purchasing (NIGP). Most of these
certifications are awarded only after work-related experience and education
requirements are met, and written or oral exams are successfully completed.

CAREER DEVELOPMENT AND COMPENSATION

Advancement is possible in all areas of operations and production for those
with drive, ability, and the proper educational background. Operations is
a critical function in manufacturing, and operations managers can earn
high salaries and have excellent possibilities for advancement. The vice
president of operations is one step from the top. Figure 7.1 shows how
operations and production in a manufacturing firm might be organized.

Today, advancement and salary within operations are determined not
only by the ability to make critical decisions, but also by technical knowledge and experience. Many of the critical decisions involve using technology, such as information and telecommunication systems, in the
production process. The greater technical expertise operations managers
have, the greater their value to their organization.

Depending on the degree of importance placed on materials and the way
the firm is structured, materials management may offer job mobility. Some
firms may assign a vice president of materials who functions at the same
level as the production vice president. Because of the growing importance
of the purchasing function and the necessary role of the materials manager
in market forecasting, production planning, and inventory control, the
materials orientation in firms has increased.

Figure 7.1

Operations/production positions and mobility

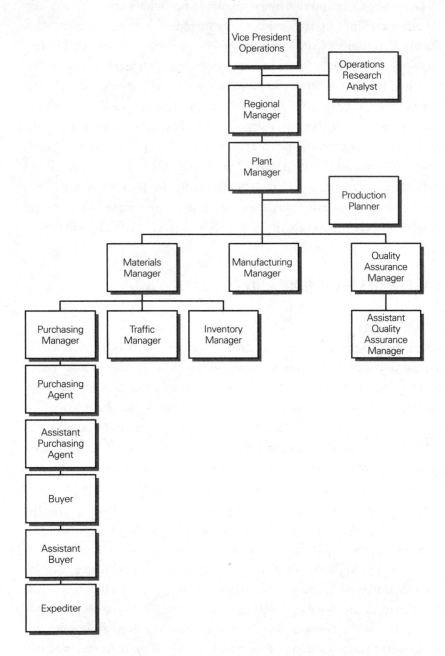

To advance from purchasing to materials management, an individual must gain a deeper knowledge of the operations of other departments and be proficient in the use of computers and quantitative techniques. This knowledge makes manufacturing line managers viable and quality assurance specialists candidates for a move into the key materials management slot. The greater emphasis on strategic planning and critical decision making in manufacturing firms, coupled with advanced technology, have catapulted the operations research analyst into a position of major importance.

Median annual earnings of operations research analysts were $56,920 in 2002; the middle 50 percent earned between $43,220 and $74,460. Top operations research analysts in large corporations can earn more than $100,000 a year. Greater recognition, greater salary, greater risks, and greater opportunity to move into top management positions are all characteristics of positions in operations research.

Median annual earnings for industrial production managers were $67,320 in 2002, with the middle 50 percent earning between $50,710 and $88,880.

In purchasing, median annual earnings of managers were $59,890 in 2002. The middle 50 percent earned between $43,670 and $81,950 a year. Median annual earnings for wholesale and retail buyers were $40,780 in 2002. The middle 50 percent earned between $30,040 and $55,670.

SOURCES OF ADDITIONAL INFORMATION

There is much information available through the many organizations for operations, production, and materials management professionals. Listed here are the names and addresses of organizations to which you may write for career information.

For careers in production planning, contact:

American Production and Inventory Control Society/The Association
for Operations Management
5301 Shawnee Road
Alexandria, VA 22312
apics.org

National Association of Manufacturers
1331 Pennsylvania Avenue, NW
Washington, DC 20004
nam.org

For careers in quality assurance, contact:

American Society for Quality
600 North Plankinton Avenue
Milwaukee, WI 53203
asq.org

For careers in physical distribution, contact:

Council of Chain Management Professionals
2805 Butterfield Road, Suite 200
Oak Brook, IL 60523
cscmp.org

For careers in operations research, contact:

Institute for Operations Research and the Management Sciences
    (INFORMS)
7240 Parkway Drive, Suite 310
Hanover, MD 21076
informs.org

Mathematical Association of America
1529 18th Street, NW
Washington, DC 20036
maa.org

Society for Industrial and Applied Mathematics
3600 University City Science Center
Philadelphia, PA 19104
siam.org

For careers in purchasing, contact the following:

National Association of Purchasing Management
P.O. Box 22160
Tempe, AZ 85285
napm.org

National Association of State Purchasing Officials
167 West Main Street, Suite 600
Lexington, KY 40507
naspo.org

National Institute of Governmental Purchasing
151 Spring Street
Herndon, VA 20170
nigp.org

Sources of Additional Information in Canada

APICS/The Association for Operations Management
1370 Don Mills Road, Suite 300
Toronto, ON M3B 3N7
apicis-toronto.com

Canadian Manufacturers and Exporters
1 Nicholas St., Suite 1500
Ottawa ON K1N 7B7
cme-mec.ca

National Quality Institute
2275 Lake Shore Boulevard West, Suite 307
Toronto, ON M8V 3Y3
nqi.ca

CAREER DECISION-MAKING MODEL

It is now time to consider a career in operations, production, or materials management. Using the career decision-making model, complete the following forms according to the directions. Figures 7.2a and 7.2b are forms with the factors included in the career decision-making model described in Chapter 1. Follow these directions in completing them.

1. Enter the position that interests you most on the line titled Job.
2. Enter any additional factors used to personalize your model (from Chapter 1) in the blank spaces provided.

Figure 7.2a

Career evaluation for operations, production, and materials management

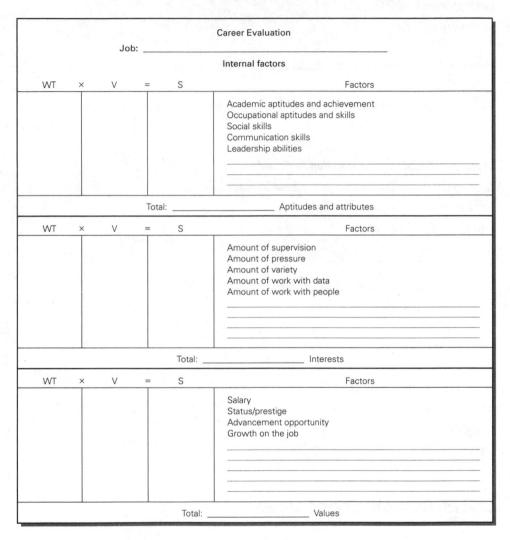

3. Enter the weights that you assigned to the factors (from Chapter 1) in the column WT. (It would be wise to review the explanations of these factors in the description of the model in Chapter 1 before going on to step 4.)

4. Assign a value from 1 (lowest) to 10 (highest) to each factor, based on the information in this chapter and on your personal self-assessment, entering the value in column V. If you feel that you have a certain aptitude or attribute needed for success in this

career area, you should assign a fairly high value. If a certain interest, such as amount of variety, is desirable to you and you feel the area provides the variety you enjoy, assign a fairly high value. If not, assign a low value. Use this technique to assign values to all factors in the model. If you cannot assign a value based on the information in the chapter for some of the factors in the model, either use other sources to acquire the information or leave the space beside the factor blank.

5. Multiply the weight times the value, entering the score in column S.
6. Add the scores in column S for each group of factors, entering the number in the space labeled Total.

Figure 7.2b

Career evaluation for operations, production, and materials management

| \multicolumn{5}{c}{External factors} | |
WT	×	V	=	S	Factors
					Overall economic conditions
					Employment trends
					Job market information
					_____
					_____
					_____
					_____
\multicolumn{5}{c}{Total: _____}	Family influence
WT	×	V	=	S	Factors
					Overall economic conditions
					Employment trends
					Job market information
					_____
					_____
					_____
					_____
\multicolumn{5}{c}{Total: _____}	Economic influence
WT	×	V	=	S	Factors
					Perceived effect of race, sex, or ethnic background on success
					Perceived effect of physical or psychological disabilities on success
					_____
					_____
					_____
\multicolumn{5}{c}{Total: _____}	Societal influence

You will use this evaluation in Chapter 11 in combination with evaluations of each career explored in this book.

WHAT DID YOU LEARN?

You learned about the various careers in operations, production, and materials management in this chapter. Now you know what jobs are involved, what salaries can be earned, what some of the trends are, what the job outlook is, what education and skills are required to enter operations research, production, and materials management careers, and where to get additional information. You also completed the career evaluation model for operations research, production, and materials management.

In Chapter 8, "Careers in Human Resources Management," you will explore the people-oriented area that is growing in scope and importance.

NOTES

1. Timothy Aeppel, "The Outlook: Manufacturing's Fortunes Tied to Exports," *Wall Street Journal* (October 25, 2004), A2.
2. Michael Caplinger, "Foreign Targets: Wholesalers and Manufacturers on the Top 50 Exporters Directory Show How to Win in a Competitive Global Economy," *Hispanic Business* (July/August 2004), 48.
3. Gene Bylinsky, "Not Your Grandfather's Assembly Line," *Fortune* (July 12, 2004), 136D.
4. Ibid., 136F.
5. International Organization for Standardization, iso.org/iso/en/iso900-14000/index.html, (accessed March 8, 2005).

CHAPTER 8

CAREERS IN HUMAN RESOURCES MANAGEMENT

After reading this chapter, you will be able to:

- Describe the work of human resources management specialists
- Discuss trends in human resources management and their impact on careers
- Diagram career paths for those in human resources management
- Discuss job opportunities in the field of human resources management
- List the educational preparation and skills needed for entry and advancement in human resources management careers
- Evaluate careers in human resources management according to your individualized career decision-making model

The most valuable assets of an organization are its people and its technology, the two components that help any company achieve its goals. It is therefore necessary for organizations to attract, train, and keep employees with the required skills and technological training. The professionals who help an organization achieve this goal are the human resources management staff, who provide the link between top management and employees.

In the past, human resources staff were primarily involved with an organization's administrative functions, such as handling employee benefits questions or recruiting, interviewing, and hiring new personnel in accordance with policies established with top management. In addition to these tasks, today's human resources workers also increasingly consult with top executives regarding strategic planning. They have moved from behind-the-scenes staff workers to leading the company in suggesting and changing policies. The human resources department is vital to a company's financial success.

Those who work in human resources management must excel at working with people. This field includes well-defined functional areas that afford many career options. This chapter will cover these options and includes such information as:

- What type of work is done in the area of human resources management
- Where human resources management specialists are employed
- Salaries and career paths
- Latest trends
- Job opportunities
- Education and skills needed to pursue careers in human resources management
- Sources of additional information

HUMAN RESOURCES MANAGEMENT

In a small organization, all aspects of human resources work might be handled by a human resources generalist. The responsibilities of human resources generalists can vary widely, depending on the employers' needs. Therefore, a generalist needs a broad range of knowledge in the various aspects of human resources management. In a large corporation, the human resources management department comprises specialists in several fields who work together to implement the organization's policies.

Director of Human Resources

The director of human resources generally presides over several divisions, each headed by an experienced manager who most likely specializes in one personnel activity, such as employment, compensation, benefits, training and development, or employee relations.

The top position is a demanding one, requiring the director to hold conferences with managers of other departments to ascertain future personnel needs, define training and development needs, develop and implement performance appraisal programs, and suggest guidelines for promotion and firing. Within the department of human resources management, the director establishes departmental procedures, organizes the areas of work, supervises subordinates, and personally handles administrative details in hiring executive personnel. The director is usually active in professional organizations and keeps up with current trends in all areas of human resources management. Human resources managers can rise through the ranks as generalists or as specialists in one of the following areas.

Employment. The area of employment and placement involves numerous jobs and a variety of duties. The employment manager has overall responsibility for the selection of qualified employees throughout the organization. Working under the manager are the employment interviewers, who evaluate applicants on the basis of personal interviews, and the test administrators, who conduct and score tests designed to measure an applicant's competence to do a job. Test administrators may also coordinate assessment centers in which employees are given various performance-based activities to determine their qualifications for specific positions. The employee orientation specialist provides newly-hired employees with information needed for smooth integration into company life.

In addition, the employment and placement professionals work with the manager to develop sources of potential employees to fill current and future human resource needs, to counsel employees should job-related problems or needs arise, and to administer the promotion and transfer system within the company. They may also provide outplacement activities, such as job counseling and résumé preparation, should an employee be terminated.

Recruitment. Recruiters maintain contacts within the community and may travel extensively, often to college campuses, to search for promising job applicants. Recruiters screen, interview, and sometimes test applicants. They also may check references and extend job offers. Recruitment specialists need thorough knowledge of the organization and its personnel policies in order to discuss wages, working conditions, and promotional opportunities with prospective employees. They also must keep informed about equal employment opportunity (EEO) and affirmative action guidelines and laws, such as the Americans with Disabilities Act.

Equal Employment Opportunity. Equal employment opportunity (EEO) officers, representatives, or affirmative action coordinators handle EEO matters in large organizations. They investigate and resolve EEO grievances, examine corporate practices for possible violations, and compile and submit EEO statistical reports. Responsibilities of the EEO staff may include writing the organization's affirmative action plan, assisting managers in developing affirmative action programs, advising management of legal requirements, investigating employee complaints and charges of discrimination, acting as liaison with minority and women's organizations, and representing the company in government investigations.

Training and development. Training and development managers and specialists conduct and supervise training and development programs for employees, either in classrooms or on-site. Training specialists plan, organize, and direct a wide range of training activities, often in response to corporate and employee service requests. They consult with on-site supervisors regarding available performance improvement services, conduct orientation sessions, and arrange on-the-job training for new employees.

Trainers help rank-and-file workers maintain and improve their job skills, and possibly prepare for jobs requiring greater skill. They help supervisors improve their interpersonal skills in order to deal more effectively with employees. They may set up individualized training programs to strengthen an employee's existing skills or teach new ones. Training specialists in some companies set up leadership or executive development programs among employees in lower-level positions. These programs are designed to develop potential executives to replace those leaving the organization. Trainers also lead programs to assist employees with transitions due to mergers and acquisitions, as well as technological changes.

Compensation. Establishing and maintaining a firm's pay system is the principal job of the compensation manager. Assisted by staff specialists, compensation managers devise ways to ensure fair and equitable pay rates. Members of the compensation division include job analysts, who analyze job duties, write job descriptions, and assist in developing job specifications or responsibility areas. Jobs are evaluated by a wage and salary specialist to determine the proper pay range. An aspect of the compensation manager's job is conducting compensation surveys to see how competitive the company's pay range is with similar jobs in other companies. In addition, compensation managers often oversee their firm's performance evaluation system, and they may design reward systems such as pay-for-performance plans.

Benefits. Benefits management includes a variety of tasks involving programs for employees. The benefits manager develops and administers the organization's medical, disability, stock ownership, retirement, and pension plans. The benefits planning analyst may research new benefits options for the organization as well as review competing organizations' compensation packages.

Employee relations. The employee relations director, sometimes called employee assistance plan manager or employee welfare manager, works with employee relations specialists to coordinate and offer a wide range of services to employees. Services and programs may deal with employee issues such as alcohol and drug abuse treatment; maternity leave for mothers and fathers and availability of child care centers; relocation assistance; and recreation, health, and fitness opportunities.

The objective of employee relations is to take a positive and proactive approach to retaining employees and improving their productivity. Employee relations specialists must monitor changing lifestyle preferences and needs of employees to develop programs and services consistent with those preferences and needs. For example, many companies provide on-site fitness centers where employees can work out during lunch breaks, and host company-sponsored recreational events to foster good employee relations and high morale.

Safety. The safety director, with the assistance of plant safety specialists, works with management in developing and administering safety programs, conducts safety inspections, maintains accident records, and submits required governmental health and safety reports. This job has become more complicated as new regulations have been added and old ones changed. The safety director is responsible for insuring that the organization complies with local and federal safety regulations that govern the workplace.

Industrial relations. An organization's director of industrial relations forms the labor policy, oversees industrial labor relations, negotiates collective bargaining agreements, and coordinates grievance procedures to handle complaints resulting from management disputes with unionized employees. The director of industrial relations also advises and collaborates with the director of human resources, other managers, and members of the staff, because all aspects of personnel policy, such as wages, benefits, pensions, and work practices, may be involved in drawing up a new or revised union contract.

Labor relations. The labor relations manager and staff implement industrial labor relations programs. When a collective bargaining agreement is up for negotiation, labor relations specialists prepare information for management to use during negotiation—a process that requires knowledge of economic and wage data, labor law, and collective bargaining trends. The labor relations staff interprets and administers the contract with respect to grievances, wages and salaries, employee welfare, health care, pensions, union and management practices, and other contractual stipulations. As union membership continues to decline in most industries, industrial relations personnel are working more often with employees who are not members of a labor union.

CURRENT TRENDS

The elimination of levels of management over the last decade posed a dilemma for human resources managers. In today's flattened organizational hierarchy, with fewer rungs on the proverbial career ladder, how does a corporation reward its most productive employees? The answer is to create horizontal opportunities with challenge and performance-related monetary reward.

Broadbanding

Many companies have employed broadbanding as a way to create broader salary ranges or bands within fewer levels. By developing new skills, employees can use lateral moves among departments to broaden their experience. With a de-emphasis on titles and latitude to pay individuals what they are worth to the company, employees are more willing to move into new areas, acquire new skills, and increase their value to the company. To implement broadbanding, human resources professionals must create more development and educational opportunities and supply career planning information so that individuals will be aware of these new opportunities.

New Technologies

Acquisitions, mergers, divestitures, and bankruptcies have resulted in a rash of corporate restructuring and layoffs, and the responsibility for handling the employee upheaval is left to human resources professionals. Technology has streamlined record keeping in all areas of human resources management. Human resources information systems provide computer assistance in calculating and storing figures required for payroll and for compliance with government regulations. Maintaining accurate records of hirings, firings, and layoffs, especially in periods of large employee turnover, is also aided by computer applications.

Corporate recruiters increasingly use the Internet—posting jobs on websites, and even maintaining their own websites to communicate with potential job applicants. Nonetheless, they also continue to use print advertisements and job fairs.

Training

Management has increasingly recognized that training offers a way of developing skills, enhancing productivity and quality of work, and building employee loyalty to the firm. Training is widely accepted as a method of improving employee morale, but this is only one of the reasons for its growing importance. Other factors include the complexity of the work environment, the rapid pace of organizational and technological change, and the growing number of jobs in fields that constantly generate new knowledge. In addition, advances in learning theory have provided insights into how adults learn, and how training can be organized most effectively.

Technology has also had a great impact on both the topics of training sessions and how the training is conducted. Continuing education is now required for all technical employees. Both computer-assisted instruction and computer-based training programs are increasing. A trainer's methods and responsibilities may differ depending on the size, nature, and goals of the organization. Training methods include on-the-job training; operating schools that duplicate shop conditions for trainees prior to putting them on the shop floor; apprenticeship training; classroom training; and electronic learning, which may involve interactive Internet-based training, multimedia programs, distance learning, satellite training, other computer-aided instructional technologies, videos, simulators, conferences, and workshops.

Organizations facing change now or in the future need employees who are skilled and able to meet new responsibilities. Training is not limited to new or lower-level employees. Executive management development requires creative and challenging programs, which can be seen on public broad-casting stations. Quality circles engage employees at all levels in problem-solving and productivity sessions. International training is now imperative as many corporations begin and expand international operations. (Employees terminated as a result of restructuring and downsizing often receive assistance in finding new positions through the outplacement efforts of employment and career development specialists.)

Alternative Reward Systems

Although money continues to be a prime motivator, many companies also use other forms of reward. It is the human resources professionals who identify workers' needs and manage alternative reward systems. "Wellness" programs with on-site gymnasiums are becoming more common as companies accept more responsibility for the well-being of their employees. Workers want more flexibility to fit both work and family into their lives, and flexible work schedules are one way to meet this need. These efforts to meet the needs of employees pay off in employee retention and loyalty.

Other emerging specialties include international human resources managers, who handle human resources issues related to a company's foreign operations; and human resources information system specialists, who develop and apply computer programs to process personnel information, match job seekers with job openings, and handle other personnel matters.

Dispute Resolution

Dispute resolution—attaining tacit or contractual agreements—has become increasingly important as parties to a dispute attempt to avoid costly litigation, strikes, or other disruptions. Dispute resolution has also become more complex, involving employees, management, unions, other firms, and government agencies. Specialists involved in this area must be highly knowledgeable and experienced, and often report to the director of industrial relations. Conciliators, or mediators, advise and counsel labor and management to prevent and, when necessary, resolve disputes over labor agreements or other labor relations issues. Arbitrators, sometimes called umpires or referees, decide disputes that bind both labor and management to specific terms and conditions of labor contracts. Labor relations specialists who work for unions perform many of the same functions on behalf of the union and its members.

Outsourcing

Like many other areas of business, human resources management has been affected by outsourcing. Unlike other fields, however, in human resources outsourcing can be an advantage. A survey by the Society for Human Resource Management indicates that approximately 60 percent of companies contract out some human resources functions. The most commonly outsourced functions are health care benefits, pension benefits, and payroll. While the majority of respondents said that their top reason for outsourcing was to reduce operating costs, 41 percent said the reason is to reduce the number of staff and staff-related expenses.[1]

Human resources professionals are divided on what this outsourcing trend means for workers in this field. While many see outsourcing as causing a decrease in the number of jobs for human resources workers, others believe that the trend creates jobs in companies that offer human resources services to other organizations. Professionals interested in working for these service companies should fine-tune their business skills, particularly in negotiations, contracts, and general management. Outsourcing companies also report a high rate of advancement opportunities for skilled human resources specialists.[2]

JOB OPPORTUNITIES

Workers in the field of human resources management are employed throughout the private and public sectors in every industry. The private sector accounts for almost eight out of ten salaried jobs, including 11 percent in professional, scientific, and technical services and 10 percent each in manufacturing industries; health care and social assistance; finance and insurance firms; and administrative and support services.

The government employs about 18 percent of human resources managers and specialists. They handle the recruitment, interviewing, job classification, training, salary administration, benefits, employee relations, and other matters related to the nation's public employees.

Overall, employment in the field of human resources is expected to increase up to 35 percent by 2012. The demand for human resources, training, and labor relations experts will increase due to standards set by legislation and court rulings in various areas, such as occupational safety and health, equal employment opportunity, wages, health, pensions, and family leave, among others. Rising health care costs should continue to spur demand for specialists to develop creative compensation and benefits packages that firms can offer prospective employees. Employment of labor relations staff, including arbitrators and mediators, should grow as firms become more involved in labor relations, and attempt to resolve potentially costly labor-management disputes out of court. Additional job growth may stem from increasing demand for specialists in international human resources management and human resources information systems.

Demand may be particularly strong for certain specialists. For example, the increasing complexity of many jobs, the aging of the workforce, and technological advances that can leave employees with obsolete skills will cause many employers to devote greater resources to job-specific training programs. This should result in particularly strong demand for training and development specialists. Increasing efforts throughout the industry to recruit and retain quality employees should create many jobs for employment, recruitment, and placement specialists.

Many job opportunities should become available in firms involved in management, consulting, and employment services. As businesses increasingly contract out personnel functions or hire personnel specialists on a temporary basis to deal with the increasing cost and complexity of training and development programs, jobs in these firms will be readily available. Demand also should increase in firms that develop and administer complex employee benefits and compensation packages for other organizations.

Job growth could be limited by the widespread use of computerized human resources information systems that make workers more productive. As in other areas, employment of human resources specialists, particularly in larger firms, may be adversely affected by corporate downsizing, restructuring, and mergers.

APTITUDES AND ATTRIBUTES NEEDED FOR SUCCESS

The educational backgrounds of human resources specialists vary considerably, based on the diversity of duties and levels of responsibility in different areas. In filling entry-level jobs, many employers prefer college graduates who have majored in human resources, personnel administration, or industrial and labor relations. Other employers look for college graduates with a technical or business background or with a well-rounded liberal arts education.

Many colleges and universities have programs leading to a degree in personnel, human resources, or labor relations. Some offer degree programs in personnel administration or human resources management, training and development, or compensation and benefits.

An interdisciplinary background is appropriate for this field, so a combination of courses in the social sciences, business, and behavioral sciences is most useful. Courses in the main areas of human resources management, such as compensation, recruitment, training and development, and performance appraisal, will benefit prospective human resources specialists. Other relevant courses include business administration, public administration, psychology, sociology, political science, economics, and statistics. Courses in labor law, collective bargaining, labor economics, labor history, and industrial psychology also provide a valuable background for the prospective labor relations specialist. Knowledge of computers and information systems is also needed.

Some positions require a graduate degree. Many labor relations jobs require graduate study in industrial or labor relations. A strong background in industrial relations and law is highly desirable for contract negotiators, mediators, and arbitrators; in fact, many people in these specialties are lawyers. A master's degree in human resources, labor relations, or in business administration with a concentration in human resources management is highly recommended for those seeking general and top management positions.

While previous experience is an asset for many specialist positions in human resources, it is essential for such advanced positions as managers, arbitrators, and mediators. Experience gained through an internship or work-study program is also valuable for any entry-level positions. Clerical workers can sometimes advance to professional positions, but a bachelor's degree is generally preferred in these cases.

Human resources specialists must be able to work with individuals and maintain a commitment to organizational goals. Both written and oral communications skills are important, as are supervisory ability and teaching skills. Given the increasing diversity of the workforce, human resources specialists must be able to interact with or supervise people with various cultural backgrounds, levels of education, and experience. They must have a persuasive, congenial personality; demonstrate discretion, integrity, and fair-mindedness; be able to cope with conflicting points of view; and function well under pressure.

Responsibilities of entry-level workers vary depending on educational level and experience. Entry-level employees commonly learn the profession by performing administrative duties, such as entering data into computer systems, compiling employee handbooks, researching information for a supervisor, or answering the phone and handling routine questions. Entry-level workers often enter formal or on-the-job training programs in which they learn how to classify jobs, interview applicants, or administer employee benefits. Afterward, they are assigned to specific areas in the department to gain experience. Later, they may advance to a managerial position, overseeing a major element of the personnel program, such as compensation or training.

Exceptional human resources workers may be promoted to director of personnel or industrial relations, which can eventually lead to a top managerial or executive position. Others may join a consulting firm or open their own business. A Ph.D. is an asset for teaching, writing, or consulting work.

Most organizations specializing in human resources offer classes intended to enhance the marketable skills of their members. Some organizations offer certification programs, which are signs of competence and can enhance one's advancement opportunities. For example, the International Foundation of Employee Benefit Plans confers a designation to persons who complete a series of college-level courses and pass exams covering employee benefit plans. The Society for Human Resources Management has two levels of certification; both require experience and a passing score on a comprehensive exam.

CAREER DEVELOPMENT AND COMPENSATION

Jobs in human resources management have fairly specific duties. However, well-trained individuals can handle a number of the positions seen in Figure 8.1. With experience comes increased salary and advancement into one of the key positions that report to the director of human resources management. Salary is dependent upon company size, location, and a number of other factors. For example, a company with a complicated labor man-

Figure 8.1

Human resources management positions and mobility

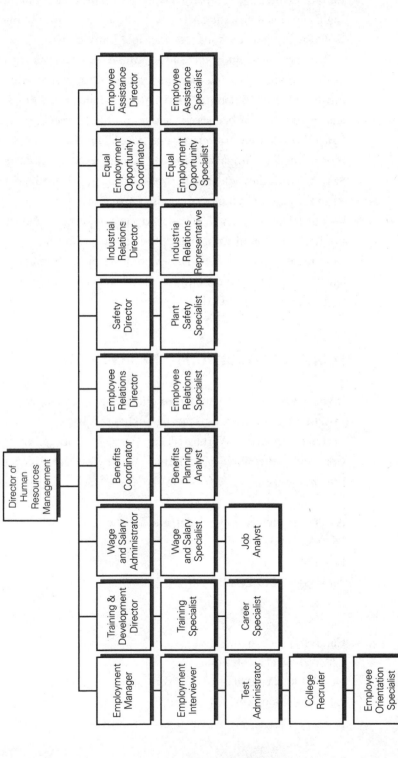

agement situation might offer a large salary for a highly qualified labor relations director. Or, a company investing a sizable amount of money in training programs will want the best training director on the market and will be willing to pay top dollar for the right individual.

The increased importance of the human resources management field has resulted in above-average salary increases over the past several years. According to the Fall 2004 National Association of Colleges and Employers (NACE) Salary Survey, new bachelor's degree candidates received offers averaging $36,425 for human resources positions. The Bureau of Labor Statistics reports median annual earnings of human resources managers in 2002 as $64,710, with the middle 50 percent earning between $47,420 and $88,100.

In the past, individuals advancing through the personnel ranks have had very little opportunity to advance to the chief executive position and have not had the level of influence in the organization that managers of other functional areas have had. The expanding role of human resources management has changed the outlook for advancement to some extent, particularly in services industries.

SOURCES OF ADDITIONAL INFORMATION

If you are interested in human resources management, you can gain much insight into the field by reading such professional journals as Human Resource Magazine, Workforce, and Human Resources Executive. In addition, the professional associations listed here are excellent sources of information.

American Society for Training and Development
1640 King Street
Box 1443
Alexandria, VA 22313
astd.org

Catalyst
120 Wall Street, 5th Floor
New York, NY 10005
catalystwomen.org

International Association for Human Resources Management
P.O. Box 1086
Burlington, MA 01803
iahrm.org

National Human Resources Association
P.O. Box 7326
Nashua, NH 03060
humanresources.org

Society for Human Resource Management
1800 Duke Street
Alexandria, VA 22314
shrm.org

Sources of Additional Information in Canada

For information about specific provincial associations in Canada, contact:
Canadian Council of Human Resources Associations
2 Bloor Street W, Suite 1903
Toronto ON M4W 3E2
cchra-ccarh.ca

CAREER DECISION-MAKING MODEL

Use the career decision-making model to help determine whether a career
in human resources management is a likely alternative for you. Figures 8.2a
and 8.2b are forms with the factors included in the career decision-making model in Chapter 1. Follow these directions in completing them.

1. Enter the position that interests you most on the line entitled Job.
2. Enter any additional factors used to personalize your model in
   the blank spaces provided (from Chapter 1).
3. Enter the weights that you assigned to the factors (from Chapter
   1) in the column WT. (It would be wise to review the
   explanations of these factors in the description of the model in
   Chapter 1 before going on to step 4.)

4. Assign a value from 1 (lowest) to 10 (highest) to each factor
   based on the information in this chapter and on your personal
   self-assessment, entering the value in column V. If you feel that
   you have a certain aptitude or attribute needed for success in this
   career area, you should assign a fairly high value. If a certain
   interest such as amount of variety is important to you and you
   feel the area provides the variety you enjoy, assign a fairly high
   value. If not, assign a low value. Use this technique to assign

Figure 8.2a

Career evaluation for human resources management

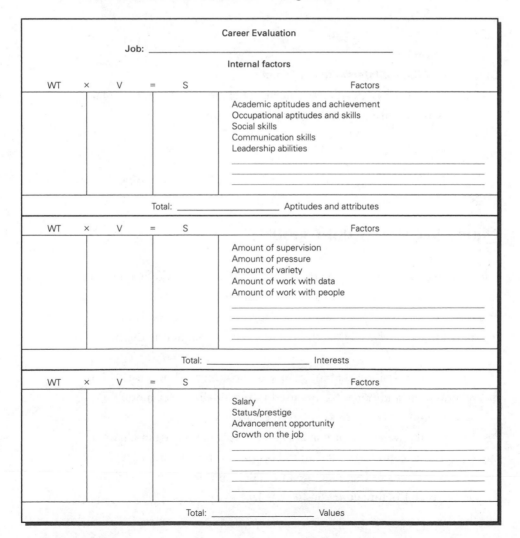

Figure 8.2b

195
Careers in
Human Resources
Management

Career evaluation for human resources management

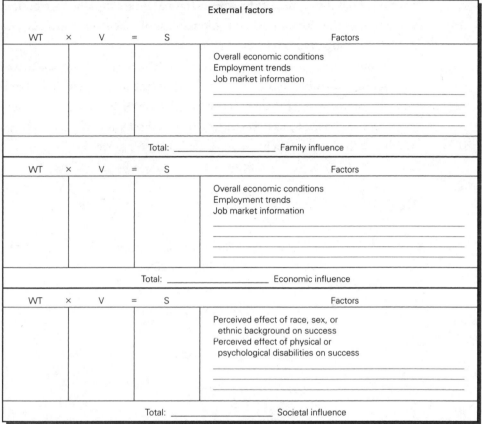

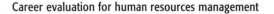

values to all factors in the model. If you cannot assign a value
based on the information in the chapter for some of the factors in
the model, either use other sources to acquire the information or
leave the space beside the factor blank.

5. Multiply the weight times the value, entering the score in
   column S.
6. Add the scores in column S for each group of factors, entering
   the number in the space labeled Total.

You will use this evaluation in Chapter 11 in combination with evaluations
of each career explored in this book.

WHAT DID YOU LEARN?

This chapter described careers in human resources management. You learned about the nature of the work, salary and career path information, some trends, the job outlook, education and skills needed for success, and where to obtain additional information.

Although many specific managerial positions have been discussed throughout this book, you will gain real insight into management and supervision by reading the next chapter. Chapter 9, "Careers in Management and Supervision," is devoted entirely to a discussion of the challenges and headaches of the much-sought-after leadership positions.

NOTES

1. Kris Maher, "The Jungle: Focus on Recruitment, Pay and Getting Ahead," *Wall Street Journal* (July 20, 2004), B4.
2. Ibid., B4.

CHAPTER

9

CAREERS IN MANAGEMENT AND SUPERVISION

After reading this chapter, you will be able to:

- Describe the work of managers and supervisors
- Discuss trends in management and their impact on careers
- Explain career paths in relation to management levels
- Discuss job opportunities in management and supervision
- List some resources helpful for success in management and supervision
- Evaluate careers in management and supervision according to your individualized career decision-making model

Management of corporations has been streamlined over the past two decades. In the 1970s it was customary to have as many as twelve to fifteen levels of supervision in large corporations. In the 1990s five or six levels was the norm. This streamlining, which has continued into the 2000s, is the result of major restructuring brought about by a wave of acquisitions and divestitures, increased global competition, management information and decision support systems, and an attempt at creating a more entrepreneurial environment to foster new product development. The reduction of middle-level managers has increased both the complexity and the pressures of management positions.

This chapter will discuss the careers of managers and supervisors. The discussion will be general rather than specific, and it will include the following information:

- What activities managers and supervisors perform
- How to advance in management
- Latest trends
- Job opportunities
- Resources helpful for success in management and supervisory careers

THE RESTRUCTURING OF CORPORATE MANAGEMENT

For nearly three decades, companies have undergone thousands of mergers, acquisitions, divestitures, and bankruptcies. As companies and pieces of companies were bought and sold, hundreds of thousands of managers and professionals were forced to change jobs or retire early. In many cases, middle-level management positions were never refilled. Major reorganizations took place within companies. Top management realized that if the firm was to compete in a more competitive, rapidly changing business environment, it had to respond more quickly to change. Though reducing costs was a factor in not replacing many middle-level managers, an even more important factor was introducing products into the market more efficiently.

For years, primarily small companies have been credited with introducing new technology into the marketplace. One reason for this is the efficiency of less-formal corporate structure. While new products were still being discussed as possibilities through fifteen levels of management in large companies, small companies functioning as entrepreneurial teams moved a product from the drawing board to the marketplace. The message was clear—until large corporations began to be more entrepreneurial both in philosophy and in practice, they would be unable to beat the small competitors into the marketplace with new technology-oriented products.

So big companies responded to the challenge. As a result of reorganization within these companies, more project or product development teams emerged. These teams were given the authority to operate fairly autonomously both in fulfilling goals and competing for company resources, as was described in Chapter 6 on product development. Product managers now reported directly to marketing managers at top levels in the company. The term "entrepreneuring" was coined to describe these teams that were entrepreneurial in spirit yet part of a large corporation.

With fewer levels of management and tighter budgets, companies are unable to reward managers with promotions and raises as they once did.

However, fewer job titles and pay grades make it easier to base raises on performance rather than seniority. One way that companies motivate promising young managers is with a lateral, or sideways, move that offers a new challenge and enables managers to learn another part of company operations. Giving more responsibility and autonomy to subordinates is another way to keep young managers interested and productive. As companies expand their global operations, overseas assignments for managers are more common. Finally, more companies are offering up-and-coming executives midcareer breaks by sending them to management development programs designed by business schools especially for executives.

MANAGING TODAY

The work of managers today is complex, to say the least. The organization exists as part of a larger system, and managers are concerned not only with employees and customers, but also with the social, political, economic, and technologic influence of the greater environment in which the organization operates.

Managers must make decisions that protect shareholder interests in light of the wealth of information and restrictions that come from politicians, economists, labor leaders, environmentalists, scientists, engineers, consumers, and, in fact, society as a whole. Yet, they are the decision makers who influence the lives and directions of all these groups.

So, who would want such a job? The answer is, many people—and competition for promotion into management positions permeates the organization at all levels. Many seek the higher status, greater salaries, and authority, but usually there is much more to it. Many employees have a strong sense of commitment to their organizations and want to contribute to the positive change or growth that takes place within them. Others want to utilize their full potential in business. All want to protect their careers and ensure their futures. Survival of an organization depends on the ability of its managers to cope with change and renew the organization so that it remains strong and healthy.

Management Functions

Although each managerial position in every organization is unique in terms of its specific activities, managers generally perform the same functions. In broad terms, managers devise strategies and formulate policies to ensure that the objectives of the organization are met. They work to determine the best techniques to maximize productivity and keep their organizations competitive with planning, implementation, and control.

Planning involves establishing goals, defining objectives, and developing long- and short-range strategies for accomplishing these objectives. Planning is becoming more and more important; it assures that an organization will be able to survive in the future in a dynamic and competitive business environment. Using numerous managerial tools to forecast future developments in the economy, the industry, and the company is essential to the planning process.

Implementation involves such activities as organizing, staffing, directing, and coordinating the organization's resources. Organizing involves establishing a structure that enables individuals to work together productively. The establishment of departments, the design of jobs, the assignment of responsibility, and the delegation of authority are important factors in the company's success. Setting up the guidelines and conditions under which employees perform the jobs that enable the organization to reach its goals is also important. Implementing also involves staffing the company with competent employees and motivating them with good working conditions, fair compensation, challenging work, good training, and counseling. Directing and coordinating the work of employees and the use of all resources are vital parts of this area of management.

Controlling provides feedback to management about how well actual performance measures up to planned objectives. If productivity falls below management expectations, the reasons are determined and either strategies for improving productivity are developed or the objective is changed. This is part of the controlling process.

Different branches of management are responsible for different management tools and techniques. Operations research and production is where quantitative tools used in management are developed. Informations sciences emphasizes the use of computers and technology in management. Organizational behavior and theory is the branch in which techniques relating to organizational structure and employee behavior are developed and taught.

CORPORATE MANAGERS

Outstanding individuals advance to management levels throughout the functional areas of a company—marketing, finance, accounting, information, and production. The top position in each of these areas is corporate vice president, who has authority over the activities in a specific functional area of a corporation. These vice presidents are commonly called chief officers, such as chief financial officer (CFO) or chief information officer (CIO). Often a vice president advances to the position of chief executive officer (CEO), the top management position in an organization. Figure 9.1 is an example of a corporate hierarchy showing the chain of command and levels of authority. This hierarchy varies from firm to firm depending on the number of levels of management and how various functions are organized within the firm.

Top-level executives determine an organization's mission and create policy in a dynamic, sometimes turbulent, business and economic environment. All managers are involved in planning, implementing, and controlling activities and decisions, but managers at the top of the organization are primarily involved in planning. Decisions pertaining to mergers, acquisitions, and divestitures, what markets to enter, what products to produce, when to conduct work in-house or to use outsourcing, when consultants are needed, how to best use company resources, and what finances will be needed to meet goals and how best to arrange them are all crucial to the success and survival of the firm. Objectives and strategies are communicated to managers working under top-level executives who develop the detailed strategy required to implement the plans.

MIDDLE MANAGERS AND SUPERVISORS

All managers perform some degree of implementation activities. But unlike top managers, who spend most of their time in strategic planning, middle-level managers, such as department heads and project team leaders, are primarily involved in implementing policies and strategies from top-level managers. Hiring staff, assigning duties, directing and overseeing projects, and distributing the budget throughout the department are the responsibility of department heads.

Middle-level managers and the supervisors they appoint to assist in these activities are responsible for controlling the efforts of personnel by measuring performance to see that objectives are met, and taking corrective action if they are not. Specific objectives related to deadlines for projects, planned budgets, and sales quotas are measurable. If objectives are not met, it is up to middle managers and supervisors to determine whether they were

Figure 9.1

Levels of management

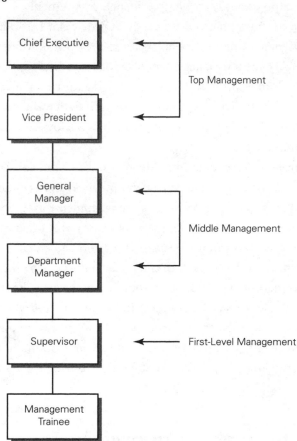

unrealistic, or whether external unpredictable factors or worker performance is responsible. Corrective action may involve revising objectives, making adjustments to allow for external factors, or working with staff to solve problems.

The work of middle managers and supervisors has been discussed throughout the chapters of this book. They manage staffs of professionals and technicians working in the various activities of business. With fewer levels of middle managers, these managers operate their departments more autonomously and have more authority over both activities and budgets. Their offices are usually located close to top management, and communications are considerably less formal than in the huge bureaucracies of the past. Though chain of command is still intact in many organizations, where managers at every level formally report to a designated individual, communications are considerably more relaxed and pragmatic in most organizations today.

Technology has changed corporate communications forever. Each manager has a personal computer, usually hooked into a central computer through local area network (LAN) technology. Branch computers are hooked into the central computer through wide area network (WAN) technology. This improved communications technology has enabled the free flow of information throughout the organization. Management information systems (MIS) and decision support systems (DSS) provide a systematic way of disseminating information needed for management decisions. A system is a collection of people, machines, programs, and procedures organized to perform a certain task. Information systems provide managers a steady flow of timely, accurate information from a variety of sources both inside and outside the firm that they can use to make decisions. In the past, many levels of management were necessary for organizing and communicating this type of information alone. Today, computer and communications technology has reduced this need dramatically.

ADVANCEMENT INTO MANAGEMENT

To succeed on the job and advance into management, professionals should choose the right company, find a mentor, and use whatever resources are available. Choosing the right company is a complicated issue. Position offers to new college graduates may be evaluated in terms of salary, benefits, and growth potential. Chapters 11 and 12 address issues that will help graduates evaluate the job market and company offers they will receive after college. But very little of the internal working of the company will be gleaned from company literature or job interviews. Only when working for a company can an individual learn the intricacies of how decisions are made and where the power lies.

Finding a Mentor

The single most important action that a new employee takes is finding a mentor. A mentor is an older professional in the same field, preferably making steady career progress up the company ladder. Good mentors offer introductions to people higher up and insights into the unspoken rules of the company. Every company has a unique corporate culture and its own way of doing things, which are not readily visible to a new employee. Finding a mentor is not easy. Any mentor worth having is extremely busy and not out looking for protégés. Any beginning employee who shows persistence yet flexibility, works hard to obtain recognition, listens to everything going on in the company before taking strong positions or forming alliances, has clearly stated career goals, and displays confidence and pride as well as ability will attract attention before long. Many employees have followed their mentors right up the hierarchy by filling the mentors' vacated positions on the way up.

Diversity in Management

The advancement rate of women and minorities in management has been slow. Although 40 percent of the workforce is female, and the U.S. population is 15 percent Hispanic and 13 percent African American, the majority of the board members of *Fortune* 1000 companies are Caucasian men in their fifties and sixties.[1] According to Catalyst, a research and advisory organization that works for the advancement of women in business, in 2003 women held 13.6 percent of board seats at *Fortune* 500 companies, up from 12.4 percent in 2001 and 9.6 percent in 1995. For the first time, all of the top 100 companies in the *Fortune* 500 have at least one female board member. However, while non-Caucasians make up about 30 percent of the U.S. population, they hold well below 10 percent of the director positions on corporate boards.[2] Studies indicate that of the 7,892 available director positions among the *Fortune* 1000 companies, African Americans hold 392 board seats, or 5 percent, and Latinos hold only 86 seats, or 1 percent.[3]

It is particularly important for female and minority managers to have mentors, since they are underrepresented in top levels of management in larger companies. Catalyst reports that although only eight CEO positions in *Fortune* 500 companies are held by women, there is a large and growing number of women working under them, running multi-billion dollar divisions. These women are not generally well known outside of their companies and industries, but they are considered major players in the future of business leadership.[4]

Following scandals involving the boards of corporations such as Enron, Arthur Andersen, and Tyco, in 2002 Congress passed the Sarbanes-Oxley

Act. While the primary intent of Sarbanes-Oxley is to provide better disclosure of public corporations' financial records, the legislation has also led to more diversity among corporate boards. The Sarbanes-Oxley Act requires boards of publicly traded companies to include more financial experts and independent directors. For example, the New York Stock Exchange requires its members to use nominating committees of independent directors to name new board members. The committees generally turn to recruiting firms which compile pools of about twenty qualified candidates.[5]

What does this mean for women and minorities? It has put a damper on the traditional practice of corporate boards filling vacancies by inviting friends and colleagues to join, a practice that reinforced the "old boy network" idea of corporate leadership and made it difficult for others the move into positions of power. The Sarbanes-Oxley Act has led to increased diversity, and diversity is increasingly seen as good for business.

According to Korn/Ferry International, a New York-based executive recruiting firm, clients who have invited a woman or a minority to join the board report positive feedback as a result of the appointment. Corporations benefit from the perspectives of minorities and women, whose understanding of the marketplace is likely to be vastly different from that of a middle-aged white male.[6] This idea is reinforced by Sharon Allen, chairman of the board of directors for Deloitte & Touche, which has sponsored seminars on "Diversifying the American Board." Allen believes that a diverse board encourages better ideas and results, and states that companies "need to understand the broadening and ever-changing constituency we serve—and we need the talent to do it." To accomplish this, Allen suggests that companies rethink their traditional patterns of recruiting and start at the bottom, ultimately filling the board with "homegrown diverse talent."[7]

The idea that board diversity should be treated as a grass-roots project is also evident at Xerox Corporation. Ernest Hicks, Xerox's corporate diversity manager, says that the company has worked steadily for the past thirty-five years to achieve diversity from the board down. One-third of Xerox's board members are women, and one-quarter are people of color.[8]

Although women and minorities have had to work very hard to prove themselves in business, those who have achieved success can have a strong impact on others who follow them. Women and minorities have formed networks within companies to help others learn the ropes. It is important for young women and minority members aspiring to management positions to know how others fare at the companies making them offers. Job candidates should determine what percentage of women and/or minorities hold middle- and top-management positions. Women might inquire about company benefits such as parental leave, flex-time, and day care assistance. The best offer for a new graduate might not come from a company that offers all of these opportunities, but rather from one that offers excellent training and development opportunities that can help build one's career. Trade-offs are always present in job offers. It is important for all candidates to carefully articulate their short- and long-range goals before entering the job market.

THE TOP CHIEF EXECUTIVE OFFICERS TODAY

Chief executive officers (CEOs) have come up from a variety of functional areas including finance/accounting, merchandising/marketing, engineering/technical, production/manufacturing, and the legal department. In the past most CEOs worked for one or two companies. Today there is greater movement from one company to another as boards attempt to find executives to lead companies through restructuring.

Despite differences in their professional backgrounds, the CEOs of large U.S. corporations share some common characteristics. Most CEOs are married with children. A large number enjoy sports, particularly golf and tennis. The top CEOs are multitalented, versatile people. This descriptive data offers some insight into those who reach the top of the management pyramid. There is little room at the top, and most new graduates hardly expect to become CEOs of large corporations. Still the backgrounds of these current CEOs give some hints about the types of people who have made it to the top in the past.

OPPORTUNITIES FOR MANAGERS

Demand for general managers and top executives will vary considerably from industry to industry. Regardless of the industry, however, the best opportunities will be for experienced managers with proven leadership qualities and the ability to improve the efficiency or competitive position of an organization. In an increasingly global economy, experience in international economics, marketing, information systems, and knowledge of several languages may also be beneficial.

Employment of top executives in management positions is expected to increase up to 20 percent through 2012. Because top managers are essential to the success of any organization, they should be less affected by automation and corporate restructuring than lower level managers. Employment growth is expected to be faster than average in professional, scientific, technical, administrative, and support services. However, employment is projected to decline in some manufacturing industries.

A recent report indicates that top-level job openings and new hires in management positions are on the rise. Within the past year Burger King Corp., Starwood Hotels & Resorts Worldwide, Inc., CMGI, Inc., Old National Bancorp, ArvinMeritor, Inc., Champion Enterprises, Inc., and ITT Industries, Inc., have all recruited new CEOs from outside the company. Some positions arise from succession planning or corporate scandal. However, many companies are hiring new management because of anticipated growth. After holding off through economic uncertainty and turmoil in Iraq, many corporate leaders can no longer wait to upgrade management and add new positions.[9]

The reputation of the corporation is a factor to consider in accepting a position at any level in management. Though new executives expect to be hired to solve existing problems and improve a corporation's performance, lower-level managers should consider a stable company in which to hone their skills and prove what they can do. The most admired American companies in 2005 are ranked by *Fortune* as follows: (1) Dell, (2) General Electric, (3) Starbucks, (4) Wal-Mart, (5) Southwest Airlines, (6) FedEx, (7) Berkshire Hathaway, (8) Microsoft, (9) Johnson & Johnson, and (10) Proctor & Gamble.[10]

Fortune's 2004 list of best companies for minorities is as follows: (1) McDonald's, (2) Fannie Mae, (3) Sempra Energy, (4) Union Bank of California, (5) Denny's, (6) U.S. Postal Service, (7) PepsiCo, (8) Southern California Edison, (9) Freddie Mac, and (10) PNM Resources.[11]

MANAGEMENT COMPENSATION

In a recent survey of the annual salaries of CEOs of 243 companies with revenue of $5 billion or more, the average salary was $12 million. The salaries ranged from Warren Buffett's $336,000 per year for running Berkshire Hathaway to Steve Jobs' whopping $219 million as CEO of Apple

Computer. Of course, when it comes to CEO salaries, money isn't everything. Jobs' compensation includes a personal jet valued at $84 million, and the largest stock option grant in history.[12]

If you feel "there oughta be a law," be assured that there is one. The federal government has imposed a $1 million cap on corporate deductibility of executive salaries. The irony is that the law established a standard of sorts so that companies that used to pay less than $1 million have upped CEO salaries to that level. Others award higher salaries and suffer the tax consequences, or rather the stockholders suffer the consequences. However, executive compensation is undergoing change. Boards of directors are hiring pay consultants to help determine what their people are worth. A trend to link CEOs' paychecks to corporate performance has definitely taken hold. Management compensation varies widely depending on the level of management, length of service, size and location of firm, and scope of responsibility.

Female executives in sales and management earn roughly 75 percent of what men earn by some estimates. Benefits such as stock options and long-term compensation vary greatly as well. Each management position and its compensation package must be evaluated individually. In general, an average salary range for middle-level managers would be from $36,000 to $52,000, plus bonuses. An average salary range for upper-level managers is from $68,000 to $105,000, plus bonuses.

RESOURCES FOR SUCCESS IN MANAGEMENT

Three major areas of resources for professional managers are company training and continuing education, professional organizations, and management newsletters and journals.

Management Training and Development

Management training and development is an important part of any manager's success. Without good training and development opportunities, a career can hit an early dead end. The first question that a job applicant should ask is, "What kind of training and development will the company provide if I accept this position?" To meet training needs, some companies allow employees to select the pace of training that takes place both inside and outside the work environment. This partnership enables ambitious employees to have more control over training opportunities and to advance at their own rate. In addition to the traditional stand-up lecture, company training programs employ more educational technologies such as interactive video, computer-based training, television courses, and numerous others.

Major restructuring in corporations has shifted the emphasis of executive training to organizational transformation. Business schools are offering more custom programs designed for specific corporations. These programs as well as in-house programs are geared to meet specific goals or to transform corporate culture.

Working for a company that offers its employees training and development programs and support should be an important career objective. Continuing education programs offered through colleges and universities will enable you to increase your chances of promotion. Many companies pay tuition costs for job-related courses, and sometimes entire M.B.A. programs. An M.B.A. can be a great asset as you advance through management ranks. Regardless of the training and continuing education opportunities provided by employers, as a business professional you must assume ultimate responsiblity for your training and career development.

Professional Management Associations

Professional organizations also offer training opportunities to their members. Joining such organizations as a student can provide an advantage of some early training opportunities that will help you to gain a competitive edge. Participation in professional organizations is very beneficial to both managers and students. The organizations provide an opportunity for communication among members at meetings and conferences, and a tremendous amount of current information is disseminated through advanced training and seminars. Through their websites, many organizations offer placement services for new college graduates as well as job listings and career guidance resources for all members. In most cases, the cost of student membership is greatly reduced.

A good source for names and addresses of professional organizations is the *Encyclopedia of Associations,* an annual publication found in the library reference section. Information includes names, addresses, phone numbers, and URLs of professional associations; the date they were founded; the number of current members; a description of the membership; and publications, if any. In addition to the organizations related to specific areas of management listed in the various chapters, many managers hold memberships in the following associations:

American Management Association
1601 Broadway
New York, NY 10019
amanet.org

American Society for Public Administration
1120 G Street, NW, Suite 700
Washington, DC 20005
aspanet.org

Canadian Women's Business Network
5765 Turner Road, Suite 280
Nanaimo, BC, V9T 6M4
cdnbizwomen.com

National Association for Female Executives
60 East 42nd Street, Suite 2700
New York, NY 10165
nafe.com

National Management Association
2210 Arbor Boulevard
Dayton, OH 45439
nma1.org

Women in Management, Inc.
P.O. Box 1032
Dundee, IL 60118
wimonline.org

Management Publications

Many professional associations publish newsletters and journals. Management periodicals are excellent sources of general information. An impressive list can be found in *Ulrich's International Periodicals Directory* in the reference section of the library or at ulrichsweb.com. A good many management periodicals can be found in public and university libraries. Most managers subscribe to a number of periodicals to keep current and gain professional insights. Also included in many newsletters and journals are classified ads posting job openings.

CAREER DECISION-MAKING MODEL

Would you like to be a manager? Evaluate management as a career. Figures 9.2a and 9.2b are forms with the factors included from the career decision-making model described in Chapter 1. Follow the directions in completing them.

1. Enter the position that interests you most on the line entitled Job.
2. Enter any additional factors used to personalize your model in the blank spaces provided (from Chapter 1).
3. Enter the weights that you assigned to the factors (from Chapter 1) in the column WT. (It would be wise to review the explanations of these factors in the description of the model in Chapter 1 before going on to step 4.)
4. Assign a value from 1 (lowest) to 10 (highest) to each factor based on the information in this chapter and on your personal self-assessment, entering the value in column V. If you feel that you have a certain aptitude or attribute needed for success in this career area, you should assign a fairly high value. If a certain interest such as amount of variety is important to you and you feel the area provides the variety you enjoy, assign a fairly high value. If not, assign a low value. Use this technique to assign values to all factors in the model. If you cannot assign a value based on the information in the chapter for some of the factors in the model, either use other sources to acquire the information or leave the space beside the factor blank.

5. Multiply the weight times the value, entering the score in column S.
6. Add the scores in column S for each group of factors, entering the number in the space labeled Total.

You will use this evaluation in Chapter 11 in combination with evaluations of each career explored in this book.

Figure 9.2a

Career evaluation for management and supervision

Career Evaluation

Job: _____

Internal factors

WT	×	V	=	S	Factors
					Academic aptitudes and achievement
					Occupational aptitudes and skills
					Social skills
					Communication skills
					Leadership abilities
					_____
					_____
					_____

Total: _____ Aptitudes and attributes

WT	×	V	=	S	Factors
					Amount of supervision
					Amount of pressure
					Amount of variety
					Amount of work with data
					Amount of work with people
					_____
					_____
					_____
					_____

Total: _____ Interests

WT	×	V	=	S	Factors
					Salary
					Status/prestige
					Advancement opportunity
					Growth on the job
					_____
					_____
					_____
					_____
					_____

Total: _____ Values

Figure 9.2b

213

Careers in
Management and
Supervision

Career evaluation for management and supervision

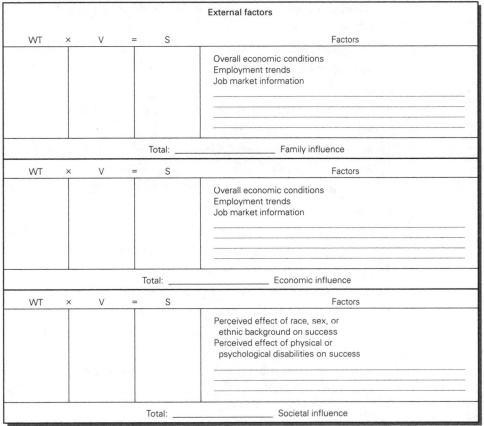

WHAT DID YOU LEARN?

You have gained some very general knowledge of management and supervision, which, when used in conjunction with the information provided in other chapters, should give you some ideas about your own future career development. An understanding of managerial functions and levels, development, trends, opportunities, and resources needed for success in management is valuable in career planning. You also completed a career evaluation for management and supervision.

To give you some interesting alternatives that might appeal to the more independent individual, Chapter 10 describes careers in business education, consulting, entrepreneurship, and franchising.

NOTES

1. Julie Bennett, "For Women and Minorities, Reaching the Boardroom Remains a Rough Ride," *Wall Street Journal* (October 12, 2004), B11.

2. Michelle T. Johnson, "Breaking the Boardroom's Glass Ceiling," *Minority MBA* (Spring 2004), 11.

3. Ibid., 11.

4. Carol Hymowitz, "Through the Glass Ceiling," *Wall Street Journal* (November 8, 2004), R1.

5. Bennett, B11.

6. Ibid., B11.

7. Johnson, 12–13.

8. Ibid., 13.

9. Kris Maher and Erin White, "Executive Ranks See Surge in New Hires, Openings," *Wall Street Journal* (October 5, 2004), A1.

10. "America's Most Admired Companies," *Fortune* (March 7, 2005), fortune.com/fortune/mostadmired/subs/2005/topten.

11. "Best Companies for Minorities," *Fortune* (June 28, 2004), fortune.com/fortune/diversity/subs/fulllist/0,20548,,00.html.

12. Graef Crystal, "U.S. CEO Pay Averages $12 Million Annually; Jobs No. 1," Bloomberg.com, http://quote.bloomberg.com/apps/news?pid=10000039&refer=columnist_crystal&sid=a2lC5UYqKkSI, (accessed March 7, 2005).

C H A P T E R 10

CAREERS IN BUSINESS EDUCATION, CONSULTING, ENTREPRENEURSHIP, AND FRANCHISING

After reading this chapter, you will be able to:

- Discuss the advantages and disadvantages of a career as a business educator, a consultant, and a business owner
- Describe the educational background, experience, and special abilities needed to be successful in business education, consulting, and business ownership
- Discuss the activities involved in owning and operating one's own business
- Explain the pros and cons of franchise ownership
- Evaluate your interest in business education, consulting, and business ownership

One of the United States' assets is its entrepreneurial youth and their love of technology. An entrepreneur is one who takes on the personal and financial risk of starting a business, an endeavor that is tremendously important to the U.S. economy. The growth of small companies provides a large number of new jobs every year. Books and magazines cover the topic in great detail. Special features in established newspapers and magazines provide readers with how-to information and profiles of successful entrepreneurs and their businesses. Colleges and universities offer special classes and even degrees in entrepreneurship. Large organizations, recognizing the value of an entrepreneurial approach, look for employees who will function as part of "entrepreneurial teams" to develop new products. Americans of all ages possess the entrepreneurial spirit, which in combination with knowledge and experience contributes to business success.

The fields of education and consulting also provide challenging career options for business professionals with the right experience and ambitions. These areas, along with business ownership, provide opportunities for individuals who value individuality, freedom, and variety. On the other hand, the work can be more demanding and require greater knowledge and skills than other areas of business. For these reasons, the careers described in this chapter may not be for beginners!

The purpose of this chapter is to help you decide whether education, consulting, or business ownership are viable career options for you. You may decide that your interests are strong, but you presently lack some of the requirements for success. In this case, any of these options can be incorporated into your career plan, but as a medium- or long-range rather than an immediate goal. This chapter will make you aware of the challenges and risks involved in these careers and describe how to prepare for entering these fields.

BUSINESS EDUCATION

College and university teaching is very satisfying to those who value flexible schedules and the ability to identify and pursue their own areas of research. Teachers at this level generally teach classes for twelve to sixteen hours each week, attend faculty and committee meetings, and hold office hours for student consultations. Aside from these commitments, they are free to establish their own schedules regarding course preparation, grading, research, writing, and other activities.

Instructors in two-year schools primarily teach, but may be expected to write books and articles as well. University professors normally have lighter teaching loads but are required to publish articles in their field as a requirement for promotion and tenure. The "publish or perish" edict is in force in most colleges and universities.

Educational Requirements

A master's degree in a business discipline or an M.B.A. is usually sufficient for teaching at a community college. However, many two-year colleges now prefer applicants to have either direct teaching experience or experience with distance learning. As competition for jobs grows, more colleges are looking for candidates with a Ph.D.

A doctorate is always required for tenure-track positions in four-year colleges and universities. Earning a doctorate requires a large commitment of both time and money. After a four-year bachelor's degree program, one must undertake a master's program requiring at least two years of full-time study and usually a master's thesis. Successful completion of a master-level program does not guarantee admission to a doctoral program.

Applicants to graduate business programs must have earned a specified grade point average in undergraduate courses, obtained a required score on the Graduate Management Admissions Test (GMAT), and demonstrated the potential for conducting original research. Doctoral programs require at least two years of full-time course work and seminars along with the design and completion of a doctoral dissertation. This can be a lengthy process, and each step must be approved by a committee before the candidate may go on. A review of the literature, design of the project, data gathering or laboratory experimentation, and an analysis of results can take well over a year to complete.

Graduate Assistantships

It might seem like a catch-22 situation that you need teaching experience in order to get your first teaching job. One way to gain the necessary experience is by working as a graduate teaching assistant. To qualify for an assistantship, candidates must be enrolled in a graduate school program, and are usually required to complete some training before teaching a course.

Graduate teaching assistants usually work in the department where they are earning their degree. However, teaching or internship positions for graduate students at institutions that do not grant a graduate degree have become more common in recent years. For example, a program called Preparing Future Faculty, administered by the Association of American Colleges and Universities and the Council of Graduate Schools, has led to the creation of many now-independent programs that offer graduate students at research universities the opportunity to work as teaching assistants at other types of institutions, such as liberal arts or community colleges. While working with a mentor, graduate students teach classes and learn how to improve their teaching skills. They may attend faculty and committee meetings, develop a curriculum, and learn how to balance the teaching, research, and administrative responsibilities of faculty. These programs provide valuable learning opportunities for graduate students interested in teaching at the postsecondary level, and also help to make these students aware of the differences among the various types of institutions at which they may someday work.

Attaining Tenure

Attaining tenure is a major part of the career path for most college teachers. New tenure-track faculty members are usually hired as instructors or assistant professors, and must serve for a specified period under term contracts. At the end of this period, usually seven years, their record of teaching, research, and overall contribution to the institution is reviewed. Tenure is granted only if the review is favorable; those denied tenure usually must leave the institution.

Tenured professors cannot be fired without just cause and due process. Tenure protects the faculty's academic freedom, allowing them to teach and conduct research without fear of being fired for advocating unpopular ideas. It also gives both faculty and institutions the stability needed for effective research and teaching, and provides financial security for faculty. Some institutions have adopted post-tenure review policies to encourage ongoing evaluation of tenured faculty.

Advancement

Often college professors enter administrative positions such as department chair or dean. Such posts as Dean of Undergraduate or Graduate Business Studies or Dean of the College of Business Administration are usually filled by former professors, as are other deanships on a college campus. Figure 10.1 shows the hierarchy of a typical university College of Business. It is not unusual for professors to earn money outside the university as consultants, writers, and sometimes entrepreneurs.

Demand

As the demand for business professionals increases, so does the demand for educators. Demand may vary with the area of specialization; for example, professors in accounting, finance, and management information systems

Figure 10.1

219

Careers in Business
Education, Consulting,
Entrepreneurship, and
Franchising

University college of business hierarchy

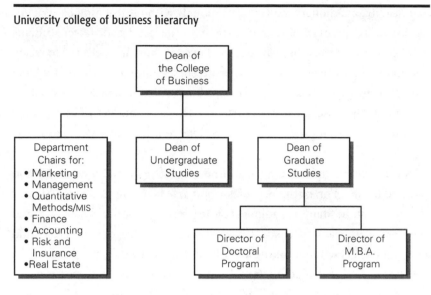

are in high demand. Doctoral candidates may concentrate in one or more specific areas within their chosen field, such as accounting in not-for-profit businesses or marketing research in service industries. New doctoral graduates are considered for positions as assistant professors. Selection criteria can include dissertation and other research publications, evaluations of professors, and experience outside the doctoral program such as previous employment in business. In addition, teaching evaluations may be considered, since most doctoral students teach undergraduate business classes as part of their graduate assistantships.

The reputation of the university and its doctoral program as well as the student's assigned major professor are factors that come into play when recent recipients of doctorates apply to prestigious and well-known universities. Therefore, those seeking doctorates should carefully evaluate a school and its program before entering. Finding a major professor who shares a student's research interests and who is well known in the field can make doctoral study more valuable, thus making the student more marketable when applying for a job. Similar to the mentor in business organizations, the major professor can help a student develop the research interests and abilities to guarantee success in the academic community. At the same time, the student works hard for the major professor, enhancing that professor's productivity.

In recent years, a growing number of business schools have begun rely-ing heavily on adjunct faculty: professionals without teaching experience or doctoral degrees who teach part-time. In the last decade fewer students have gotten doctorates in business, and fewer of those have elected to teach, leading to a shortage of full-time professors. Adjuncts can bring a "real world" quality to the classroom, sharing business experiences that students might not otherwise learn about firsthand. However, the lack of educational training of most adjuncts is seen as a deterrent by many who study the field.[1]

Some schools have managed to find a balance between adjuncts and tenured faculty. For example, professors at Yale help adjuncts with syllabus development. At Stanford, adjuncts co-teach with experienced faculty, and mentoring programs offer students exposure to executives in meetings and corporate visits without taking away from time with their professors.[2]

The employment of adjuncts will continue to be an issue, since the num-ber of tenure-track positions is expected to decline as institutions seek flex-ibility in dealing with financial matters and changing student interests. The total number of tenured faculty is expected to decrease as colleges and uni-versities rely more heavily on limited-term contracts and part-time faculty. Some institutions offer limited-term contracts to prospective faculty. These contracts, generally for two-, three-, or five-years of full-time employment, may be terminated or extended upon expiration. Institutions are not obli-gated to grant tenure to the contract holders. In addition, some institutions have limited the percentage of faculty who can be tenured.

Compensation

Earnings for college faculty vary according to rank and type of institution, geographic area, and field. Faculty in four-year institutions generally earn higher salaries than those in two-year schools.

In business, depending on the institution and years of experience and tenure, starting salaries for professors range from $65,000 to $150,000 for the nine-month academic year. Additional support, usually 22 percent of the nine-month salary, is generally available during the summer months.[3]

Many faculty members have significant earnings, in addition to their base salary, from consulting, teaching additional courses, research, writing for publications, or other employment. In addition, many college and uni-versity faculty members enjoy some unique benefits, including access to campus facilities, tuition waivers for dependents, housing and travel allowances, and paid sabbatical leaves.

New Technologies

As in all areas of business, advances in technology have changed the way most college professors work and interact with students. Most faculty extensively use computer technology, including the Internet, e-mail, software programs, and CD-ROMs. They often use computers in the classroom as teaching aids and may post course content, class notes, class schedules, and other information on the Internet. A growing number of professors use telecommunications and videoconferencing equipment and the Internet to teach courses to students at remote sites. The use of e-mail has improved communication between students and professors, and among students. Many college professors find their workloads increased by the requirement to teach online courses, which involves developing course material, answering e-mail, and using sophisticated technology.

Diversity

In an ongoing effort to foster diversity in business, some of the nation's leading corporations have sponsored The PhD Project. For over ten years this multimillion dollar diversity effort has helped African American, Hispanic, and Native American business professionals earn Ph.D.s and become professors. The PhD Project helps people evaluate the pros and cons of leaving their jobs to pursue full-time study, and supports them throughout their studies with mentoring and peer support networks.[4]

Sources of Additional Information

Further information on careers in postsecondary education is available from individual state departments of education. Information also is available from the following organizations:

Association of American Colleges and Universities
1818 R Street NW
Washington, DC 20009
aacu-edu.org

Council of Graduate Schools
One Dupont Circle NW, Suite 430
Washington, DC 20036
cgsnet.org

International Society for Business Education
P.O. Box 20457
Carson City, NV 89721
isbeusa.org

National Business Education Association
1914 Association Drive
Reston, VA 20191
nbea.org

The PhD Project
3 Chestnut Ridge Road
Montvale, NJ 07645
thephdproject.com

CONSULTING

In good humor, consultants have been defined as professionals who have been out of work for more than two months. Regarding their work—consultants borrow your watch, then tell you what time it is. Humor aside, consultants provide a valuable service in a constantly changing business environment. Business consultants are problem solvers with extensive experience and an area of expertise. Specializing in various areas of business such as strategic planning, information systems, feasibility studies, and market and product research, consultants are widely used throughout business and industry to help plan strategies and solve problems when strategies go awry.

As competition heats up at home and abroad, management must focus on making operations more efficient. With the downsizing of staff and the elimination of departments, consultants must use outsourcing to restructure the company and to perform activities that had been previously done in-house. Consultants are listed in such reference books as the *Consultants and Consulting Organizations Directory* found in the reference section of many libraries.

What Consultants Do

The primary work of consultants is to provide structure and solve problems. Since consultants work for many clients, they are exposed to different methods of solving problems and a variety of valuable sources of information. Having the knowledge of what works and what doesn't work in a variety of situations, the consultant makes recommendations that can save time and money.

Most consultants have tremendous freedom over their time and other resources. Whether they freelance, work in small companies, or work for large consulting firms, they work very independently with individual clients. In order to be rehired for additional work by a client, a consultant must demonstrate the ability to help solve the client's problems in creative and cost-effective ways. Consulting is not the job for someone who wants to work less and avoid the nine-to-five routine. Longer, though less routine, hours are required for successful consulting, since client companies often impose difficult-to-meet deadlines and expect unrealistic results.

Unless a company is rehiring a consultant who has worked for it previously, sometimes several consultants are scheduled for interviews. A number of factors determine who is hired. The first is how well the interviewer and consultant get along personally, since they will usually be working together. Another factor is the quality of the consultant's references, including companies for whom the consultant has completed an assignment similar to the one proposed. Though consultants may work for competing companies, often consulting contracts stipulate that they may not disclose privileged company information or work for a competing firm for a certain time period. A final consideration is the consultant's number of years of experience and the quality of that experience. Consulting fees vary greatly depending on the scope and complexity of the project and the reputation of the consultant. Well-established, successful consultants rarely lack employment. However, building a reputation as a consultant requires hard work over a number of years.

Opportunites in Consulting Firms

Top consulting firms hire the most talented graduates and then train them. These firms also offer summer internships to promising candidates. Since people are the greatest resource in consulting companies, everyone in large consulting companies gets involved in recruiting new employees. In general, consultants enter the field with two to four years of experience and a college degree, often an M.B.A. or doctorate. Firms offer summer internships to promising candidates, enabling them to evaluate recruits performing typical tasks before offering them permanent employment.

Work in large consulting firms is characterized by pressure, long hours, travel, and high turnover. These firms are partnerships with an up-or-out policy, that is, consultants have from five to seven years to make partner. If they fail, they are out. Only one in five who begins work with a large company is expected to make partner. Many opt for consulting with large firms for the training and experience, then go out on their own by choice. Most consulting firms are based in the Northeast and California. Larger firms have branches throughout the country.

Clients generally retain consultants on a continuing basis, so the work tends to be long-term oriented. Entry-level consulting work in large companies is primarily research-oriented. As junior consultants or associates demonstrate the analytic, interpersonal, and motivational skills required for success in the job, they are promoted to the position of case team leader or senior consultant. In this capacity, a consultant supervises a small team, normally working on one or two cases at a time. After three or four years, a senior consultant who performs well is promoted to consulting manager. As manager, a consultant leads a consulting team on important client projects. Once promoted to junior partner and finally senior partner or director, the consultant's work is primarily marketing the firm and its services. Figure 10.2 shows a career path in a large consulting firm.

Independent Consulting and Contracting

The vast majority of establishments in this industry are fairly small, employing fewer than five workers. Many of these firms are operated by self-employed consultants. Independent consulting may be done on a full-time or part-time basis. Many university professors consult as a sideline to supplement their teaching salaries. Retired executives or executives between jobs find their experience and insights very marketable as consultants. Successful managers in high-level positions in an organization might find success as strategic planning consultants. Although consultants are well paid when they work, paying the bills requires steady work. Self-employed consultants must earn 50 percent more money to pay for the costs of doing business and for the benefits normally provided by the company such as

Figure 10.2

Career path in a large consulting firm

health insurance, holidays and vacations, travel expenses, office space, supplies and equipment, clerical help, telephone expenses, and so on.

The image projected through the consultant's dress, manners, and office will have a great impact on landing jobs. Recall that when people pay a consultant considerably more than they pay the average manager, they expect a high degree of professionalism. Even though consultants are self-employed, they are still governed to some extent by the behavior and dress codes of the particular industry for which they consult. For example, consultants are better received in the banking and insurance industries if they are conservatively dressed and clean shaven. It is unlikely that one can be a rugged individualist and a successful consultant at the same time.

The successful consultant is aggressive and willing to go out and hustle business. This alone is hard work. One way to do this is to become known through publishing articles in trade journals. Still another way is to become actively involved in professional organizations, thus meeting many potential clients. Efforts can't end there, however. Using former clients to identify potential clients, consultants must sell their services to executives with the power to hire them. Consultants who want to run their consulting as a small business and maintain independent contractor status in the eyes of the Internal Revenue Service may use broker firms (which operate somewhat like headhunters) to find consulting jobs. The broker earns a percentage of what the consultant is paid on the initial contact with the hiring company, and less in subsequent contacts.

Independent consulting is not for everyone. But if one has expertise in a sought-after area of specialization, can sell himself or herself, is financially stable enough to survive the lean times, and wants the challenge and freedom of consulting, our advice is to go for it! Those who are unsuccessful can always give up the business and find a salaried job. It is easier to recover from a loss of self-esteem if a person is gainfully employed.

A subset of consultants who provide a specific service are contractors. Some people make the following distinction between consultants and contractors: Consultants analyze a situation, propose a solution, but do not implement it. Contractors, used predominantly for programming, implement predefined solutions. From teenagers to those with years of experience, from the physically handicapped to the most athletic, from totally self-employed to moonlighters—any creative individual with good computer programming skills can be a contractor. Industry experts believe that one-half of the nation's full-time programmers moonlight as contractors.

Education and Certification

While very few universities or colleges offer formal programs of study in management consulting, many fields provide a suitable background. These fields include most areas of business and management, such as marketing and accounting, as well as economics, computer and information sciences, and engineering. Though exceptional beginners may be hired out of college with undergraduate degrees, an M.B.A. is required by many firms for advancement.

Professional certification is available through The American Consultants League (ACL). The Certified Professional Consultant (CPC) certificate is conferred upon ACL members who pass a certification exam. The designation of Accredited Professional Consultant (APC) is granted to more tenured ACL members. The Institute of Management offers the Certified Management Consultant (CMC) for members who meet education, experience, and competence criteria.

Compensation

According to a 2002 survey by the Association of Management Consulting Firms, the average total cash compensation (salary, plus bonus or profit sharing) for research associates was $47,826; for entry-level consultants, $61,496; for management consultants, $78,932; for senior consultants, $112,716; for junior partners, $168,998; and for senior partners, $254,817.

According to a 2003 survey conducted by Abbot, Langer, and Associates, a firm that monitors salary and benefits information, the median annual cash compensation for junior consultants was $48,248; for consultants, $58,817; for senior consultants, $80,000; for principal consultants, $98,000; and for senior or executive vice presidents (with an ownership interest in the firm), $144,200.

Besides earning a straight salary, many workers receive additional compensation, such as profit sharing, stock ownership, or performance-based bonuses. In some firms bonuses can constitute one-third of annual pay.

Demand

Jobs in management consulting services are expected to grow by 55 percent through 2012, ranking consulting fifth among the most rapidly growing industries. However, job competition should be strong because the independent nature of the work and generous salary and benefits attract a great many applicants. Candidates with the most education and job experience will have the best prospects.

The anticipated job growth can be attributed primarily to economic growth and the continuing complexity of business. All areas of business will require planning advice as the number of businesses increases. For example, the expansion of franchised restaurants and retail stores will increase demand for marketing consultants to determine the best locations and develop marketing plans. Logistics consulting firms will also be in demand to link new suppliers with producers and to get the final product to consumers. Finally, businesses will continue to need advice on compliance with government workplace safety and environmental laws. Clients need consultants to keep them up-to-date on the latest changes in legislation affecting their businesses, including changes to tax laws, environmental regulations, and policies affecting employee benefits, health care, and workplace safety. As a result, firms specializing in human resources, environment, and safety consulting should be in strong demand.

The continuing advances in technology and computer software will also lead to opportunities in all areas of consulting. Management consulting firms help clients implement new accounting and payroll software. Consulting firms might also help design new computer systems or online distribution systems. One of the biggest areas impacted by technology is logistics consulting. The Internet has greatly increased the ability of businesses to link with their suppliers and customers, which increases productivity and decreases costs. Technology-related consulting projects have become so important that many traditional consulting firms are now merging with or setting up joint ventures with technology companies. This way each firm has access to another's resources in order to serve clients better.

The trend toward outsourcing and mergers will also create new opportunities in consulting. In order to cut costs, many firms are outsourcing administrative and human resources functions to consultants specializing in these services. This should provide opportunities in human resources consulting for the management of clients' payroll systems and benefits programs.

Globalization also will continue to provide numerous opportunities for consulting firms to expand their services and those of their clients into foreign markets. Consulting firms can advise clients on strategy, foreign laws, taxes, employment, worker safety, and the environment. The growth of international businesses has created numerous opportunities for logistics consulting firms, because now businesses have an international network of suppliers and consumers, which requires more coordination.

As consulting firms continue to expand their services, they will be forced to compete with a more diverse group of firms that provide similar services. For example, increasing competition from investment banks, accounting firms, and technology firms might affect opportunities in management consulting.

Sources of Additional Information

Numerous publications are available to those interested in consulting as a profession. Consultants are listed in a number of directories, including

Consultants and Consulting Organizations Directory, found in the reference section of many libraries. *Management Consultant International* and *Journal of Management Consulting* are periodicals covering up-to-date information in the field. Some associations for consultants are listed below:

Association of Management Consulting Firms (AMCF)
380 Lexington Avenue, Suite 1700
New York, NY 10168
amcf.org

AMCF provides a referral service for members to organizations seeking consulting services.

Institute of Management Consultants USA (IMC)
2025 M Street NW, Suite 800
Washington, DC 20036
imcusa.org

Members of IMC include AMCF firms, public accounting firms, small firms, and independent consultants. The organization offers its members certification as Certified Management Consultants (CMC).

The American Consultants League
c/o ETR
245 NE Fourth Avenue, Suite 102
Delray Beach, FL 33483
consultants-league.com

The ACL confers certification for members who pass the required exams.

Canadian Association of Management Consultants
BCE Place
181 Bay Street
Heritage Building, Floor 2R
Toronto, ON M5J 2T3
camc.com

ENTREPRENEURSHIP AND FRANCHISING

Two major areas of business that appeal to a growing number of people are entrepreneurship and franchising. Both of these areas offer possibilities for those who desire to be self-employed. Whether an individual has business training and specific skills, or no training and a desire to make an investment, many options are available.

Entrepreneurship

The current generation of entrepreneurs, like their predecessors, runs the gamut from well-educated people opening sophisticated businesses to business novices taking a chance on a simple idea. Some new business start-ups are begun by those who lost their jobs as a result of corporate restructuring, but most are started by individuals seeking a better quality of life than they were able to have while working for someone else. Among the increasing number of women starting businesses, many cite the desire for a flexible schedule as a primary reason for leaving corporate jobs and striking out on their own.[5]

Most of today's small businesses provide only a modest living for their owners; the majority will go out of business within the first three years. Entrepreneurs are those who are willing to assume huge personal and financial risks to change their lives. Most see self-employment as a way to gain control of their lives, to build for their families' futures, to live the way they want or in the place they want, to gain respect or recognition, to earn lots of money, or to fulfill their expectations.

Succeeding as an entrepreneur. It is amazing to think of small businesses that started out in a garage—where Walt Disney drafted his first cartoons, Steve Jobs and Stephen Wozniac assembled the first personal computer that grew into Apple, Lila and DeWitt Wallace conceived the Reader's Digest, Buddy Holly and the Crickets rehearsed the music that helped create rock-and-roll, C. E. Wollman turned his crop-dusting business into Delta Airlines, and Ruth and Elliot Handler together with friend "Matt" Matson founded Mattel toys and Barbie.

From small beginnings arise *Fortune* 500 companies. Entrepreneurs find a market niche and develop a product. The entrepreneur has the freedom to run the company in his or her own way. However, small businesses are built on more than dreams of money and independence. A tremendous amount of knowledge and effort is involved. The entrepreneur needs total commitment to the business, support from family members, a tolerance for hard work, good health, and strong financial backing. Starting a business is difficult; staying in business is harder still.

The aspiring entrepreneur must secure financing for the proposed venture, usually from relatives, friends, and lending institutions. Normally entrepreneurs put a good bit of their own money into their businesses, often borrowing against home equity or other capital. If they have developed an impressive business plan, they may be successful in getting financial backing from outside sources such as banks or venture capitalists. Venture capital firms are groups of investors who extend financial backing to start-up companies in return for part ownership of the company. Usually the venture capital firm wants to protect its investment by having considerable say in how the company is run.

If the idea is good, raising capital for high-tech businesses is somewhat easier than for other small businesses. This is not to say that many high-tech businesses do not go bankrupt. But the growth and potential profits in high-tech areas are appealing enough to venture capitalists to offset the risk. Many fledgling businesses fail because they are underfinanced and lack sufficient capital to remain in business long enough to turn a profit.

Once the financial backing is secured, the entrepreneur begins planning, accounting, purchasing, producing, marketing, staffing, and managing. This requires a good general knowledge of the activities of business. Such attributes as a willingness to face risk, to work long hours, to tolerate the uncertainty of success during the early stages of the business, and to keep very thorough records in order to fill out the innumerable forms required by the government are all needed to be a successful entrepreneur.

A tremendous amount of sales ability is needed, not only to raise the capital but to attract employees willing to risk job security in a newly formed company, and to sell the product to consumers being constantly bombarded with ideas for new and better products. The entrepreneur is of a rare breed, both resilient and tough—flexible enough to change plans when advantageous, and strong enough to handle the disappointments and problems that plague all who go into business for themselves.

Franchising

Many people want to own small businesses, but have neither an original idea nor the business acumen to start an enterprise from scratch. When this is the case, an entrepreneur may choose to buy a franchise. A franchise can be defined as an agreement between a small business owner and a parent company that gives the owner the right to handle the company's products or services under conditions agreed upon by both. The store itself is also called a franchise. There are 1,500 franchise brands in the United States, generating hundreds of billions in sales every year. Many small retail stores, including fast-food eateries, gas stations, print shops, cleaning services, shipping centers, and others selling almost every type of good or service are run almost exclusively as franchises.

And the number continues to grow, as more entrepreneurs take a chance on an idea that others can then invest in and grow with. Take Brian Scudamore, for example, a thirty-three-year-old from Vancouver with no formal training, but with the business savvy to turn an idea into 1-800-Got-Junk?, one of the fastest-growing franchises in North America. Scudamore didn't plan on starting a franchise; he began his company as a way to pay his college tuition. Today the company has seventy-four territories, and posted revenues of $12.6 million in 2003. One of Scudamore's recent investors has said, "This is like joining the McDonald's chain in 1955."[6]

Experience in the business area of the franchise is not necessarily a requirement. Franchisees are given training by the parent company, during which they learn all aspects of the business. With this in mind it can be easier for a potential investor to decide on a franchise to buy into. There are a number of ways prospective franchisees learn about business opportunities. Some conduct online searches and work with franchise consultants, some depend on recommendations from others, and some already have a specific brand or product in mind. The International Franchise Association offers a free online database of 850 franchises, which can be searched by industry or investment required.[7]

Buying into a franchise has certain advantages that help minimize the risk of failure. Training and assistance from the parent company in choosing a location, setting up shop, estimating potential sales, and designing successful marketing strategies are very helpful to the new owner. Another advantage to franchises is the benefit of having a nationally known name and tested products—giving the business owner instant brand recognition. Cooperative buying power enables the franchisee to get supplies at lower costs, and sometimes credit assistance. These advantages do not guarantee success, however. Even parent companies sometimes fail, bringing down all franchise stores as well.

Costs associated with a franchise include some or all of the following: a franchising fee, a percentage of the profits of the business going to the parent company, and an agreement that products or equipment will be purchased from the vendors specified by the franchiser. In the relationship between franchiser and franchisee, the franchiser holds more bargaining power, so the franchisee should exercise caution before entering into an agreement.

There are some general guidelines for those interested in starting a franchise. Before entering into an agreement, a potential owner should carefully read the prospectus provided by the parent company and get legal advice as well. Potential profits should be assessed by questioning other franchisees and objective sources. The Federal Trade Commission requires that franchisers divulge any litigation in which they are involved. The franchisee should obtain his or her own land and lease-hold improvement costs, and not rely solely on the franchiser's estimates. Return on investment should be calculated using the prospective franchisee's figures. Remember that the franchiser is in business to sell franchises and is bound to make them look as attractive as possible.

Growth in Small Businesses and Franchises

Small businesses contribute greatly to the health of the U.S. economy, creating both products and jobs. Whether begun from the ground up by an entrepreneur or by a franchisee willing to make an investment, small businesses spur larger ones to make innovations in products and to create new markets. Incentives for businesses owned by women and minorities are in place in the federal government and throughout the country.

As mentioned earlier, starting a small business is a great risk, whether it involves an original idea or an investment into an established franchise. One cannot help but wonder if it is worth the time, effort, money, and risk to take the chance on being self-employed. In a recent survey conducted by the Gallup Organization for Wells Fargo, 86 percent of small business owners said they would still choose to own their own companies if given the chance to do it again. Only 14 percent said they would do something else. Seventy-six percent of the respondents said they believe they are better off financially than they would be if they worked for another company; 20 percent think they would have more financial reward working for another employer.[8]

Franchising has grown in recent years. According to FranChoice, a franchise consulting company, the company sees 2,000 to 3,000 potential franchisees a month, and anticipates that the number will double by 2006.[9]

New Technologies

As in so many areas of business, technology has created new opportunities for small businesses. Many entrepreneurs are engaged in "e-tailing," that is, selling items on Internet auction sites. Over 430,000 people earn a full- or part-time living selling items on eBay; the highest earners gross up to $1 million a month. Selling on the Net is particularly attractive to women, who make up 48 percent of eBay's regular sellers. Many of these women have left corporate careers to raise their families, and e-tailing provides a way to earn money and maintain a healthy balance between work and home.[10]

Sources of Additional Information

The Small Business Administration (SBA), with offices in all major cities, is an excellent source of information for those who want to start their own businesses or need help once they have set up shop. A wealth of information is available at the SBA website, covering topics such as start-up, planning, marketing, and staffing. Information also is available on taxes and legal topics. A special interest section includes information for women, minorities, Native Americans, veterans, young entrepreneurs, and international trade. The site also includes a free online entrepreneurship course. There are also many books and periodicals that deal with starting and managing small businesses. Small business consultants also offer services to business owners.

Any franchise should be thoroughly checked out by contacting both the Better Business Bureau and the International Franchise Association. Many excellent books on franchising are on the market; a number of them are available through the International Franchise Association itself.

Information and assistance for small business and franchise owners can be obtained by contacting some of the following:

Chamber of Commerce of the United States
1615 H Street, NW
Washington, DC 20062
uschamber.com

International Franchise Association
1350 New York Avenue NW, Suite 900
Washington, DC 20005
franchise.org

Minority Business Development Association
U.S. Department of Commerce
1401 Constitution Avenue NW
Washington, DC 20230
mbda.gov

National Association of Small Business Investment Companies
666 11th Street NW, Suite 750
Washington, DC 20001
nasbic.org

National Association of Women Business Owners
8405 Greensboro Drive, Suite 800
McLean, VA 22102
nawbo.org

National Minority Business Council, Inc.
25 West 45th Street, Suite 301
New York, NY 10036
nmbc.org

U.S. Small Business Administration
1441 L Street, NW
Washington, DC 20416
sba.gov

The following directories offer advice and information on opportunities:

Franchise Annual Directory On-Line
728 Center Street
P.O. Box 128
Lewiston, NY 14092
infonews.com

FranchiseOpportunities.com
1085 Powers Place
Alpharetta, GA 30004
franchiseopportunities.com

ieFranchise.com
8260 Greensboro Drive, Suite 550
McLean, VA 22102
iefranchise.com

Sources of Additional Information in Canada

Canadian Franchise Association
2585 Skymark Avenue, Suite 300
Mississauga, ON L4W 4L5
cfa.ca

Canadian Venture Capital Association
234 Eglinton Avenue East, Suite 200
Toronto, ON M4P 1K5
cvca.ca

Canadian Youth Business Foundation
123 Edward Street, Suite 1404
Toronto, ON M5G 1E2
cybf.ca

Entrepreneurship Institute of Canada
P.O. Box 40043
75 King Street South
Waterloo, ON N2J 4V1
entinst.ca

INTEREST ANALYSIS CHART

Consider what you have just learned about education, consulting, and business ownership—both as an entrepreneur and as a franchisee. In an effort to analyze your interest in these areas as options along your career path, complete Figure 10-3, the interest analysis chart. In identifying the pros and cons of education, consulting, and business ownership, think in personal terms. Focus on what appeals or does not appeal to you in terms of your identified aptitudes, interests, and values.

WHAT NEXT?

You have learned a great deal about careers in business. Chapter 11 is designed to help you examine trends in the job market and select a good field using the career evaluations at the ends of the chapters.

NOTES

1. Erin Chambers, "Too Much of a Good Thing," *BusinessWeek* (October 18, 2004), 94.
2. Ibid., 94.
3. Bernard J. Milano and Lisa King, "Navigating the Path to Your Ph.D.," *Minority MBA* (Spring 2004), 34.
4. Ibid., 35.
5. Michelle Conlin, "The Rise of the Mompreneurs," *BusinessWeek* (June 7, 2004), 70.
6. Justin Martin, "Cash From Trash," *Fortune Small Business* (November 2003), fortune.com/fortune/smallbusiness/ articles/0,15114,516204,00.html, (accessed March 12, 2005).
7. Sarah Max, "Instant Entrepreneur," *CNN Money* (March 5, 2004), http://money.cnn.com/2004/03/05/pf/franchise/index.htm, (accessed March 14, 2005).
8. Richard Breeden, "Small Talk: Reflecting on Ownership," *Wall Street Journal* (November 2, 2004), B6.
9. Les Christie, "Franchises: How Much Can You Earn?," *CNN Money* (July 1, 2004), http://money.cnn.com/2004/04/29/ pf/howmuchfranchise, (accessed March 14, 2005).
10. Michelle Conlin, "The Rise of the Mompreneurs," *BusinessWeek* (June 7, 2004), 70.

Figure 10.3

Interest analysis chart

Education	
Personal pros	Personal cons
1.	1.
2.	2.
3.	3.
4.	4.
Consulting	
Personal pros	Personal cons
1.	1.
2.	2.
3.	3.
4.	4.
Business ownership	
Personal pros	Personal cons
1.	1.
2.	2.
3.	3.
4.	4.

CHAPTER 11

TRENDS IN THE JOB MARKET AND YOUR CAREER SELECTION

After reading this chapter, you will be able to:

- Explain how a service-oriented economy, the restructuring of corporations, changing technology, and changes in lifestyles and values affect business careers
- Identify some of the best cities for business
- Describe supply and demand projections for future jobs
- Use the career decision-making model to select a business career choice

Understanding trends in the job market is particularly important for entry-level job seekers. As you have seen in previous chapters, major transformations in American business over the past two decades have strongly impacted careers. The types of products offered, the nature of jobs, the demand for employees with certain skills, the salaries offered workers, even the sizes and locations of businesses themselves have been affected by a growing service economy, the globalization of business, the restructuring of corporations, the impact of technology, the diversification of the workforce, and the changing lifestyles of American families.

In January 2005, the national unemployment rate fell to 5.2 percent, the lowest it had been since the terrorist attacks of September 11, 2001. The overall national income of households and businesses rose nearly 8 percent in 2004, the fastest increase in 15 years.[1] Part of this upturn can be attributed to effective strategies employed by workers who lost jobs due to restructuring, downsizing, outsourcing, and other factors. Many found employment in new industries; moved to smaller, more entrepreneurial firms; started their own businesses; or worked as consultants.

However, anyone who is about to enter the job market should look at all sides of the situation. Although 1.7 million new jobs were added to the economy in 2003, that number is well below the 2.2 million average annual gain of the 1990s. Many experts believe that this slow job growth is a short-term problem caused by high oil prices and political uncertainty. Others cite intense global competition and the high cost of health care as reasons for the slump. Whatever the reason, it is important to look at the areas most affected by this trend. These include retail trade, education, telecommunications, computer services, finance and insurance, and business support services, among other industries. The reality seems to be that job creation has become more difficult in light of the changes that business has undergone in the last several years, and it has been proposed that it will take the introduction of a major innovation to revitalize job growth, such as occurred with the introduction of the Internet.[2]

The impact of the slow growth rate of new jobs is mitigated by other factors, however. The Bureau of Labor Statistics anticipates a shortage of ten million workers through 2010. It is projected that U.S. companies will need to fill fifty-five million jobs over the next ten years, but there won't be enough workers. Changing lifestyles and demographics, which will be discussed later in this chapter, will impact the number of workers.

A SERVICE-ORIENTED ECONOMY

We live in a service-oriented economy, and the long-term shift from goods-producing to service-producing employment is expected to continue. By 2012 service industries are expected to account for approximately 20.8 million of the 21.6 million new wage and salary jobs.

The service sector of education and health services is expected to grow faster than any other, at 31.8 percent. About one of every four new jobs created will be in either the health care and social assistance or private educational services sectors. Professional and business services should grow by 30.4 percent, adding nearly five million new jobs. Some of the fastest growing industries in the U.S. economy are included in this group.

Management of companies and enterprises will grow by 11.4 percent through 2012, adding 195,000 new jobs. The information sector is expected to add 632,000 jobs, growing at a rate of 18.5 percent.

The quality of a service is contingent on the performance of the worker and can vary considerably within a firm. For this reason, more firms are realizing the importance of quality and are emphasizing and rewarding excellence. The traits most valued in new workers today are communications skills, technical and computer-related expertise, teamwork abilities, and work experience.

THE RESTRUCTURING OF AMERICAN CORPORATIONS

The last two decades were a turbulent period in American business, causing major restructuring in corporations. Acquisitions and buyouts changed many corporate identities. Recession and competition from abroad forced downsizing and restructuring. Assigning limited resources in a vastly more complex marketplace is the challenge confronting managers today.

The business environment of the next decade will be characterized by continued restructuring and downsizing of corporations, outsourcing of jobs, global competition, shortened product life cycles, and customers demanding more quality and convenience. More and more work in America is project-oriented. With shorter product life cycles, new products must be produced faster. These projects are completed by combinations of in-house staff, contract workers, and consultants who work together as teams, complete projects, then disband. Such projects as port expansions, hospital restructuring, and nuclear-waste cleanups are done by teams. Information technology has spawned many new high-tech contractors.

The reduction in numbers of mid-level managers is good news and bad news. First the bad news: Advancement in the corporate hierarchy will become increasingly more competitive, and most college graduates will remain in the same jobs for longer periods of time—perhaps five years or more. Also, fewer types of positions will be available to new graduates. Now the good news: Even entry-level jobs will be more varied and challenging. Managers with too much to do will be forced to delegate many tasks to lower-level and beginning employees. Project teams will be more widely used as companies attempt a more entrepreneurial approach to product development. Work will be less structured. More freedom, as a result of reduced numbers of supervisors, will enable employees to show what they are able to do.

THE IMPACT OF CHANGING TECHNOLOGY

Advances in information and communications technology have revolutionized the workplace, and created opportunities for companies and individuals that simply did not exist a decade ago. Computers are faster, cheaper, smaller, and more versatile than ever before. New information technology has enabled managers to make better decisions faster. Sophisticated marketing research analysis, such as multivariate statistical analyses too complex to do manually, can be done readily on computers. Monitoring the economic and business environments is also easier. Responding more rapidly to competition can be accomplished through technological advances in manufacturing equipment. Sales campaigns can be run more efficiently and effectively with improved distribution and inventory techniques made possible through new technology. Improved graphics technology has greatly affected the field of advertising. Breakthroughs in telecommunication technology have furthered the development of branch or satellite offices and the expansion of global operations. The World Wide Web and Internet have fueled the knowledge explosion by making information ever more available.

Telecommuting

Many companies use telecommuting programs as a means to enhance productivity, keep valuable employees, and increase employee loyalty. Companies such as Xerox, Hewlett-Packard, and Perkin-Elmer have instituted telecommuting programs that enable members of the sales force to work at home. Other companies such as American Express, Apple, AT&T, Chase Manhattan, Compaq, Ford Motor, General Electric, GTE, IBM, Merrill Lynch, Prudential Insurance, and Sears also have structured telecommuting programs.

In reality, telecommuting has grown more slowly and in different ways than was first anticipated. U.S. businesses employ 12.2 million telecommuters, and the growth rate of telecommuters is expected to rise just over 2 percent a year through 2008, a figure well below the initial projection of 5 to 6 percent. Although some companies have formal policies governing telecommuting, many others permit informal arrangements between individual managers and employees. It does seem that telecommuting works best for those in technology and financial industries, as opposed to manufacturing workers or service employees who must interact with customers.[3]

CHANGES IN LIFESTYLES AND VALUES

The last ten years have seen a marked shift in American values and lifestyles. The family is taking central importance in the choices people make, both in their careers and as consumers. People are marrying and having children later in life when careers are already in place. Because of economics, in the great majority of marriages both the husband and wife work. In these two-career couples, both partners share in family responsibilities and the divorce rate is decreasing. Though studies show that it is still the woman who misses work more frequently when children are ill, men are definitely doing more of the shopping.

According to a 2002 study by the Families and Work Institute, working men born between 1965 and 1979 spend about three-and-a-half hours a day with their children, the same amount of time as working women. Seventy percent of the men surveyed reported that they would take a pay cut to spend more time with their families, and nearly half would turn down a promotion if it meant less family time. Companies are responding to this major trend by providing more flexible work schedules and child-care resources.[4]

A growing number of women are choosing family over formal careers. Many women desire greater flexibility in their schedules than a corporate career allows. Time with children is becoming more important to women at all levels of management. Some enterprising women who leave corporate jobs work independently as consultants. Many have become involved in "e-tailing"—developing flexible careers selling items on the Internet.[5]

Many workers are also reconsidering retirement. More people are putting off full retirement, opting instead to move from full-time careers to part-time, flexible jobs that suit their lifestyles. The Bureau of Labor Statistics reports that by 2012 the number of workers over age fifty-five will increase by 51 percent, and those ages sixty-five and older by 43 percent. According to a 2004 study conducted by the American Association for Retired Persons

(AARP), 80 percent of baby boomers plan to work in retirement. Many people continue to work for the enjoyment of being involved in something they like to do; still others continue to work for financial reasons.[6]

What does this growing trend, called phased retirement, mean to businesses? According to some observers, companies are realizing that it is beneficial to keep older, skilled workers on the job. Given the projections for labor shortages over the next several years, it would be in the best interest of a company to develop strategies to keep experienced workers on the payroll. In addition to flexible schedules, tuition reimbursement, and telecommuting, more companies are offering phased retirement, skills training, and health and finance workshops to older employees.[7]

Contingent workers are self-employed or work part-time, and include those who do not work forty hours a week, year-round, for the same employer. They range from highly paid management consultants who choose to work on a contingent basis to low-paid service workers who do not receive benefits and would prefer full-time employment. It is difficult to estimate the number of contingent workers because there is not a specific consensus as to which categories of workers should be included, but some estimates put the number as high as 30 percent of the workforce.

The benefit of hiring contingent employees is lower costs and easy layoffs. The Economic Policy Institute, a Washington DC research organization, has found that employees in "nonstandard" work arrangements are nearly twice as likely to be unemployed one month later than traditional full-time workers. Despite this potential job uncertainty, however, contingency work appeals to many. It is often a good transition from a postcollege internship to full-time employment, and can provide useful experience to those considering a career change. The downside to employees, aside from lack of job security, is that contingent workers do not receive health insurance, sick days, or paid vacation.[8]

GEOGRAPHY

Although career opportunities in business occur everywhere in the world, certain cities emerge as the best locations for business. *Fortune* magazine ranks cities based on four criteria: overall business environment (new business growth, diversity of industries); the cost of doing business (commercial real estate prices, tax and fiscal policies); the quality of the local workforce (education level, management experience); and quality of life (housing, schools). The top five U.S. cities in the ranking are New York, San Francisco, Chicago, Greater Washington DC, and San Jose.[9]

In a separate study *Forbes* ranked the best metropolitan areas outside of big cities. The survey found that many revolve around universities that offer a diverse, well-educated workforce and a relatively low cost of living. The top cities are Madison, Wisconsin; Raleigh-Durham, North Carolina; Austin, Texas; Washington, DC; Atlanta, Georgia; Provo, Utah; Boise, Idaho; Huntsville, Alabama; Lexington, Kentucky; and Richmond, Virginia.[10]

SUPPLY AND DEMAND PROJECTIONS

The overall demand for business majors has been consistently strong. Demand has increased in the areas of sales and marketing, particularly for business-to-business marketers. High-tech knowledge is very much in demand in all areas today and will improve a beginner's chances of securing a good job. The increased number of recruiters on college campuses signals increased demand and will greatly help new graduates in their job searches. Most job offers are within the service sector, in areas such as public accounting, operations research, information systems, merchandising, and consulting.

The rate of job creation has been slow in this recovering economy. Some explanations for this are that the productivity gains experienced by many companies reduce the need for more employees, downsizing is eliminating many positions, outsourcing certain parts of operations is more efficient than performing the work in-house, and employers are more cautious about adding new positions because hiring and firing costs are growing.

Demand is half of the job market picture; supply is the other half. The birth rate has risen, new mothers are slower to return to work, women are staying in school longer, and baby boomers are reaching retirement age. Employers will have to compete for qualified workers in this atmosphere. With competition from businesses, universities, and the military, there will not be enough entry-level workers to go around. This bright picture for young, entry-level personnel has a more somber side for older workers. Promotions will continue to be more competitive because of larger numbers of middle-aged workers with obsolete skills, the need to staff lower-level jobs, and the current trend to reduce middle-management positions. Increasing demand and limited supply will enable more women and minorities to enter the workforce. Advances in technology will increase opportunities for the handicapped to enjoy more employment opportunities.

INNOVATION

Experts have suggested that it will take the launching of a major new innovation to bolster the struggling economy. If this is true, where might the next big thing in innovation come from? In what area will it bring the most change? In recent years, change has occurred more rapidly in information processing and health care than in energy, transportation, and manufacturing. Advances in electronics, medications, surgical techniques, and financial systems far outweigh those in areas such as nuclear power, transportation, and manufactured products.[11]

One issue that affects innovation is the lack of agreement among economists about how to encourage it. Some of this difficulty can be attributed to the fact that the innovation economy has many components. Government, universities, corporations, start-ups, venture-capital firms, and stock market investors all play a role in innovation. Add to this the fact that innovation is now global, and the issue is even more complex. Although the United States was seen in the late 1990s as mature and slow-growing, the country defied expectations by surpassing others in adapting Internet technology into products and services. Economists have suggested that governments around the world, and the United States in particular, should be able to continue building on this success by following a few steps for progress. The suggestions for innovation progress are to invest in research and education for the future, to take advantage of the global economy, to provide protection for intellectual property, and to emphasize innovation as a high priority.[12]

What will innovation mean for those seeking to enter the job market? Companies working toward innovation in various areas will need employees with the best technological skills and the ability to work as members of teams. *BusinessWeek* rated companies from the *Standard and Poor*'s 500 based on a combination of research and development and capital spending to come up with the *BusinessWeek Investing for the Future Index*. The index offers insight into which companies and industries are devoting the largest share of resources to projects with future payoffs. High-tech companies outnumber all others in the index, with all but one of the top thirty U.S. companies involved in drugs and biotechnology, semiconductors, software and IT services, technology gear, or health care.[13]

It is also important to consider the impact of globalization on innovation. The United States has been a technological giant for years, but other countries are emerging as strong competition. One concern is that America does not invest enough capital in innovative science or in educating citizens in science and technology. New immigration policies in the wake of terrorism fears are seen as a deterrent to foreign-born students, scientists, and engineers. With over ten million people with degrees in science or engineering, the United States leads the world in scientific papers and patents. However, other nations are beginning to catch up. China, Korea, India, Britain, Singapore, and Taiwan are all exhibiting rapid advances in innovation research. One upside of this is that U.S. researchers are working collaboratively with companies and universities throughout Europe and Asia in fields such as microelectronics.[14]

Whatever the next big innovation, American workers are sure to be part of it, whether in its design, implementation, or sale.

SELECTING YOUR BUSINESS CAREER

The culmination of your decision-making process occurs in this chapter. You are now ready to put together the pieces of your career puzzle. After that, the rest will fall into place for you. Your career decision-making model and the career evaluations that you completed throughout the book, will enable you to select a career in business that will satisfy your personal career requirements.

You have systematically investigated a number of career areas and focused on some specific jobs in those areas. This chapter offered some general information about trends in the job market. Use the Job Rank form in Figure 11.1 to reconsider those jobs according to the following instructions.

1. Look back at Figures 2.2a and 2.2b, Career Evaluation for Accounting, near the end of Chapter 2. Examine the completed Career Evaluation form. You entered a specific job at the top of the form. Write this job in the column entitled "Job" on the Job Rank form in the space to the right of the word "Accounting." Follow this procedure for entering jobs from each Career Evaluation form for the remaining chapters through Chapter 9.

Figure 11.1

Job rank form

Chapter	Career area	Job	Subjective Rank	Objective Rank
2	Accounting			
3	Computers and information technology			
4	Finance			
5	Insurance and real estate			
6	Marketing			
7	Operations research, production, and materials management			
8	Human resources management			
9	Management and supervision			

2. Examine the jobs you have listed. In the column entitled "Subjective rank," rank the jobs in the order of your preference from 1 to 8, with 1 entered beside the job you most prefer and 8 the job you least prefer. Use only your gut feeling to do this!

3. Now look at the Career summary form in Figure 11.2. Enter the jobs from the Job column on the Job rank form into the Job column on the Career summary form.

4. Turn to the completed Career Evaluation form in Chapter 2 again. Enter the totals from each of the six groups of factors into the appropriate columns ("Aptitudes and attributes," "Interests," and so on) on the Career summary form. Repeat this step for each chapter through Chapter 9.

5. Sum up the points for each job by adding points for all factors across the row horizontally. Enter the sum in the column entitled "Overall total" on the Career summary form. Do this for each of the nine jobs.

6. Return to the Job rank form and the column entitled "Objective rank." Rank the jobs from 1 to 8 according to the overall total points that you entered for each job on the Career summary form. Let 1 indicate the job with the most points and 8 the job with the least points.

7. Carefully compare the subjective rank and the objective rank for each job.

If this book were a novel, the activity you have just completed would be considered the climax. Now let's see if you have resolved the career dilemma. Does each job that you have listed carry the same subjective and objective rank, or do the ranks differ? What about the number 1 job you prefer at gut level? Is this job also number 1 in the objective analysis resulting from the use of the career decision-making model? If both your gut feeling and the objective analysis produced the same number 1 job, you have very likely ended up with a solid basis for planning your career. But don't be disappointed if a discrepancy occurred. Probably more often than not, the ranks will differ, even on the number 1 job. This does not mean that you have wasted your time. It simply means that you have to do a little more analysis before selecting your career area.

Consider how most people choose careers. They act on a few pieces of information and gut feeling or intuition. Few engage in the systematic analysis that you have done in the course of this book. Even your subjective rank for each job was based on the evaluation of a considerable amount of information. The job ranked number 1 according to your gut feeling may be the one for you even though it differs from the number 1 job in the objective analysis. At this point, you must be sure because your career decision may well be the most important decision of your life so far.

One reason many people change college majors or make drastic career changes that require complete retooling is that their career choices have been too subjective, often unrealistic for them personally. Look at your

Figure 11.2

Career summary form

| Chapter | Career area | Job | Internal factors | | | External factors | | | |
			Aptitudes and attributes	Interests	Values	Family influence	Economic influence	Societal influence	Overall total
2	Accounting								
3	Computers and information technology								
4	Finance								
5	Insurance and real estate								
6	Marketing								
7	Operations research, production, and materials management								
8	Human resources management								
9	Management and supervision								

number 1 job from subjective rank and your number 1 job from objective rank. If they differ use the Career summary form to compare the two jobs. It is possible that you are weighing certain factors in your mind as being more important than the weights that you assigned to them in your model and some factors as less important. You may have to return to the Career Evaluation forms at the ends of the chapters for each of the jobs and compare them.

It is up to you to reconcile your job choice now. You may want to reread some chapters. You may want to look more closely at the job that ranked number 2 in your objective analysis. You may want to consider some of the individual factors in the model and weigh them again in your mind. If you haven't already requested additional information from some of the sources listed in each chapter, you may want to do that before making a career decision.

Before planning your educational program, you should feel fairly comfortable with your career choice. You should then begin to look at various types of organizations and specific industries so that you can tailor your career preparation for entry into an organization or industry that interests you and is likely to provide opportunities for you in the future.

Chapter 12, "Preparing Yourself for a Career in Business," contains many tips for planning your education, gaining valuable experience while still in college, researching industries and companies, and finding your first job.

NOTES

1. James C. Cooper and Kathleen Madigan, "Finally for Workers, A Bigger Piece of the Pie," *BusinessWeek* (June 14, 2004), 29.
2. Michael J. Mandel, "Jobs: The Lull Will Linger," *BusinessWeek* (October 25, 2004), 40–41.
3. Robert Weisman, "Home Work," *Rocky Mountain News* (June 21, 2004), 2B–3B.
4. Diane Brady, "Hopping Aboard the Daddy Track," *BusinessWeek* (November 8, 2004), 100–101.
5. Michelle Conlin, "The Rise of the Mompreneurs," *BusinessWeek* (June 7, 2004), 70.
6. Mary Quigley and Loretta E. Kaufman, "Hire Calling," *AARP* (November/December 2004), 69–70.

7. "Best Employers for Workers Over 50," *AARP* (November/ December 2004), 72.

8. Daniel Nasaw, "Companies Are Hedging Their Bets by Hiring Contingent Employees," *Wall Street Journal* (September 14, 2004), B10.

9. Mark Borden, "The Best Cities for Business," *Fortune* (November 27, 2000), fortune.com/fortune/subs/article/0,15114,368137,00 .html, (accessed March 1, 2005).

10. Kurt Badenhausen, "Best Places for Business," *Forbes* (May 7, 2004), forbes.com/2004/05/05/04bestplacesland.html, (accessed March 1, 2005).

11. Michael J. Mandel, "This Way to the Future," *BusinessWeek* (October 11, 2004), 93–94.

12. Michael J. Mandel, "How to Sharpen the Innovation Edge," *BusinessWeek* (October 11, 2004), 225–226.

13. Peter Coy, "The Search for Tomorrow," *BusinessWeek* (October 11, 2004), 216–218.

14. John Carey, "Flying High?" *BusinessWeek* (October 11, 2004), 116–118.

C H A P T E R

12

PREPARING YOURSELF FOR A CAREER IN BUSINESS

After reading this chapter, you will be able to:

- Plan a college program that will prepare you for the career that you selected
- Identify sources for job openings
- Research companies and industries to determine where the best opportunities are
- Prepare a résumé that will appeal to prospective employers
- Conduct yourself in a job interview so that you make a positive impression on the interviewer

Job market statistics can be frightening and can shake a graduate's confidence. The likelihood of success in a business career depends on two things: proper preparation and finding a good entry-level job. Preparing yourself for a career in business involves getting the best possible education and gaining experience through involvement in campus activities, part-time jobs, and internships. Once you are prepared to enter the job market, you should use a variety of resources to acquire some job-finding skills and locate the best jobs. Sometimes opportunities exist where they are not expected, and many of the best jobs may be in companies graduates have never heard of.

GETTING THE BEST EDUCATION

Depending on your career goal, you may gain the required background for a career in business in high school, vocational school, technical school, community college, college, or a university. Educational requirements were discussed throughout this book as part of the specific job descriptions, so this chapter will focus on where to obtain this needed education and training. The majority of the careers discussed in this book require college or university degrees and, in some cases, graduate study.

Probably the most useful source of educational information on programs nationwide is *The College Blue Book*. This five-volume set is particularly useful to those seeking highly specialized programs. The volume entitled "Occupational Education" includes a listing of available programs of study in technical schools and community colleges, organized alphabetically by state or by subject area. Another volume, "Degrees Offered by College and Subject," includes degree programs offered by two-year colleges, four-year colleges, and universities. Other volumes offer narrative descriptions of schools, costs, accreditation, enrollment figures, scholarships, fellowships, grants, loans, and a great deal of other information.

The College Blue Book is found in the reference section of the library along with many other educational resources. Most college and university libraries also carry a variety of college catalogs enabling one to compare curricula of different schools offering the degree or program of interest. Education is important and expensive, and you should shop for it the way you would for any other important, expensive item. Gaining information from counselors, teachers, local colleges and universities, people working in the field, and potential employers is very advisable before selecting an educational program.

Another valuable source of information is the Peterson's online guide (petersons.com). This website offers a searchable database of two- and four-year colleges, graduate schools, career programs, and study abroad, among other options. Information is available on test preparation, financial aid, admissions essays, and résumé writing. Peterson's also offers books and materials for sale on various educational and career topics.

One important consideration when choosing a program is whether it has established national accreditation. National bodies that accredit these schools are the Accrediting Council for Independent Colleges and Schools, International Association for Management Education, Association of Collegiate Business Schools and Programs, and the Accrediting Commission of Career Schools and Colleges of Technology.

GAINING THE NECESSARY EXPERIENCE

As stressed throughout this book, experience is required for many of the more desirable business careers. This experience can be gained through internships and cooperative programs, part-time jobs, and involvement in campus activities.

Internships and Cooperative Programs

Traditional internships are usually three-month summer positions, while cooperative programs (co-ops) last a college quarter, semester, or longer. Internships are sometimes arranged by an interested faculty member and a company manager, and the intern is not always paid. Co-ops, on the other hand, are part of an on-going college program for which students receive both credits and pay. These distinctions aren't as clear any more since companies want interns for longer periods as well, and they frequently offer paid internships. Many organizations hire their brightest interns and co-op students.

Smart students start looking for internships during their freshman year, and competition can be stiff. Professors, older students who have had internships, and family contacts in a student's chosen field can be great sources of information and referral.

Annual publications such as *Internships 2005* (*Peterson's Internships*) and *The Princeton Review's Internship Bible* are excellent sources of information. Internships may be advertised in campus newspapers and may also be advertised on college campuses through placement offices, on billboards, through faculty members, campus newspapers, and books. Many professional associations offer information on internships available with member companies. Student membership in a number of professional associations is available at a reduced cost and is worth investigating.

Interviews for internships are essentially job interviews, so students should learn everything they can about a company prior to the interview. Often interview sign-up sheets are posted on campus bulletin boards. The best time slots are first, last, or right after lunch—never right before lunch.

A number of organizations assist students in arranging international internships, including the following:

Association for International Practical Training (AIPT)
10400 Little Patuxent Parkway, Suite 250
Columbia, MD 21044
aipt.org

Association Internationale des Étudiants en Sciences Économiques
    et Commerciales
AIESEC International
Teilingerstraat 126
3032-AW Rotterdam
The Netherlands
aiesec.org

Institute of International Education
iie.org

Part-Time Jobs

Apart from intern and co-op programs, many students find part-time jobs on their own that offer both pay and experience. Though part-time jobs often pay a low wage, this work experience is very important to prospective employers. Former employers can give important recommendations for full-time jobs after graduation, attesting to an individual's reliability, initiative, and ability to work with others.

Many on-campus jobs can be obtained through student financial aid and job placement services. Every college campus has job boards and student publications advertising openings. Graduate assistantships are available to qualified students. Any opportunity for work experience prior to graduation should be considered important because of the strength it lends to the job search for that first, very important, full-time job.

Involvement in Campus Activities

An option for all students is involvement in campus activities and organizations. By joining student business associations and taking a role in student government, students can develop the interpersonal skills needed in most business professions. Though grade point average and work experience are very important, they do not always reveal the potential for leadership. Corporations particularly look for students who hold leadership positions in campus organizations, often hiring them over scholars in many fields of business. The very charisma that helps students gain elective offices also scores high marks in job interviews. Participation in organized sports by both men and women also increases the strength of their résumés. How to be a good team player is an important lesson learned through participation in team sports. This, along with the acceptance that the coach may not always be right but is never wrong, has probably influenced promotion in corporations as much as scholarly preparation.

FINDING A GOOD JOB

Competition for the best jobs in most areas is stiff, so developing good job-finding skills should become part of your education. The first full-time job out of college is particularly important because it sometimes sets the direction for an entire career. The first step in the job search is to decide what attributes you want in the job and how the job fits into your overall career objectives.

Defining Career Objectives

Not everyone defines a good job in the same way, so it is important for you to define what you want in a job before beginning the search. For example, to an entry-level employee, a good job may be one offering growth through a formal company training program or company-financed continuing education; to a physically handicapped person or to a parent with young children, a good job may be one that can be done in the home; to a student, a good job may be part-time or have flexible working hours; to a partner in a dual-career marriage, a good job may be one available locally; to an ambitious woman, a good job may be one in a company employing women managers in key positions. It is very important, however, for you to have your individual requirements and career goals clearly in mind prior to launching the job search.

Locating Jobs

The task of finding a good job is twofold in that you must identify companies with existing openings and companies for which you would like to work. The fact that a company does not have an advertised opening does not mean that the company would not create an opening for an outstanding applicant. This makes the job search more complicated, but it also offers considerably more opportunities. It is helpful to build a network of family, friends, and associates who can refer you to others who might be able to help with your career.

Many maintain that the way to find excellent jobs is through direct contact with the person who has the authority to hire. One of the best and most widely used books on the subject of job finding is *What Color Is Your Parachute?* by Richard Nelson Bolles. A new edition of the book is subtitled, "A Practical Manual for Job Hunters and Career Changers." This book can help you to organize your time and energy and avoid tactics that rarely, if ever, pay off.

Various avenues for locating job opportunities include college placement offices, published job openings, recruiting firms, and computerized search services. These are discussed below.

The college placement office. Prospective college graduates should take advantage of the on-campus interviews arranged by their college placement office. These interviews provide an opportunity for a first contact with major representatives of companies that are willing to hire beginners. It is best to sign up early because the company representatives have time for only a limited number of interviews. To prepare for these interviews, review the information on file in the college placement office. This information, provided by the interviewing companies, often includes annual reports and recruitment materials from which students can glean facts about a particular company and the career opportunities it offers.

Published job openings. A number of sources of listed job openings in business include *The Career Guide*, *Career Visions*, and *NACE's Job Choices* series. These books can usually be found in the career planning and placement offices of most colleges and universities. They contain a tremendous amount of information, including listings of career opportunities, locations of employment, special training programs available with the companies, benefits, employer profiles, and addresses to write for further information.

Professional journals provide another source of published job openings. Many journals devote a section near the end to advertising job openings. The *Wall Street Journal,* the *New York Times*, and other big-city and local newspapers advertise openings, but responding to newspaper advertisements is rarely the way to obtain good first jobs.

Recruiting firms. Some job opportunities are listed with recruiting firms. These firms provide needed services to organizations and applicants. Although it is unusual for a beginner to find a highly desirable job through a recruiting firm and often a sizable chunk of the first month's salary must be paid as a commission, these firms offer some entry-level jobs that enable beginners to get much-needed experience. Some organizations seeking employees assume the charges for the service.

Computerized search services. Computerized search services have gained popularity in recent years. The services vary among schools, but may include some of the following: Students may call up a list of job openings in their chosen field. Some systems place student résumés online for companies to review, others allow students to sign up for on-campus interviews by computer. Other online services include America's Job Bank (the Department of Labor service), Monster.com, CareerPath, Help Wanted USA, Career City, and NationJob Network.

New job seekers can find entry-level job listings and career guidance for improving résumés, cover letters, and interviewing skills on the World Wide Web. JobDirect (jobdirect.com) is free to student job hunters who enter résumé information and interest areas into the database. The service matches résumés to job postings and the student may be e-mailed by the service or a prospective employer. JobWeb (jobweb.org) is maintained by the National Association of Colleges and Employers and contains thousands of postings, but does not allow users to enter their résumés. MonsterTRAK (monstertrak.com) lets students and alumni search for jobs, internships, and part-time work. The site also offers job search tips and alumni networking.

The College Grad Job Hunter (collegegrad.com) is yet another service for new graduates, offering job searches, salary information, interview help, and a relocation center.

An excellent guide to job searching on the Internet is *The Guide to Internet Job Searching*, copublished by McGraw-Hill and the Public Library Association. This comprehensive guide gives clear directions on how to find and use online bulletin boards, job listings, résumé-posting services, and cooperative education and internship opportunities.

Professional association placement services. Many professional associations have placement services. As a job seeker, you should become affiliated at the outset of your career planning with one or more of the professional organizations for individuals in your area of expertise.

Even if associations have no placement service, many provide directories of their members free or at a minimal cost on request. They can often recommend or supply sources of information to help research and contact companies. Many of the professional associations listed throughout this book provide information on job searches, salary, and continuing education.

Job fairs or career days. Job fairs are held in large cities around the country. At these events, company representatives talk to professionals about opportunities within their organizations. In addition, job-search seminars are offered. There is no charge to job seekers for either participation in the seminars or placement in jobs. Job fairs are generally advertised locally, as well as promoted at colleges and universities.

Temporary employment services. If the job search becomes discouraging, consider gaining experience and access to companies by signing up with a temporary employment service. No longer just placement for clerical and lower-level positions, temps are catering more and more to companies that are outsourcing segments of their operations. White-collar technical and professional workers are being hired for special projects and long-term assignments. Many workers are hired for permanent positions by companies where they work as temps. Once inside a company as a temp, an employee's abilities may be noticed and rewarded.

GAINING COMPANY INFORMATION

As you begin your job search, it is very important for you to have knowledge about the specific companies by which you will be interviewed.

Industry information is extremely valuable to the job seeker, and is available from numerous sources. The current *U.S. Industrial Outlook* analyzes two hundred industries with projections into the future. It is published by the Bureau of Industrial Economics of the U.S. Department of Commerce and can be found in the government documents section of the library. *Standard & Poor's Industry Surveys* include current and basic analyses for the major domestic industries. The current analysis includes latest industry developments; industry, market, and company statistics; and appraisals of investment outlook. The basic analysis includes prospects for the particular industry, an analysis of trends, and problems; spotlights on major segments of the industry; growth in sales and earnings of leading companies in the industry; and other information over a ten-year span. Another excellent source of up-to-date industry information is the *Value Line Investment Survey*.

Many sources focus on specific companies. The *Dun & Bradstreet Directories* (dnb.com), *Moody's Investor Services* (moodys.com), and *Thomas's Register* (thomasnet.com) all provide specific company information, such as the contact information, what each business produces, its annual sales, and the names of officers and directors. If you are interested in the backgrounds of those who make it to the top in a particular company, *Standard & Poor's Register of Corporations, Directors, and Executives* and *Dun & Bradstreet's Reference Book of Corporate Managements* both provide this type of information. These resources are found in public and college libraries in the reference section. Annual and quarterly corporate reports are usually housed in the college career placement offices. In addition, business publications such as *Fortune* and *Forbes* publish many articles about successful businesspeople.

Information on companies can help you to prepare a list of employers to contact, to eliminate companies with low growth potential, to identify a job target for your résumé, and to compile a list of intelligent questions that will impress any interviewer.

One way to gain information about what is happening in companies is by reading professional journals. Along with advertised job openings, these resources provide a wealth of information that will help you to ask timely and well-informed questions during the interview and to make a final decision on what company would be the best employer.

THE RÉSUMÉ

Your résumé is likely to be the first contact that you have with a company. It has to be good or you won't even be granted an interview. Every statement should show how you are qualified for the position you seek. As a reflection of your skill in written communication, it is a perfect way to bias the interviewer in your favor before you even walk through the door. In this sense, a résumé is basically a sales device. As such, it should do three things. First, it should emphasize the most positive features in your background, such as maintaining an A average in college. Second, it should stress your work experience and positive contributions to former employers. Third, it should describe positive personal attributes and abilities. The best résumés are written by job seekers themselves rather than by professional résumé preparation services. Only you can present yourself in the best light and sound truthful doing it. It is wise, however, to get some editorial help from a career counselor or other skilled individual since the résumé should make the best possible impression.

The following are some basic hints for writing a good résumé:

1. People usually skim résumés. Too many numbers, too much verbiage, poor spacing, and unclear headings all make a résumé difficult to skim. The strongest positive points should be made first.

2. A résumé for a new college graduate should not exceed one page, regardless of your experience and abilities. A résumé should include two pages only when your experience is sufficient to qualify you for a management position and/or after excluding information such as volunteer activities, sports, and hobbies. Although unnecessary, these items may be included on a scanty résumé, but should never be the reason for an additional page. Stay with the facts and eliminate unnecessary words such as I, he, or she. Résumés are usually written in phrases—not complete sentences.

3. Use action words such as coordinated, supervised, and developed. A résumé should be oriented toward results and accomplishments rather than duties. The tone should be as positive as the content.

4. The résumé should be free of spelling or grammatical errors and should be printed on white or ivory rag paper. No fancy typesetting or binders should be used.

5. Salaries, reasons for termination, and supervisors' names should be excluded. This also applies to any personal information such as religion, race, ethnic background, sex, height, weight, health, age, marital status, children, and photos. References should not be included, but a line on the résumé should state that references are available upon request.

6. An individually typed cover letter should be used each time a résumé is sent to a prospective employer. The letter should be addressed to a specific person rather than "Personnel Director"

whenever possible. The cover letter is how you will introduce yourself, name the position for which you are applying, describe your potential contributions to the company, and request an interview. Keep a file of all the letters that you send, as well as one for responses that require action on your part. Rejection letters should be filed as well.

With the above basics clearly in mind, you should write a résumé that is a summary of your education, work experience, interests, career goals, and qualifications.

Different formats may be used in developing a résumé, depending on your background.

Chronological Résumés

A commonly used format is a chronological arrangement of educational and work experiences, each listed separately with the most recent experience first. If you seek a job that is a natural progression from former jobs and has a good work history with growth and development, this is a good format to use. However, if your work history consists of part-time jobs while in college, there is a better format—the functional arrangement.

Functional Résumés

A résumé organized around functional or topical headings stresses competencies. Such headings as "Research" and "Marketing" enable you to include course work, special projects, and work experience in these areas. These headings are geared to the type of position you are seeking. Actual work experience is included at the bottom of the résumé. Both functional and chronological résumés can be used for broad career objectives.

Targeted Résumés

Jobs have become more highly defined and specific than they used to be. Beginners who are aware of the job market will have developed some special areas of expertise in order to make themselves viable applicants for some of the best positions. In this résumé, your job target is clearly stated along with specific areas of expertise related to your ability to do the job.

Digital Résumés

Many employers now require the digital submission of résumés, due in large part to the high volume of résumés received by most companies. There are two types of digital résumés. Electronic résumés are sent by e-mail or posted to a website. Scannable résumés can be read by a computer. An electronic résumé can be sent to a specific employer by e-mail, or submitted to an online job search site, such as Monster.com or CareerBuilder.com. Some companies use technology to scan and store résumés in a database, which can then be scanned for keywords and phrases that match the job descriptions. There are specific rules for preparing both types of digital résumés. Most of the job search websites offer résumé preparation guidance. Your college library or guidance center should have books on the topic as well.

Which résumé format is best for you will be determined by your experience and career objectives. Whichever format you choose, remember that a good résumé increases your chances of being called for an interview. Be sure to include all of your contact information, such as an e-mail address and cell phone number, if you have them. You may be contacted by phone or by e-mail, so be prepared to check messages and respond quickly if you are called. The more organized and in control an applicant appears, the more impressed prospective employers will be.

PREPARING FOR THE INTERVIEW

Preparing for a job interview involves a lot more than putting on proper clothes. An earlier section described sources of information on specific companies. It is sometimes possible to obtain a schedule of your visit to the company in advance, including the names and titles of the interviewers. If any are senior managers, their backgrounds can be researched in an industry *Who's Who* or one of the earlier sources mentioned, and some aspect of this background could be casually referred to during the interview. You may also request a sample copy of the company's employee newsletter, relevant company publications, or the company's annual report to stockholders.

Since you will have an opportunity during the interview process to ask questions, it is best to have developed a list of critical questions, some based on your preinterview research. Examples of such questions include the following: what type of performance appraisal system is used? How is the company's career development system set up, and what are some common career paths within the company? How are new workers trained and developed? How long has the prospective supervisor held that position? What is the management style of the company? In what direction is future growth anticipated? In short, any information that you have been unable to gain in advance that might heavily affect your career development should be learned in the interview, if possible.

Conservative dress—without looking uniformed—is usually safe attire for a job interview. Women might wear a simply tailored suit, a neat hairstyle, plain jewelry, and moderate makeup. Men might wear a conservative suit, shirt, and tie. Polished shoes, trimmed and styled hair, and clean fingernails are all important.

Posture is significant, as are all types of body language. A firm handshake, eye contact, poise, ease, and manners all contribute to a positive interview. It might even be helpful to practice beforehand in front of a mirror.

A portfolio of college experiences might be useful to show to a prospective employer at the job interview. This portfolio might include best class papers; descriptions of projects completed for class, internships, or jobs; and fliers from events that you participated in or helped organize such as seminars or club fundraising events. Anything related to the job sought should be put in the portfolio.

THE INTERVIEW

Each corporation has a culture of its own, and an applicant's ability to fit into this culture is often the key to being hired. Sizing up the corporate culture is something you can do by walking into a lobby. Is there elaborate security or a clublike atmosphere? Is the coffee served in fine china or plastic cups? Do the executives sometimes pick up their own phones? Are only degrees and certificates displayed in the offices, or family photos as well? Your ability to pick up on the degree of formality or informality and modify interview behavior accordingly might make the difference between a job offer or disappointment. The fact is that managers are looking not only for levels of experience but also for types of people who would fit comfortably into the organization. In other words, chemistry between candidate and interviewer is critical. Both need to determine whether or not they would like to work together daily. This is a highly subjective factor.

The applicants most likely to be hired are effective communicators both on professional and personal levels. Business graduates have an edge because most of them know how to sell things—including themselves. They are warm, outgoing, enthusiastic, self-confident, and have many other good qualities. Both the applicant and interviewer are under stress. The more relaxed both manage to be during the interview, the better the interview will be and the more information will be exchanged. The interviewer is looking at both substance, which is basically a person's past performance, and style, which includes communication skills, poise, self-confidence, and motivation. Broad questions such as "How would you describe yourself as a person?" and "How can you contribute to our organization?" reveal the applicant's values and personality and how the applicant organizes his or her thoughts. How a person fields questions also shows performance under pressure, quickness, energy, and sense of humor.

In general, employers regard specific skills and experience as more important qualifications than educational background. Such skills as written and verbal communications, related work experience, and knowledge of the functions of the company are very important. This is not to say that grade point average and course work are not scrutinized also. The point is that most employers care more about what you can do for their company than what you have learned in college, so in both the résumé and the interview, job seekers should focus on the skills they possess and the value of these skills to the company.

The preliminary interview is generally conducted by a member of the human resources department who is skilled in interview techniques. This interview determines whether or not a candidate will fit into the corporate culture. If it goes well a second interview is conducted by the manager of the department in which the applicant would work. You should work in questions as the interview progresses or, if the interviewer shows a high need for structure, wait until you are asked if there are any questions. Your questions should emphasize professional growth and work-related activities. Such topics as salary and benefits should be discussed after the job is offered. Some bargaining may then occur, particularly if you have another offer in hand.

Ironically enough, most applicants forget to ask for the job. You should ask for the job and thank the interviewer, and you should leave with some indication of when you will hear from the company. The interest that an interviewer shows in an applicant does not mean that a job will be offered.

It is standard operating procedure; the interviewer is building goodwill and keeping the applicant interested. It is best to go on as many interviews as possible and carefully compare companies and offers, no matter how well a first interview goes or how certain you are that a job will be offered. Additional offers not only provide you with choices but also give you some leverage to bargain for salary and benefits.

THE BEST RESOURCE

You are your own best resource. By using good judgment in choosing and planning a career, by gaining information from a variety of sources, by relying on well-formulated questions as well as intuition in accepting a job, you can increase chances of success in finding a good job and beginning a wonderful business career.

ABOUT THE AUTHORS

Lila B. Stair is a professional author in the areas of careers and business. She holds an M.A. in counseling from the University of New Orleans and an M.B.A. from Florida State University. As an instructor of business courses at both community college and university levels, she has had the opportunity to teach business concepts and to assist students in selecting business careers. Formerly a career counselor, Lila Stair has worked with students in developing job search, résumé writing, and interviewing skills. In addition to counseling and providing students with career information, she has worked with employers in job development and placement.

Leslie Stair graduated from Tulane University with a double major in business and communications. While in college, Leslie served as an officer of the Alpha Kappa Psi business fraternity arranging speakers for the group and learning from these professionals the importance of internships and networking. An internship with the Denver Broncos provided valuable insights into working in professional sports. An internship with Charles Schwab led to a position in client services after graduation through which she obtained a broker's license. Leslie is currently a treasury bond trader in Chicago.